graphis annual 79|80

79|80 graphis annual

The International Annual of Advertising and
Editorial Graphics

Das internationale Jahrbuch der Werbe-
graphik und der redaktionellen Graphik

Le répertoire international de l'art graphique
publicitaire et rédactionnel

Edited by / Herausgegeben von / Réalisé par:

Walter Herdeg

Graphis Press Corp., Zurich (Switzerland)

Distributed in the United States by

Hastings House

Publishers
10 East 40th Street, New York, N.Y.10016

PUBLICATION No. 157   [ISBN 8038-2704-0]

Contents

Inhalt

Sommaire

Abbreviations

Abkürzungen

Abréviations

Argentina	ARG	Argentinien	ARG	Afrique du Sud	SAF
Australia	AUS	Australien	AUS	Allemagne occidentale	GER
Austria	AUT	Belgien	BEL	Argentine	ARG
Belgium	BEL	Brasilien	BRA	Australie	AUS
Brazil	BRA	Dänemark	DEN	Autriche	AUT
Canada	CAN	Deutschland (West)	GER	Belgique	BEL
Cuba	CUB	Finnland	FIN	Brésil	BRA
Czechoslovakia	CSR	Frankreich	FRA	Canada	CAN
Denmark	DEN	Grossbritannien	GBR	Cuba	CUB
Finland	FIN	Hongkong	HKG	Danemark	DEN
France	FRA	Irland	IRL	Espagne	SPA
Germany (West)	GER	Israel	ISR	Etats-Unis	USA
Great Britain	GBR	Italien	ITA	Finlande	FIN
Hong Kong	HKG	Japan	JPN	France	FRA
Ireland	IRL	Jugoslawien	YUG	Grande-Bretagne	GBR
Israel	ISR	Kanada	CAN	Hongkong	HKG
Italy	ITA	Kuba	CUB	Irlande	IRL
Japan	JPN	Niederlande	NLD	Israël	ISR
Netherlands	NLD	Norwegen	NOR	Italie	ITA
Norway	NOR	Österreich	AUT	Japon	JPN
Poland	POL	Polen	POL	Norvège	NOR
South Africa	SAF	Schweden	SWE	Pays-Bas	NLD
Spain	SPA	Schweiz	SWI	Pologne	POL
Sweden	SWE	Spanien	SPA	Suède	SWE
Switzerland	SWI	Südafrika	SAF	Suisse	SWI
Turkey	TUR	Tschechoslowakei	CSR	Tchécoslovaquie	CSR
Uruguay	URU	Türkei	TUR	Turquie	TUR
USA	USA	Uruguay	URU	Uruguay	URU
Yugoslavia	YUG	USA	USA	Yougoslavie	YUG

In this annual graphic design work appears, as our introduction says, divested of its "real-world problems" and judged primarily on the basis of its originality and artistic quality. We believe most designers appreciate this form of recognition – especially as good design is mostly effective design – and we are grateful to them for enabling us, by sending in their entries, to provide an annual touchstone of design quality.

Dieses Jahrbuch zeigt Graphik-Design, das nicht nur zweckmässig ist, sondern vor allem durch Originalität und künstlerische Qualität zu überzeugen vermag. Wir glauben, dass die meisten Designer und Illustratoren diese Form der Anerkennung schätzen, und wir danken Ihnen dafür, dass sie es uns durch ihre Einsendungen ermöglichen, einen jährlichen Prüfstein für Design-Qualität zu setzen.

Dans le présent annuaire, la création graphique appliquée apparaît – comme nous en avertit l'introduction – détachée de son insertion dans les problèmes du réel et appréciée en première ligne pour son originalité et sa qualité artistique. Nous estimons que la plupart des designers favorisent cette forme de reconnaissance, et ce d'autant plus que le design de qualité est la plupart du temps aussi un design efficient; nous les remercions de nous faire parvenir régulièrement leurs travaux et de nous mettre ainsi à même de préparer an pour an un compendium de la qualité suprême en matière de design.

TUDOR MIRONESCO, whose cover design for this issue shows the hands of the graphic artist weaving the colours of the rainbow into his personal vision, was born in Rumania in 1936. He was an established illustrator when he came to France in 1969. He now lives in Paris as a freelance illustrator and is at present preparing his first one-man exhibition.

TUDOR MIRONESCO zeigt in seiner Umschlagillustration für diese Ausgabe die Hände des Graphikers, die die Farben des Regenbogens in eine eigene Vision verweben. Er wurde 1939 in Rumänien geboren und war bereits ein etablierter Illustrator als er 1969 nach Frankreich kam. Heute lebt er in Paris als freier Illustrator und plant gerade seine erste Einzelausstellung.

TUDOR MIRONESCO est l'auteur de la composition ornant la couverture de ce volume où l'on voit les mains de l'artiste graphique occupées à tisser les couleurs de l'arc-en-ciel dans sa vision personnelle. Né en Roumanie en 1936, il avait déjà fait ses preuves dans l'illustration quand il s'installa en France en 1969. Illustrateur indépendant à Paris, il prépare actuellement sa première exposition personnelle.

Ralph Caplan

Introduction

RALPH CAPLAN, a New-York-based freelance writer and communications consultant, is the author of books and articles on design and related subjects. He was co-chairman of "Making Connections", the 28th International Design Conference in Aspen.

The programme notes for *Getting Out*, a new off-Broadway play, include credits not just for the design of sets and lighting but for the design of the logo by John Follis. Nobody thinks this is strange, and it isn't. But a decade ago it would have been very hard to figure out what a play was doing with a logo.

Professional design is increasingly pervasive, and for more than a quarter of a century GRAPHIS ANNUAL has been the right place to look for the best of it from all over the world. Years, to be sure, are misleading units for judgement; graphic design, unlike wine, has no vintages. But although twelve months is admittedly an arbitrary period of time, it is the arbitrary period of time that our calendar and our culture depend on. Graphic design is not timeless and by definition cannot be. It is art in the service of someone, or something, and therefore is always tied to time and place in fairly prosaic ways. Coleridge fiercely resented the intrusion of the real world during the composition of Kubla Khan, but a graphic designer would necessarily have accepted this as a standard working constraint.

Design, after all, solves "real-world problems"; but in the process of viewing (and even selecting) annual work, it is not always easy to be sure what the problems were. For our purposes here, it may be just as well not to know: there is nothing irresponsible about a concern with the quality, rather than the effectiveness, of graphics, so long as we remember that effectiveness is the major criterion in another context. This year's work (like last year's) betokens an impressive wealth of graphic talent. So much so that one hears warnings about "a surfeit of good design". I am never sure what hazard is posed by that possibility – perhaps merely the danger that in a climate characterized by nothing but good work, no work will stand out. Not to worry. The built environment does not really look like the best designs of any year. Anyone truly disturbed by the prospect of excessive excellence can relieve his distress by focusing attention on, say, most signage in most cities. The signage matters: much of our vital information comes from poorly designed signs. Conversely, as it happens, many of our trivial messages come from very well designed signs.

Design is a process of ordering information, but messages are often messy and may resist neatness with the passion of an adolescent. In communication, cleanliness is not equal to godliness. Yet cleanliness (particularly in the form of reducing word clutter) is a design obsession that, like obsessions generally, endures beyond the circumstances that initiated it. Other obsessions have comparable staying power, hanging on in the form of graphic nervous tics. Consider the tendency for designers to insert periods after headline phrases. When this was first done in advertising years ago, the period added an intelligent punch; it was a playful way of emphasizing an idea by closing the head – a graphic contradiction in terms. Today the device lingers on as an unthinking habit in the work of designers who simply do not know what periods normally are used for, or why.

But commercial designers know something more important to them than punctuation or syntax: they know a great deal about the art they depend on and steal from. As a rule, copywriters seem to know far less of their roots. For the sake of literary tone, or something equally suspect, quotations from great writers are frequently used in advertisements and brochures; but one invariably feels in such cases that they were drawn from *Bartlett's Quotations* rather than from actual books or plays. Designers are less reverential, and perhaps more truly admiring, of the sources of their craft. Consequently, something like the film director's concept of *homage* enlivens our design for print: the Mona Lisa, for example, appears in more advertisements than the *Michelin* man or Frank Perdue. This cleverness, a staple of contemporary graphics, is easy to disparage. But the quality is perfectly appropriate to the ephemeral nature of graphic design. There is always the danger that cleverness will become self-defeating, but designers are for the most part a responsible lot and reserve self-defeating cleverness for work done on their own behalf or for personal friends — business cards, letterheads, change-of-address notices and birth announcements.

As professional design becomes more important, it is less critical that any individual design, however well executed, should be significant in itself. This annual is probably a case in point. W.H. Auden wrote that an author's body of work is divided into four classes:

First, the pure rubbish which he regrets ever having conceived; second — for him the most painful — the good ideas which his incompetence or impatience prevented from coming to much... third, the pieces he has nothing against except their lack of importance; these must inevitably form the bulk of any collection since, were he to limit it to the fourth class alone, to those poems for which he is honestly grateful, his volume would be too depressingly slim.

There are of course important differences between personal art and public craft, and between work selected by the artist himself and work selected by a jury or editor. But, even allowing for such differences, the sort of composition Auden describes can be discerned in any large selection of work, including one year's worth of graphic design. The bulk must be made up of work that pleases and satisfies, rather than work that sets one's heart soaring and changes the world. This is not cause for despair. It is the way the world works, and the way we do too.

Ralph Caplan

Vorwort

RALPH CAPLAN, ein in New York lebender freier Texter und Kommunikations-Berater, ist Autor von Büchern und Artikeln über Design und verwandte Themen. Bei der 28. Internationalen Design-Konferenz in Aspen, «Making Connections», war er einer der Vorsitzenden.

Das Programm für *Getting Out*, ein neues Theaterstück, das in New York gespielt wird, enthält nicht nur die Namen des Bühnenbildners und des Beleuchters, sondern auch den des Designers des Logos. Niemand wundert sich heute darüber, aber noch vor zehn Jahren hätte man sich kaum vorstellen können, was ein Logo mit einem Theaterstück zu tun hat.

Professionelles Design setzt sich auf immer mehr Gebieten durch, und seit über einem Vierteljahrhundert kann man in GRAPHIS ANNUAL die besten Arbeiten aus aller Welt finden. Natürlich lässt sich Design nicht wie Wein nach Jahrgängen beurteilen, aber obwohl zwölf Monate eine willkürlich festgesetzte Zeitspanne sind, so hängt doch von ihr auch unsere Zeitrechnung und unsere Kultur ab. Graphik-Design ist nicht zeitlos und kann es auch nicht sein, denn es ist Kunst im Dienste einer Firma oder Institution oder einer Sache und somit immer an Zeit und Ort gebunden. Während Coleridge an seinem Gedicht über Kubilaj Khan arbeitete, wurde er durch das Eindringen der realen Welt (in Gestalt eines Vertreters an der Haustür) so gestört, dass er es nicht beenden konnte. Ein Graphik-Designer dagegen hätte dies als eine normale Störung seiner Arbeit akzeptiert.

Design soll schliesslich reale Probleme lösen, aber bei der Durchsicht (oder sogar bei der Auswahl) der Arbeiten eines Jahres kann man nicht immer mit Sicherheit sagen, worum es eigentlich ging. Für unseren Zweck hier muss man es auch nicht wissen: man kann durchaus das Hauptgewicht auf die Qualität statt auf die Wirksamkeit der Graphik legen, solange man sich bewusst ist, dass Wirksamkeit in einem anderen Zusammenhang das wichtigste Kriterium ist.

Die Arbeiten dieses Jahres (wie die des letzten Jahres) sind ein eindrucksvoller Beweis für die Vielfalt graphischen Talents. Man warnt sogar zuweilen vor einem «Überangebot an gutem Design». Ich weiss nicht recht, wo hier die Gefahr liegt – vielleicht in der Tatsache, dass bei vorherrschend gutem Design nichts mehr hervorragen kann. Aber man braucht sich wohl kaum Gedanken darüber zu machen. Die Bauwerke, die uns heute umgeben, sehen eigentlich nicht wie das beste Design irgendeines Jahres aus. Jeder, den die Aussicht auf ein Überangebot an ausgezeichneten Arbeiten wirklich beunruhigt, wird sich vom Gegenteil überzeugen, sobald er seine Aufmerksamkeit zum Beispiel auf die Beschilderung in den Städten richtet. Beschilderung ist wichtig, aber die meisten für uns bedeutenden Informationen erhalten wir von schlecht gestalteten Zeichen. Auf der anderen Seite erhalten wir für uns unbedeutende Hinweise oft von hervorragend konzipierten Zeichen.

Design soll Botschaften übermitteln, doch diese sind oft keineswegs klar umrissen und widersetzen sich der Ordnung. In der Kommunikation ist beschränkende Ordnung aber nicht das oberste Gebot. Und doch ist sie (besonders in Gestalt einer klaren Beschriftung) zu einer Design-Besessenheit geworden, die, wie alle Besessenheiten, auch dann andauert, wenn die auslösenden Ursachen nicht mehr vorhanden sind. Auch andere Besessenheiten behaupten sich hartnäckig; sie tauchen in Form von gewissen graphischen Ticks immer wieder auf. Man denke an die Neigung der Designer, nach Schlagzeilen einen Punkt zu setzen. Als dies vor Jahren zum ersten Mal in der Werbung gemacht wurde, war der Punkt ein intelligent gesetzter Akzent; auf spielerische Weise wurde durch das Abschliessen der Schlagzeile eine Idee unterstrichen – eine Art graphischer Widerspruch. Heute ist diese Idee zur gedankenlosen Gewohnheit von Designern geworden, die einfach nicht wissen, wann und warum Punkte gesetzt werden.

Allerdings gibt es für Designer Wichtigeres als Satzzeichen oder Satzlehre: Sie wissen sehr viel über die Kunst, von der sie profitieren. Werbetexter wissen in der Regel viel weniger über ihre Wurzeln. Um einer Sache einen literarischen Anstrich zu geben oder aus ähnlich suspekten Gründen, werden in Inseraten und Broschüren häufig grosse

Dichter zitiert, aber man wird dabei das Gefühl nicht los, dass eine Zitaten-Sammlung anstelle der Bücher oder Theaterstücke konsultiert wurde. Designer sind im Umgang mit der Kunst weniger ehrfurchtsvoll, aber ihre Bewunderung für diese Quellen ihres Handwerks ist wahrscheinlich echter. Dementsprechend sieht ihre «Hommage» an grosse Meister aus: die Mona Lisa, zum Beispiel, ist in mehr Inseraten zu sehen als das *Michelin*-Männchen oder Frank Perdue (führend im Hähnchen-Geschäft der USA). Diese Art von Humor, zum Massenartikel der modernen Graphik geworden, fordert natürlich leicht Kritik heraus. Aber der kurzlebigen Natur des Graphik-Design entspricht dieser Stil ausgezeichnet. Es besteht zwar immer die Gefahr, dass Witz oder Humor das Gegenteil der beabsichtigten Wirkung hervorrufen, aber da die meisten Designer ihre Arbeit sehr ernst nehmen, reservieren sie ihre Selbstironie für Arbeiten, die sie für sich oder für Freunde machen: Geschäftskarten, Briefköpfe, Adress-änderungs-Mitteilungen und Geburtsanzeigen.

Mit wachsender Bedeutung des professionellen Designs wird es weniger wichtig, dass, abgesehen von der guten Ausführung, jede einzelne Arbeit bedeutend sein sollte. Auch das wird in diesem Jahrbuch deutlich. Nach W.H. Auden lässt sich das Werk eines Autors in vier Kategorien aufteilen:

«Die erste, der reine Ausschuss, den er lieber nicht verfasst hätte, die zweite – für ihn das Schmerzlichste – die guten Ideen, deren Ausarbeitung sein Unvermögen oder seine Ungeduld im Weg standen..., die dritte, die Arbeiten, gegen die er nichts einzuwenden hat ausser ihrem Mangel an Bedeutung; diese machen unausweichlich den Hauptteil jedes Werkes aus, denn sollte er sich auf die vierte Kategorie beschränken, auf jene Arbeiten, für die er wirklich dankbar ist, so wäre das Volumen seines Gesamtwerkes doch deprimierend klein.»

Es gibt natürlich grosse Unterschiede zwischen persönlicher und angewandter Kunst und zwischen den vom Künstler ausgewählten Arbeiten und denen, die eine Jury oder ein Herausgeber bevorzugen. Aber trotz dieser Unterschiede, ist in jedem grösseren Gesamtwerk die von Auden beschriebene Zusammensetzung erkennbar. Der Hauptteil muss zwangsläufig aus Arbeiten bestehen, die gefallen und befriedigen, aber weder die Herzen höher schlagen lassen noch die Welt verändern können. Dies ist kein Grund zum Verzweifeln. Auf diese Weise funktioniert die Welt, und wir auch.

Ralph Caplan

Introduction

RALPH CAPLAN, publiciste et conseiller en communications installé à New York, a écrit plusieurs nombre d'ouvrages et d'articles sur les questions du design et des arts et techniques annexes. Il a coprésidé «Making Connections», la 28e Conférence internationale du design à Aspen.

Les crédits inscrits au programme de *Getting Out*, une nouvelle pièce jouée *off Broadway*, ne concernent pas seulement les décors et l'éclairage, mais aussi le logo conçu par John Follis. Ce n'est là guère matière à étonnement, et pourtant, il y a dix ans encore, il aurait été bien difficile d'imaginer ce qu'une pièce de théâtre pouvait avoir à faire avec un logo.

Le design de caractère professionnel pénètre progressivement tous les médias, et depuis plus d'un quart de siècle, la publication annuelle GRAPHIS ANNUAL constitue la source majeure de renseignements sur les meilleures productions du genre au plan mondial. Le découpage par années fournit évidemment des unités de compte peu appropriées, puisque l'on ne peut guère millésimer des moissons graphiques annuelles comme on le ferait de certains grands crus. Douze mois représentent donc une période arbitraire, et pourtant c'est bien de cette tranche de vie arbitraire que dépendent et notre calendrier et notre civilisation. L'art graphique appliqué n'est pas ni ne saurait de par sa nature être intemporel. C'est un art-service, au service de quelqu'un, de quelque chose et donc lié d'une manière fort prosaïque à un lieu et à un temps déterminés. Le poète anglais Coleridge s'indignait de l'intrusion du réel social dans l'atmosphère de rêve où s'ébauchait son sublime *Kubla Khan* – un artiste graphique aurait par contre accepté comme contrainte inéluctable la marque du hic et nunc dans son œuvre.

C'est qu'après tout le design résout des problèmes relevant des réalités auxquelles nous sommes affrontés. Il est vrai qu'à parcourir ou à sélectionner après coup la production d'une année entière, on éprouve quelque difficulté à cerner les problèmes traités. Qu'importe! Ce n'est certes pas faire preuve d'irresponsabilité que de se préoccuper de la seule qualité plutôt que de l'efficacité d'une création graphique, aussi longtemps que nous restons pleinement conscients que l'efficacité représente un critère décisif dans un autre contexte.

Les travaux de cette année – tout comme ceux de l'année dernière – révèlent une somme impressionnante de réel talent graphique, au point que certains s'alarment d'un «excès de bon design». Je ne saurais dire quels périls sont inhérents à cette surabondance en bien – peut-être courons-nous juste le danger de ne pouvoir dégager des travaux pilotes de la masse des réalisations de premier plan. Je ne pense pas que ce serait risquer grand-chose. De toute façon, l'environnement construit n'a vraiment pas l'air de refléter les meilleures conceptions graphiques de quelque année que ce soit. On conseillera donc aux âmes sensibles qui souffrent de ne plus pouvoir décerner que des prix d'excellence d'orienter leur attention vers, disons, la majeure partie de la signalisation dont sont parsemées la plupart des villes: ils pourront alors éprouver un soulagement certain. Qu'on ne me dise pas que la signalisation urbaine est chose négligeable: en fait, une énorme proportion d'informations vitales nous vient de designs de conception plutôt fruste. Ce n'est guère un paradoxe, mais plutôt un juste retour des choses qu'une grande partie des messages triviaux qui nous sont destinés émanent de signes superbement conçus...

Le design est un processus d'ordonnancement de l'information; pourtant, les messages sont trop souvent désordonnés et peuvent même s'opposer à tout effort de clarification avec la passion qu'un adolescent met à s'opposer à l'environnement de ses origines. En matière de communication, la netteté et la clarté ne sont pas synonymes de vertu. Pourtant, le souci de clarté (en particulier lorsqu'il s'agit de réduire la confusion verbale) reste une obsession du design qui, tout comme les obsessions en général, persiste bien au-delà des circonstances qui l'ont engendrée. D'autres obsessions ont un caractère rémanent comparable et s'affirment alors sous forme de tics graphiques – ainsi la tendance qu'ont les graphistes de mettre un point après chaque titre élaboré. La première fois qu'on vit un point apparaître après un slogan il y a bien des années de cela, il ajoutait comme un coup de poing intelligent; c'était un moyen badin de souligner le slogan et l'idée qu'il renferme en marquant un arrêt net, ce qui est en soi une contradiction graphique. Aujourd'hui le truc fait figure d'habitude machinale chez des artistes qui ignorent à quoi sert le point et pourquoi on s'en sert.

Mais les artistes publicitaires savent quelque chose de plus important à leurs yeux que la ponctuation ou la syntaxe: ils savent un tas de choses sur l'art dont ils dépendent et où ils pillent sans discontinuer. En règle générale, les rédacteurs de textes publicitaires semblent bien moins connaître leurs racines. Pour assurer une certaine tenue littéraire (ou pour tout autre motif également suspect), ils font grand emploi de citations empruntées aux grands écrivains dans leurs annonces et brochures; pourtant, on a régulièrement l'impression qu'ils ont été puiser au *Larousse des citations* (ou, pour l'anglais, au *Bartlett's Quotations*) plutôt qu'à la source même des œuvres romanesques et théâtrales. Les artistes graphiques font moins de courbettes et vouent peut-être une admiration plus authentique aux maîtres présidant aux origines de leur art. La conséquence en est que quelque chose de comparable à la conception de l'hommage chez les cinéastes apporte vie et couleur à la création graphique imprimée: la Joconde, par exemple, hante plus d'annonces que le bonhomme des pneus *Michelin* ou Frank Perdue. Cette ingéniosité, courante dans l'art publicitaire contemporain, est évidemment facile à railler. Pourtant, la qualité à laquelle elle fait appel est parfaitement appropriée au caractère éphémère du design graphique. Même si le risque existe de voir l'ingéniosité se retourner en fin de compte contre son auteur, il faut reconnaître que la plupart des designers sont des gens responsables qui réservent ce genre de risque aux travaux qu'ils réalisent pour leur propre compte ou pour celui de leurs amis — sous forme de cartes de visite, d'en-têtes, d'annonces de déménagement et de faire-part de naissances.

Dans la mesure où le design de qualité professionnelle gagne en importance, il devient moins essentiel que tel travail individuel soit significatif en soi. La présente édition de l'annuaire en apporte probablement la démonstration. L'écrivain anglo-américain W. H. Auden a dit une fois que l'œuvre d'un auteur se répartissait en quatre catégories:

«Tout d'abord, les âneries qu'il regrette à tout jamais d'avoir écrites; puis — et c'est là pour lui une source constante de regrets douloureux — les bonnes idées que son incompétence etc. ou son impatience l'empêchèrent de réaliser... troisièmement, les œuvres auxquelles il n'a rien à objecter sauf leur manque d'importance; ce sont ces dernières qui forment inévitablement le gros de sa production et alimentent ses œuvres complètes, car s'il voulait se borner à faire connaître la production de la quatrième catégorie, les poèmes qui emplissent son cœur de reconnaissance, son volume serait bien trop mince pour que son amour-propre y survive...»

Il existe bien sûr des différences notables entre l'art personnel et celui destiné au grand public, entre l'art sélectionné par l'artiste lui-même et celles de ses œuvres qui sont retenues par un jury ou un éditeur. Pourtant, même si l'on tient compte de ces différences, on s'apercevra que la catégorisation d'Auden se retrouve dans toute sélection d'envergure, y compris la production annuelle en matière de design graphique. Le gros des travaux qui y figurent doit représenter des œuvres plaisantes et satisfaisantes plutôt que des réalisations qui font s'envoler les cœurs et changer le monde. N'y voyons aucune cause de désarroi ou de tristesse. C'est tout simplement ainsi que va le monde, et nous sommes faits de la même étoffe après tout.

Index to Artists and Designers
Verzeichnis der Künstler und Gestalter
Index des artistes et maquettistes

Index to Art Directors
Verzeichnis der künstlerischen Leiter
Index des directeurs artistiques

Index to Agencies, Studios and Producers
Verzeichnis der Agenturen, Studios und Produzenten
Index des agences, studios et producteurs

Index to Publishers
Verzeichnis der Verleger
Index des Editeurs

Index to Advertisers
Verzeichnis der Auftraggeber
Index des clients

■ Entry instructions may be requested by anyone interested in submitting samples of exceptional graphics or photography for possible inclusion in our annuals. No fees involved. Closing dates for entries:
GRAPHIS ANNUAL (advertising and editorial art and design): 31 January
PHOTOGRAPHIS (advertising and editorial photography): 30 June
GRAPHIS POSTERS (an annual of poster art): 30 June
Write to: Graphis Press Corp., Dufourstrasse 107, 8008 Zurich, Switzerland

■ Einsendebedingungen können von jedermann angefordert werden, der uns Beispiele hervorragender Photographie oder Graphik zur Auswahl für unsere Jahrbücher unterbreiten möchte. Es werden keine Gebühren erhoben. Einsendetermine:
GRAPHIS ANNUAL (Werbe- und redaktionelle Graphik): 31. Januar
PHOTOGRAPHIS (Werbe- und redaktionelle Photographie): 30. Juni
GRAPHIS POSTERS (ein Jahrbuch der Plakatkunst): 30. Juni
Adresse: Graphis Verlag AG, Dufourstrasse 107, 8008 Zürich, Schweiz

■ Tout intéressé à la soumission de travaux photographiques et graphiques recevra les informations nécessaires sur demande. Sans charge de participation. Dates limites:
GRAPHIS ANNUAL (art graphique publicitaire et rédactionnel): 31 janvier
PHOTOGRAPHIS (photographie publicitaire et rédactionnelle): 30 juin
GRAPHIS POSTERS (annuaire sur l'art de l'affiche): 30 juin
S'adresser à: Editions Graphis SA, Dufourstrasse 107, 8008 Zurich, Suisse

Editor and Art Director: Walter Herdeg
Assistant Editors: Stanley Mason, Vreni Monnier
Project Manager: Vreni Monnier
Designers: Martin Byland, Ulrich Kemmner, Klaus Schröder
Art Assistants: Willy Müller, Peter Wittwer

1

Magazine Advertisements

Newspaper Advertisements

Zeitschriften-Inserate

Zeitungs-Inserate

Annonces de revues

Annonces de presse

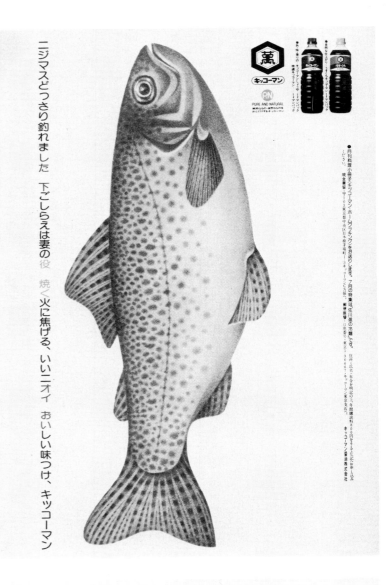

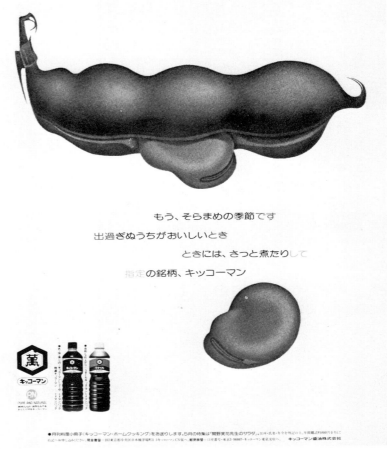

ARTIST / KÜNSTLER / ARTISTE:

1 Siegbert Reinhard
2, 4, 5 Tadashi Ohashi
3 Braldt Bralds
6 Ralph Steadman

DESIGNER / GESTALTER / MAQUETTISTE:

1 Victor Della Barba
2, 4, 5 Tadashi Ohashi
3 Atelier Pütz
6 Mike Garwood

ART DIRECTOR / DIRECTEUR ARTISTIQUE:

1 Victor Della Barba
2, 4, 5 Tadashi Ohashi
3 Robert Pütz
6 Mike Garwood

AGENCY / AGENTUR / AGENCE – STUDIO:

1 Lewis & Gilman Inc.
3 Robert Pütz GmbH & Co.
6 Benton & Bowles Ltd.

3

1 Double-spread magazine advertisement for a new distribution system initiated by *Dixie/Marathon*, a company for dispensable paper articles. Full colour, on cardboard. (USA)
2, 4, 5 From a long-running series of full-page, full-colour magazine ads for *Kikkoman Shoyu* sauces. (JPN)
3 Illustration of a double-spread advertisement for the *Siegwerk* printing inks company. The rainbow always appears as the *"Siegwerk* symbol". Full colour. (GER)
6 Example from a series of black-and-white magazine advertisements for the Joe Coral Leisure Group, to entice people to bet on horses. (GBR)

1 Doppelseitige Zeitschriftenanzeige für ein neues Verteilersystem, das ein Unternehmen für Wegwerf-Papierartikel aufzog. Mehrfarbig, brauner Karton. (USA)
2, 4, 5 Aus einer langjährigen Serie von ganzseitigen, mehrfarbigen Zeitschriftenanzeigen für Saucen von *Kikkoman Shoyu.* (JPN)
3 Illustration einer doppelseitigen Anzeige der Druckfarbenfabrik *Siegwerk.* Der Regenbogen erscheint als *Siegwerk*-Wahrzeichen auf allen Anzeigen. Mehrfarbig. GER.
6 Beispiel aus einer Serie von schwarzweissen Zeitschriftenanzeigen der Joe Coral Leisure Group, die zum Wetten an verschiedenen Pferderennen auffordern soll. (GBR)

1 Annonce de magazine double page pour un nouveau système de distribution organisé par une fabrique d'articles de papier à jeter. Polychromie sur carton brun. (USA)
2, 4, 5 Exemples d'une longue série d'annonces de magazines pleines pages en faveur des sauces *Kikkoman Shoyu.* En polychromie. (JPN)
3 Illustration d'une annonce double page d'une fabrique d'encres d'imprimerie. L'arc-en-ciel est depuis quelques années l'emblème de cette entreprise. (GER)
6 Exemple d'une série d'annonces de magazines noir et blanc pour le Joe Coral Leisure Group prônant le pari mutuel à l'occasion de diverses courses de chevaux. (GBR)

Will a dark horse 'Eclipse' Lester Piggott today?

Of the three favoured horses for today's Joe Coral Eclipse Stakes, one has the legendary Lester Piggott on his back. That alone must give the Irish horse, Artaius, an enviable advantage.

Nevertheless, there are a couple of runners who intend to test Piggott every inch of the course. Perhaps you rate their chances this time.

If you fancy a flutter on The Eclipse, the simplest way is a straight bet on your horse winning outright. This is referred to as 'a win'.

Alternatively, you can bet 'each way'. This is

two bets covering your horse to win, and/or coming first, second or third.

But if you want further help, don't hesitate to ask our staff. Having been in the business for over 50 years, there isn't much we don't know about horse racing, or punters. We want you to have fun.

To apply for your credit account, write to: Joe Coral, 252-260 Regent Street, London W.1. A member of The Coral Leisure Group.

Sorry, no postal bets.

JoeCoral
for a friendly flutter

6

7

8

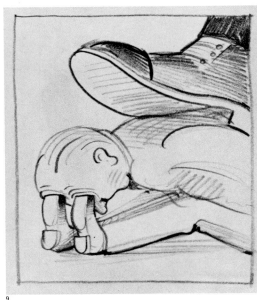

9

10

11

12

ARTIST / KÜNSTLER / ARTISTE:

7–17 Tomi Ungerer

DESIGNER / GESTALTER / MAQUETTISTE:

7–17 Atelier Pütz

ART DIRECTOR / DIRECTEUR ARTISTIQUE:

7–17 Robert Pütz

AGENCY / AGENTUR / AGENCE – STUDIO:

7–17 Robert Pütz GmbH & Co.

13

14

15

17

7–17 Full-colour and black-and-white illustrations from *Abracadabra*, the book of ideas by Tomi Ungerer and Robert Pütz, dealing here with the following themes: Demotivation (7), Stress (8), Obsession (9), Overburden (10), Anxiety (11), Contact difficulties (12), Performance pressure (13), Lack of initiative (14), Exorbitant demand (15), Inferiority complexes (17). (GER)

7–17 Illustrationen, mehrfarbig und schwarzweiss, aus *Abracadabra*, dem Ideenbuch von Tomi Ungerer und Robert Pütz, hier zu folgenden Themen: Demotivation (7), Stress (8), Zwangsneurose (9), Überlastung (10), Angstzustände (11), Kontakt-Schwierigkeiten (12), Leistungsdruck (13), Antriebslosigkeit (14), Überforderung (15), Minderwertigkeits-Komplexe (17). (GER)

7–17 Illustrations, en couleurs et en noir-blanc, du Livre d'idées *Abracadabra* réalisé par Tomi Ungerer et Robert Pütz, se référant ici à: absence de motivation (7), stress (8), névrose obsessionnelle (9), surcharge (10), angoisses (11), isolement (12), pression du travail (13), apathie (14), surménage (15), complexes d'infériorité (17). (GER)

19

ARTIST / KÜNSTLER / ARTISTE:

18 Bob Pepper
19 Stanislaw Zagorski
20 Jack Davis
21 Adelchi Galloni

DESIGNER / GESTALTER / MAQUETTISTE:

19 P. Corriston
21 Michele Goëtche

ART DIRECTOR / DIRECTEUR ARTISTIQUE:

18 Mike Callouri
19 P. Corriston
20 Bill Sweney/Dick Henderson
21 Michele Goëtche

AGENCY / AGENTUR / AGENCE – STUDIO:

18 Essie Pinsker Associates
20 Cole Henderson Drake, Inc.
21 Agenzia Italia

18 Illustration from a full-page magazine ad for printed textiles by *Cranston*. The motif is similar to Russian icons. (USA)
19 Double spread ad in a trade journal for the *Infinity* record company. Mostly in shades of blue and grey. (USA)
20 Black-and-white ad enticing customers to save. (USA)
21 Full-colour magazine ad for the new *Fiat 127*, which is guaranteed to get one quickly but surely to one's destination. (ITA)

18 Illustration einer ganzseitigen Zeitschriftenanzeige für bedruckte Textilien. Das Motiv erinnert an russische Ikonen. (USA)
19 In der Fachpresse erschienene doppelseitige Anzeige für eine Schallplattenfirma. Vorwiegend in Blau- und Grautönen. (USA)
20 Schwarzweiss-Anzeige mit Aufruf zum Sparen. (USA)
21 Mehrfarbige Zeitschriftenanzeige für den neuen *Fiat 127*, der einen schnell aber sicher ans Ziel bringt. (ITA)

18 Illustration d'une annonce pleine page en faveur de textiles imprimés. Le motif rapelle une icône russe. (USA)
19 Annonce de magazine professionnel, sur page double, publiée par un producteur de disques. Prédominance de tons bleus et gris. (USA)
20 Annonce en noir et blanc faisant appel aux clients d'une banque d'épargner davantage. (USA)
21 Annonce de magazine (en polychromie) pour la nouvelle *Fiat 127*, qui roule sûrement mais rapidement. (ITA)

Advertisements / Anzeigen / Annonces

Advertisements / Anzeigen / Annonces

ARTIST / KÜNSTLER / ARTISTE:

22 Alan Krosnick
23 John Dearstyne
24, 25 Kim Milnazik
26 Tom Hallman
27, 28 Charles Lilly

DESIGNER / GESTALTER / MAQUETTISTE:

22 Nicolas Sidjakov
24–26 Kramer Miller Lomden Glassman
27, 28 Ted Amber/Mike Psaltis/Ron Canagata

ART DIRECTOR / DIRECTEUR ARTISTIQUE:

22 Gino Icardi
23 Tom Kelly
24–26 Alan J. Klawans
27, 28 David Krieger

AGENCY / AGENTUR / AGENCE – STUDIO:

22 Somers & Icardi
23 Pawluk Adv.
24–26 Smith Kline & French Labs.
27, 28 Adelante Advertising Inc.

22 Double-spread ad in a trade journal, for toasted corn manufactured without any additional foodstuffs. Black-and-white with full-colour paper bag. (USA)
23 Double-spread ad with colour illustration for a minicomputer. (USA)
24–26 Complete, double-spread ad and two full-colour illustrations for the psychopharmaceutical *Thorazine*, to help sick people return to reality. (USA)
27, 28 From a series of full-page magazine advertisements for *Pepsi-Cola*, showing famous negroes; here: Charlie Christian and Harriet Tubman. (USA)

22 Doppelseitige, in der Fachpresse publizierte Anzeige für geröstete Maiskörner, die ohne irgendwelche Lebensmittelzusätze hergestellt werden. Schwarzweiss, mehrfarbige Tüte. (USA)
23 Doppelseitige Anzeige (Farbillustration) für Minicomputer. (USA)
24–26 Vollständige, doppelseitige Anzeige und zwei Illustrationen (mehrfarbig) für das Psychopharmakum *Thorazine*, das psychisch kranken Menschen hilft, in die Realität zurückzufinden. (USA)
27, 28 Aus einer Serie von ganzseitigen Zeitschriftenanzeigen für *Pepsi-Cola*, die berühmte Schwarze zeigen, hier den Jazz-Musiker Charlie Christian und die Freiheitskämpferin Harriet Tubman. (USA)

22 Annonce double page publiée dans la presse professionnelle en faveur de grains de maïs grillé, sans additifs nocifs. Noir et blanc, sachet en couleurs. (USA)
23 Annonce sur page double avec illustration en couleurs figurant dans une campagne publicitaire pour un mini-ordinateur. (USA)
24–26 Annonce double page complète et deux illustrations (en polychromie) pour un produit psychotropique qui facillite le retour à la réalité. (USA)
27, 28 D'une série d'annonces de magazines pleines pages pour *Pepsi-Cola*, présentant de célèbres personnes noires, telle que Charlie Christian ou Harriet Tubman, combattante pour la liberté. (USA)

23

22

Our giant kernels of corn are 100% natural, with nothing artificial added.
Just colossal kernels of corn, vegetable oil and salt. Pure, simple and delicious.

There's nothing artificial about the size of Cornnuts toasted corn either. The kernels actually grow as big as you find them. They're not artificially puffed-up or exploded. Even the color is real.

The golden hue you see on each kernel is the result of roasting, not food coloring.
Plus, they've got fewer calories than potato chips, corn chips, peanuts or sunflower kernels.

Most important, Cornnuts toasted corn contains no added sugar. And that helps us with cavity-conscious parents and school boards.
Add all these facts together and you begin to

see why Cornnuts toasted corn has made a 250% sales increase in the past five years.
The next five years promise to be even better. Even so, Cornnuts will still be offering excellent

margins and outstanding incentives on all sizes of our product.
For complete nutritional information on one of America's fastest-growing natural snacks, write us at the

address below.
You'll get the straight facts. With nothing artificial added.
Larry Martino, V.P. Sales, Cornnuts, Inc., P.O. Box 6759, Oakland, CA 94603

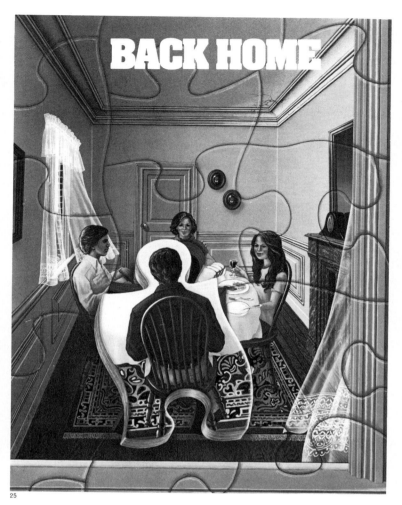

BACK HOME

GOING HOME

25

26

You can thank the late Mr. Christian for all of the music you're enjoying now. □ Today there are literally hundreds of Jazz, Blues, Pop and Rock guitarists. Some have even become Super Stars. It wasn't always that way. For a long time, the only people who had any use for the guitar were folk singers, hillbillies, and Hollywood cowboys. Jazz musicians were pretty much agreed that the guitar had no future in jazz. □ Then, in the late 30's the electric guitar was invented. And the gods of music sent someone down to play it —

kid named Charlie Christian. □ He was only 20 years old when he joined Benny "The King of Swing" Goodman. Soon Charlie was the most talked about man in music. No one had ever heard anything like him! He played the first jazz guitar solos! Charlie Christian's ideas formed the basis of Modern Jazz. □ In 1942 tragedy struck. A downhill struggle with tuberculosis ended a short but dynamic career. Charlie Christian was only 23. □ But his music still lives. And so does the electricity he created — modern jazz.

CHARLIE CHRISTIAN
THE MAN WHO ELECTRIFIED JAZZ

27

Born a slave in Maryland around 1820, Harriet Tubman rose to become one of the great freedom fighters in the history of America. □ After escaping from slavery in 1848, she spent the next ten years leading other slaves to freedom, among them, her own brothers and parents. At great risk to her own life and freedom, she went on nineteen freedom missions from the slave states to Canada. She saved more than 300 slaves and never once did one return to his master. On Harriet Tubman's railroad, desertions were forbidden. □ Her

underground railroad exploits proved good training for the work she did during the Civil War. She served the Union as a nurse, soldier, spy and scout, and led men into battle. □ When the war ended, she became a spokesman for civil rights and feminist causes until her retirement from public life in the early 1900's. □ In her lifetime, Harriet Tubman received many honors including a medal from Queen Victoria. She was known as "The General" and as "Moses." More than just a Freedom Fighter, Harriet Tubman was truly a freedom winner!

HARRIET TUBMAN
FREEDOM FIGHTER

28

33

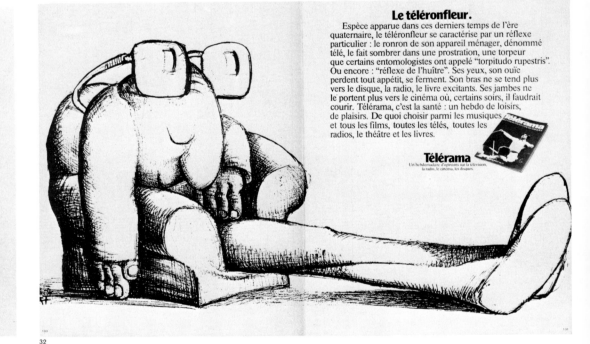

ARTIST / KÜNSTLER / ARTISTE:

29 Kenny Higdon
30, 32 André François
31 Rick Meyerowitz
33 Dorothee Walter

DESIGNER / GESTALTER / MAQUETTISTE:

33 Dorothee Walter

ART DIRECTOR / DIRECTEUR ARTISTIQUE:

29 Bill Sweney
30, 32 Yves Delacroix
31 Dick Henderson

AGENCY / AGENTUR / AGENCE – STUDIO:

29, 31 Cole Henderson Drake, Inc.
30, 32 Mirabelle
33 Deinhard & Co., Marketing Service

Advertisements / Anzeigen / Annonces

29, 31 Two examples from a series of full-page, full-colour magazine ads of the Aviation Insurance Agency directed to airline pilots who can insure themselves, without the usual complications, against inability to work. (USA)
30, 32 ''The Teleglutton.'' – ''The Telesnorer.'' From a series of double-spread newspaper ads of a weekly magazine for radio, television, cinema and music. (FRA)
33 Full-page illustration (actual size) from a public relations publication of Deinhard & Co. (GER)

29, 31 Zwei Beispiele aus einer Serie von ganzseitigen, mehrfarbigen Zeitschriftenanzeigen einer Versicherungsgesellschaft, bei welcher sich Linienpiloten ohne «wenn und noch und aber» gegen Arbeitsunfähigkeit versichern lassen können. (USA)
30, 32 «Der Televielfrass.» – «Der Teleschnarcher.» Aus einer Serie von doppelseitigen Zeitungsanzeigen einer Wochenzeitschrift für Radio, Fernsehen, Kino und Musik. (FRA)
33 Ganzseitige Illustration (in Originalgrösse) aus einer PR-Veröffentlichung von Deinhard & Co. (GER)

29, 31 Exemples d'une série d'annonces de magazines pleines pages (en polychromie) publiées par une compagnie d'assurances auprès de laquelle les pilotes de lignes peuvent s'assurer contre l'incapacité de travail, «sans si et sans mais». (USA)
30, 32 Deux annonces de presse doubles pages (en noir et blanc) figurant dans une série de Télérama, l'hebdomadaire d'opinions sur la TV, le cinéma, la radio et les disques. (FRA)
33 Illustration pleine page (grandeur nature) d'une publication de prestige de Deinhard & Cie. (GER)

34

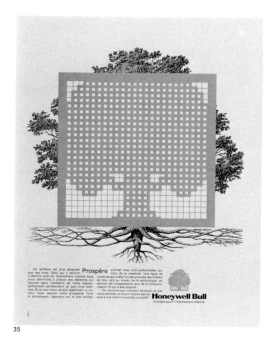

35

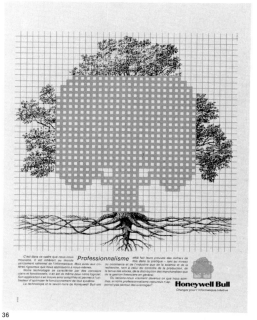

36

37

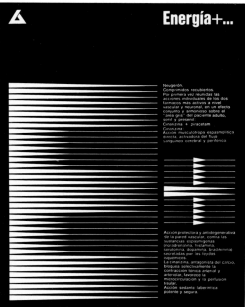

38

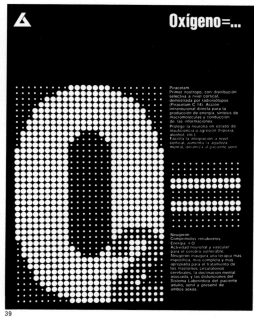

39

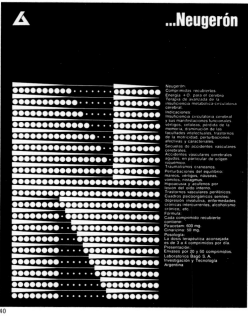

40

41

ARTIST / KÜNSTLER / ARTISTE:

34–37 J. Kunz
38–40 Javier Cafaro
41 Richard Jack

DESIGNER / GESTALTER / MAQUETTISTE:

34–37 A. Bosshard
38–40 Eduardo A. Cánovas
41 Frans Jacobs

ART DIRECTOR / DIRECTEUR ARTISTIQUE:

34–37 A. Bosshard
38–40 Eduardo A. Cánovas
41 Ian Coetser

AGENCY / AGENTUR / AGENCE – STUDIO:

34–37 Adolf Wirz AG
38–40 Estudio Cánovas
41 Ian Coetser Associates (Pty) Ltd

Advertisements / Anzeigen / Annonces

42

43

ARTIST / KÜNSTLER / ARTISTE:

42 Bill Myer
43, 45 Hanspeter Wyss
44 Haruo Miyauchi
46–48 Michel Dubré

DESIGNER / GESTALTER:

43, 45 Hanspeter Wyss
44 Seymour Chwast
46–48 John Scott

ART DIRECTOR:

42 Dick Henderson
43, 45 Th. Walser
44 Seymour Chwast
46–48 John Scott

AGENCY / AGENTUR / AGENCE:

42 Cole Henderson Drake, Inc.
44 Push Pin Studios
46–48 Homsy-Delafosse

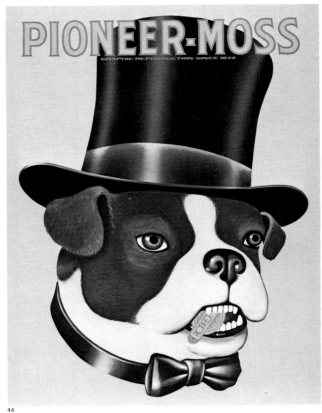

44

45

42 Full-colour newspaper advertisement of the Aviation Insurance Agency for the insuring of airline pilots unable to work. (USA)
43, 45 From a series of full-colour magazine ads with which the weekly satirical periodical *Nebelspalter* aims at new subscription-holders. (SWI)
44 Full-page magazine advertisement for *Pioneer-Moss,* lithographers. Full colour on a dull green surface. (USA)
46–48 "There is always a hint of craziness in our champagne." Illustrations (full colour) and complete magazine advertisement from a series for a French champagne. (FRA)

42 Mehrfarbige Zeitungsanzeige einer Versicherung, die Linienpiloten gegen Arbeitsunfähigkeit versichert. (USA)
43, 45 Aus einer Serie von mehrfarbigen Zeitschriftenanzeigen, mit welchen die humoristische Wochenzeitschrift *Nebelspalter* neue Abonnenten wirbt. (SWI)
44 Ganzseitige Zeitschriftenanzeige einer Litho-Anstalt. Mehrfarbig auf matt grünem Grund. (USA)
46–48 «In unserem Champagner liegt immer ein Hauch von Verrücktheit.» Illustrationen (mehrfarbig) und vollständige Zeitschriftenanzeige aus einer Serie für einen französischen Champagner. (FRA)

46

47

42 Annonce de magazine (en couleurs) par laquelle l'Aviation Insurance Agency offre une assurance aux pilotes de ligne en chômage. (USA)
43, 45 Exemples figurant dans une série autopromotionnelle lancée par l'hebdomadaire humoristique *Nebelspalter*. En couleurs vives. (SWI)
44 Annonce de magazine pleine page d'un photolithographe. En polychromie sur fond vert pâle. (USA)
46—48 «Il y a toujours eu un brin de folie dans notre champagne.» Deux illustrations (en couleurs) et annonce de magazine complète tirée d'une série pour le champagne *Mercier*. (FRA)

48

39

49, 50 Full-page magazine advertisements made up of sketches, for handbags sold at the Galerie de la Liberté. Fig. 49: Beige and blue, text in orange; Fig. 50: mostly in grey shades, text in blue. (JPN)
51, 52 From a long-standing series of full-page magazine advertisements showing frogs for *Grit,* an American weekly magazine that claims to be specially popular in small towns. Fig. 51: mostly in grey shades; Fig. 52: mostly in yellow-brown shades. (USA)
53, 54 Full-page advertisement and illustration, shown here in actual size, for *Foot-Joy* tennis shoes. (USA)

49, 50 Als Skizzen aufgemachte, ganzseitige Zeitschriftenanzeigen für Handtaschen. Abb. 49: beige und blau, Text in Orange; Abb. 50: vorwiegend in Grautönen, Text in Blau. (JPN)
51, 52 «Der grosse Frosch in kleinen Städten.» Aus einer langjährigen Serie von ganzseitigen Zeitschriftenanzeigen für *Grit,* eine amerikanische Wochenzeitschrift für kleinere Städte. Abb. 51 vorwiegend in Grüntönen, Abb. 52 vorwiegend in Gelbbrauntönen gehalten. (USA)
53, 54 «Steh dein Spiel durch.» Ganzseitige Anzeige und Illustration in Originalgrösse für eine Tennisschuh-Marke. (USA)

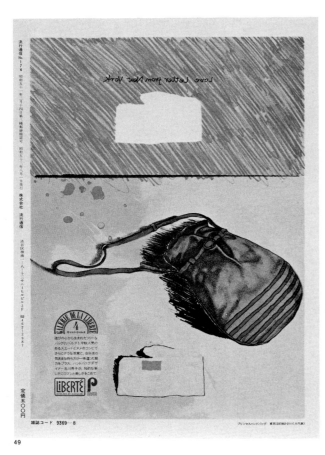

49

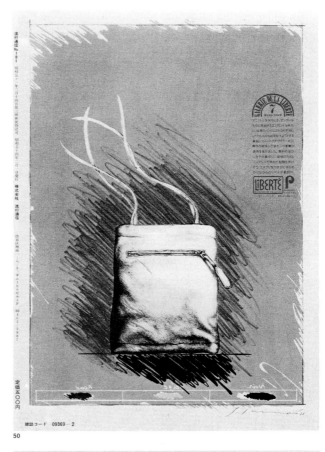

50

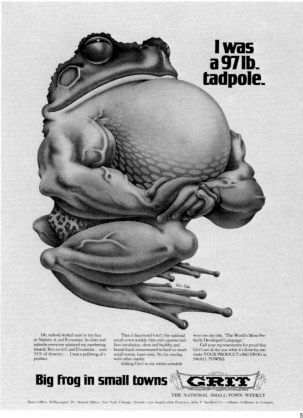

51

52

ARTIST / KÜNSTLER / ARTISTE:

49, 50 Showzoh Shinoda
51 Verlin Miller
52 Linda Gist
53, 54 Carlos Ochagovia

DESIGNER / GESTALTER:

49, 50 Yasuyuki Uno
51, 52 Elmer Pizzi

ART DIRECTOR:

49, 50 Yasuyuki Uno
51, 52 Elmer Pizzi
53, 54 L. Silvas

AGENCY / AGENTUR / AGENCE:

51, 52 Gray & Rogers
53, 54 Chester Gore Company Inc.

Advertisements
Anzeigen
Annonces

54

53

41

55

Advertisements
Anzeigen
Annonces

56

57

58

Für die Kunst des Verpackens: Die Kunststoffe von Solvay

Rund 90% aller Lebensmittel und die meisten Non-Food-Artikel werden heute über SB-Geschäfte abgesetzt. Verpackt. Verkaufen ist mehr denn je die Kunst des Verpackens. Nur eine in Form, Farbgebung und Qualität optimale Verpackung erzielt im Wettbewerb von heute auch optimalen Verkaufserfolg. Solvay, der Welt grösster Hersteller von PVC und einer der Grössten bei Niederdruck-polyäthylen, hat die Kunststoffe für die Kunst des Verpackens, für jede Verpackungsaufgabe den richtigen Kunststoff. Dazu die anwendungstechnische Beratung, damit aus guten Kunststoffen gute Verpackungen werden.

59

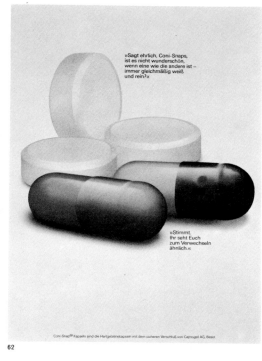

61

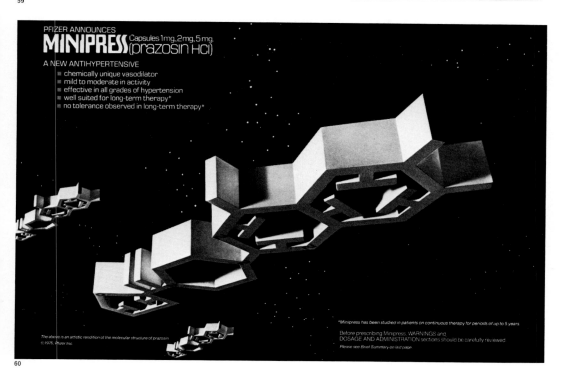

PFIZER ANNOUNCES
MINIPRESS Capsules 1 mg, 2 mg, 5 mg.
(prazosin HCl)

A NEW ANTIHYPERTENSIVE
■ chemically unique vasodilator
■ mild to moderate in activity
■ effective in all grades of hypertension
■ well suited for long-term therapy*
■ no tolerance observed in long-term therapy*

*Minipress has been studied in patients on continuous therapy for periods of up to 5 years.

The above is an artistic rendition of the molecular structure of prazosin. ©1976, Pfizer Inc.

Before prescribing Minipress, WARNINGS and DOSAGE AND ADMINISTRATION sections should be carefully reviewed. Please see Brief Summary on last page.

60

62

ART DIRECTOR / DIRECTEUR ARTISTIQUE:

55, 56 Artur Kulak
57, 58 John Dolby
59 Robert Pütz
60 Tom Haynes
62 Pierre Mendell

AGENCY / AGENTUR / AGENCE – STUDIO:

57, 58 BBDM, Inc.
59 Robert Pütz GmbH & Co.
60 Sudler & Hennessy, Inc.
61, 62 Mendell & Oberer

55, 56 Complete advertisement and illustration, in actual size, of an ad for the German Savings-Banks Organization. (GER)
57, 58 From a series of double-spread trade advertisements for the Amoco Chemicals Corporation, here for cables and cable insulation and synthetic pipes. (USA)
59 Double spread advertisement in bright colours for the synthetic packing material of the Deutsche Solvay Werke. (GER)
60 Advertisement for a *Pfizer* medicine for high blood pressure, which appeared in the medical trade press. Full colour. (USA)
61, 62 From a series of advertisements for *Coni-Snap* hard gelatine capsules. Capsules in blue-yellow and red-green. (SWI)

55, 56 Vollständige Anzeige und Illustration (in Originalgrösse) einer Anzeige der Deutschen Sparkassenorganisation. (GER)
57, 58 Aus einer Serie von doppelseitigen, in der Fachpresse erschienenen Anzeigen eines Chemiekonzerns, hier für Kabel und Kabelisolierungen und Rohrsysteme aus Kunststoff. (USA)
59 Doppelseitige Anzeige in bunten Farben für Kunststoffverpackungen der Deutschen Solvay Werke. (GER)
60 In der medizinischen Fachpresse erschienene Anzeige für ein Mittel gegen zu hohen Blutdruck. Mehrfarbig. (USA)
61, 62 Aus einer Serie von Anzeigen für *Coni-Snap* Hartgelatinekapseln. Kapseln in Blau-Gelb und Rot-Grün. (SWI)

55, 56 Annonce complète et illustration (en grandeur nature) de l'organisation des caisses d'épargne allemandes. (GER)
57, 58 D'une série d'annonces doubles pages publiées dans la presse professionnelle. Publicité d'une entreprise de produits chimiques pour des câbles et des tuyaux en matière plastique. (USA)
59 Annonce de magazine double page – en couleurs vives – pour un fabricant de conditionnements en matière plastique. (GER)
60 Annonce publiée dans les périodiques médicales en faveur d'un médicament contre l'hypertension. En polychromie. (USA)
61, 62 D'une série d'annonces pour *Coni-Snap*, des capsules de gélatine. Capsules en bleu-jaune, resp. rouge-vert. (SWI)

63

64

65

66

63, 64 From a series of double-spread advertisements to promote tourism on the islands of Hawaii. Colour photographs and illustrations. (USA)
65—68 The chances of purchasing a bad bottle of *Hirondelle* are practically nil according to this full-page magazine advertisement and illustration in actual size. From an advertising campaign for *Hirondelle* wines. (GBR)

63, 64 Aus einer Serie von doppelseitigen Anzeigen aus Farbaufnahmen und -illustrationen zur Förderung des Tourismus auf den Hawaii-Inseln. (USA)
65—68 «Die gezeigten Vorkommnisse sind genau so unwahrscheinlich, wie eine schlechte Flasche *Hirondelle*.» Ganzseitige, mehrfarbige Zeitschriftenanzeigen und Illustration in Originalgrösse aus einer Werbekampagne für *Hirondelle*-Weine. (GBR)

63, 64 Exemples figurant dans une série d'annonces doubles pages pour la promotion touristique des îles Hawaii. Photos et illustrations en couleurs. (USA)
65—68 «Ces événements sont aussi impossibles et invraisemblables qu'un défaut de qualité d'une bouteille de *Hirondelle*.» Annonces de magazines pleines pages (en polychromie) et illustration (en grandeur nature) d'une série publicitaire pour les vins *Hirondelle*. (GBR)

Advertisements / Anzeigen / Annonces

67

68

ARTIST / KÜNSTLER / ARTISTE:

65 Barry Craddock
66 Wayne Anderson
67, 68 Pauline Ellison

DESIGNER / GESTALTER / MAQUETTISTE:

63, 64 Nicolas Sidjakov

ART DIRECTOR / DIRECTEUR ARTISTIQUE:

63, 64 Gene Despard
65–68 Tony Muranka

AGENCY / AGENTUR / AGENCE – STUDIO:

63, 64 Milici Valenti Adv.
65–68 J. Walter Thompson Co. Ltd.

45

Der Hausfriede ist ausbaufähig

Rigips ist der ganze Innenausbau.

Überall gibt es 'ausbaufähiges' für Rigips. Denn Rigips hat das komplette Angebot für den Innenausbau...
für Wand- und Deckenverkleidungen, Montagewand- und Deckenkonstruktionen und den Dachgeschoßausbau, für alle Anforderungen des Brand-, Schall- und Wärmeschutzes;
für Neu- und Altbauten vom Einfamilienhaus bis zum Großobjekt.
Rigips ist universell und aktuell; Rigips hat den Service für eine ausbaufähige Partnerschaft. Fragen Sie nach Rigips oder sprechen Sie mit uns, wenn es um Innenausbau geht.
Rigips, 3452 Bodenwerder, Tel. 05533/711

Besuchen Sie uns auf der Constructa '78 in Hannover vom 12. bis 22. Februar in Halle 23.

70

Das Betriebsklima ist ausbaufähig

Rigips ist der ganze Innenausbau.

Überall gibt es 'ausbaufähiges' für Rigips. Denn Rigips hat das komplette Angebot für den Innenausbau...
für Wand- und Deckenverkleidungen, Montagewand- und Deckenkonstruktionen und den Dachgeschoßausbau, für alle Anforderungen des Brand-, Schall- und Wärmeschutzes;
für Neu- und Altbauten vom Einfamilienhaus bis zum Großobjekt.
Rigips ist universell und aktuell; Rigips hat den Service für eine ausbaufähige Partnerschaft. Fragen Sie nach Rigips oder sprechen Sie mit uns, wenn es um Innenausbau geht.
Rigips, 3452 Bodenwerder, Tel. 05533/711

Besuchen Sie uns auf der Constructa '78 in Hannover vom 12. bis 22. Februar in Halle 23.

71

Die Feuersicherheit ist ausbaufähig

Rigips ist der ganze Innenausbau.

Überall gibt es 'ausbaufähiges' für Rigips. Denn Rigips hat das komplette Angebot für den Innenausbau...
für Wand- und Deckenverkleidungen, Montagewand- und Deckenkonstruktionen und den Dachgeschoßausbau, für alle Anforderungen des Brand-, Schall- und Wärmeschutzes;
für Neu- und Altbauten vom Einfamilienhaus bis zum Großobjekt.
Rigips ist universell und aktuell; Rigips hat den Service für eine ausbaufähige Partnerschaft. Fragen Sie nach Rigips oder sprechen Sie mit uns, wenn es um Innenausbau geht.
Rigips, 3452 Bodenwerder, Tel. 05533/711

Besuchen Sie uns auf der Constructa '78 in Hannover vom 12. bis 22. Februar in Halle 23.

72

73

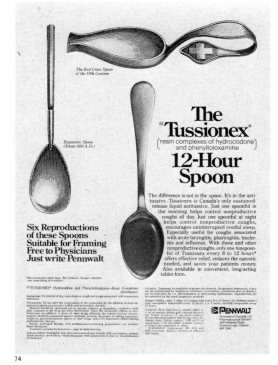

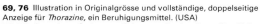

74

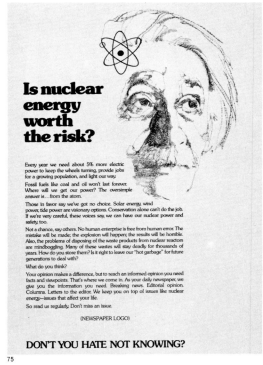

75

69, 76 Illustration in actual size and complete double-spread advertisement for *Thorazine*, a sedative. (USA)
70—72 From a series of black-and-white advertisements for *Rigips* fire, sound, and heat insulation. (GER)
73 Numbered black-and-white ad for a photo laboratory. (USA)
74 Magazine advertisement for a *Pennwalt* cough mixture. Large reproductions of the historical spoons are available. (CAN)
75 From a series of black-and-white advertisements developed by the Newspaper Advertising Bureau for self-promotional purposes of newspapers. The newspaper's heading can be inserted at will. (USA)

69, 76 Illustration in Originalgrösse und vollständige, doppelseitige Anzeige für *Thorazine*, ein Beruhigungsmittel. (USA)
70—72 Aus einer Serie von Schwarzweiss-Anzeigen für *Rigips* Brand-, Schall- und Wärmeisolationen. (GER)
73 Numerierte Schwarzweissanzeige eines Photolabors. (USA)
74 Zeitschriftenanzeige für einen Hustensirup. Grossreproduktionen der historischen Löffel sind erhältlich. (CAN)
75 Aus einer Serie von Schwarzweiss-Anzeigen, die eine Agentur als Eigenwerbung für Tageszeitungen entworfen hat. Der Schriftzug der Zeitung kann nach Belieben eingefügt werden. (USA)

69, 76 Illustration (grandeur nature) et annonce double page complète pour le tranquillisant *Thorazine*. (USA)
70—72 D'une série d'annonces en noir et blanc pour des dispositifs d'isolation acoustique et thermique. (GER)
73 Première annonce d'une série numérotée de *Photo Labs*. (USA)
74 Annonce de magazine pour un sirop contre la toux. Reproductions grand format des cuillères historiques sur demande. (CAN)
75 D'une série d'annonces en noir et blanc qu'une agence a réalisée comme autopromotion pour des journaux. L'entête du journal en question peut être inséré en bas de l'annonce. (USA)

76

ARTIST / KÜNSTLER / ARTISTE:

69, 76 Joan Landis
70—72 Tomi Ungerer
74 Dale Davidson
75 Robert Heindel

DESIGNER / GESTALTER / MAQUETTISTE:

69, 76 Bruno Mease
70—72 Atelier Pütz
73 Patrick Koeller
74 Dennis Frank
75 Lynne Anderson

ART DIRECTOR / DIRECTEUR ARTISTIQUE:

69, 76 J. Robert Parker
70—72 Robert Pütz
74 Dennis Frank
75 Tom Clemente

AGENCY / AGENTUR / AGENCE – STUDIO:

69, 76 Smith Kline & French Labs.
70—72 Robert Pütz GmbH & Co.
73 BBDM, Inc.
74 Sieber & McIntyre, Inc.
75 Newspaper Advertising Bureau

You could buy a new car, announce your daughter's engagement, sell the puppies, locate a temporary job, find the right apartment, find a Victorian hat rack, plant your garden, locate a convenient marina, bid on a Samurai sword, get help finding a job, sell your stereopticon slides, hire a programmer, find a split-level in Queens, sell your share of the business, sell your stamp collection, fix up the back porch, make a list of restaurants to try, sign up for cooking lessons, get catalogues from colleges, buy a health food restaurant.

The New New York Times

We've got what you want... right where you live.

77

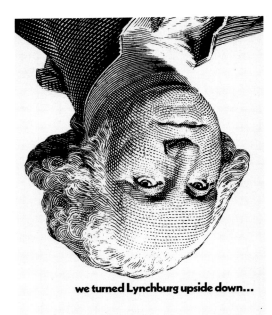

we turned Lynchburg upside down...

FIDELITY
NATIONAL BANK

78

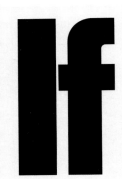

If there had never been an OPEC oil embargo, fuel might not have increased from $3 a barrel to $13.

If environmental laws had not required the conversion of generating facilities from coal to oil, the embargo wouldn't have had such a devastating effect.

If the cost of a new power station had not increased from $73 million in the early 1970's to $232 million in 1980, the rates you pay would be lower. The same size station will cost $475 million in 1987.

If the cost of borrowing money had not increased from 7% in 1968 to over 9% today, new facilities would cost less.

If wages, materials and practically everything else that goes into providing your electric service had not increased, we would be able to serve you for less.

If it only took a year or two to plan and build new generating facilities, rather than ten or more, we would not have to worry about too much or too little generating capacity.

These and other "ifs" show clearly why costs have increased and... "if" something isn't done to cut inflation, enact a sound national energy policy, and streamline time consuming regulatory procedures for power station construction, costs will continue to climb.

We need your understanding of the costs involved in providing your electric service today.

Delmarva
Power

79

---

77 Black-and-white advertisement of the *New York Times,* introducing a new regional advertising section. (USA)
78 Black-and-white advertisement of the Fidelity National Bank with an invitation to the public as well as prospective customers to come to the inauguration and look around the new branch office in Lynchburg. (USA)
79 Black-and-white newspaper advertisement of an electricity firm. (USA)
80, 81 Newspaper advertisement and illustration for *Hanson Trust,* a management company. Black and white. (GBR)

77 Schwarzweiss-Anzeige der *New York Times,* die einen neuen regionalen Annoncenteil einführte. (USA)
78 «Wir stellten Lynchburg auf den Kopf...» Schwarzweiss-Anzeige einer Bank mit einer Einladung zur Einweihung und Besichtigung der neuen Gebäude in Lynchburg. (USA)
79 Schwarzweisse Zeitungsanzeige einer Elektrizitätsgesellschaft. (USA)
80, 81 «Stellen Sie sich *Hanson Trust* so vor?» Zeitungsanzeige und Illustration einer Management-Firma. Schwarzweiss. (GBR)

77 Annonce de presse noir-blanc du *New York Times* qui introduit une rubrique régionale de petites annonces. (USA)
78 «Lynchburg sera mis la tête en bas...» Annonce de presse en noir et blanc publiée par une banque: invitation à l'inauguration de son nouveau bâtiment à Lynchburg. (USA)
79 Annonce noir-blanc d'une compagnie d'électricité. (USA)
80, 81 «C'est ainsi que vous voyez *Hanson Trust?»* Annonce de presse et illustration pour une compagnie de direction et de gestion. (GBR)

ARTIST / KÜNSTLER / ARTISTE:

77 Elwood Smith
80, 81 Ronald Searle

DESIGNER / GESTALTER / MAQUETTISTE:

77 Peter Schaefer
78 Dick Athey
79 Richard L. Downes

ART DIRECTOR / DIRECTEUR ARTISTIQUE:

77 Andrew Kner
78 Dick Athey
79 Richard L. Downes
80, 81 Charles Cooper

AGENCY / AGENTUR / AGENCE – STUDIO:

78 Webb & Athey, Inc.
79 de Martin-Marona-Cranstoun-Downes
80, 81 Allen, Brady & Marsh Ltd.

Advertisements

Is this how you see Hanson Trust?

80

82, 83 Newspaper advertisements from a campaign launched by the Toyota Motor Sales Co. for greater safety on the roads. (JPN)
84, 85 Newspaper advertisements from a safety campaign initiated by *Toyota*. (JPN)
86 Black-and-white advertisement of a packing company. (USA)
87 Newspaper ad from a prestige campaign by the Toshiba Electric Co. Ltd. (JPN)
88 Newspaper advertisement of a building and property-agent company which is looking for buyers for new houses built in colonial style. (USA)
89 "More warmth, less work." Newspaper ad for triple insulating glass. Full colour. (SWE)

82, 83 Zeitungsanzeigen aus einer von der Toyota Motor Sales Co. lancierten Kampagne für grössere Sicherheit auf der Strasse. (JPN)
84, 85 Zeitungsanzeige aus einer von *Toyota* lancierten Sicherheitskampagne. (JPN)
86 Schwarzweiss-Anzeige eines Unternehmens der Verpackungsbranche. (USA)
87 Zeitungsanzeige aus einer Prestigekampagne der Toshiba Electric Co. Ltd. (JPN)
88 Zeitungsanzeige eines Bau- und Liegenschaftenvermittlungs-Unternehmens, das hier Käufer für ein im Kolonialstil gebautes Neubauquartier sucht. (USA)
89 «Mehr Wärme, weniger Arbeit.» Zeitungsanzeige für dreifaches Isolierglas. Mehrfarbig. (SWE)

82, 83 Annonces de magazines figurant dans une campagne de sécurité routière patronnée par la Toyota Motor Sales Co. Ltd. (JPN)
84, 85 Annonces de presse d'une campagne de sécurité routière lancée par *Toyota*. (JPN)
86 Annonce en noir et blanc publiée par une fabrique de conditionnements. (USA)
87 Annonce de journal tirée d'une campagne de prestige lancée par *Toshiba Electric*. (JPN)
88 Annonce de presse d'une compagnie de construction et de gérance immobilière qui vend des maisons situées dans un quartier construit dans le style colonial. (USA)
89 «Plus de chaleur, moins de travail.» Annonce pour un verre d'isolation. (SWE)

ARTIST / KÜNSTLER / ARTISTE:

82, 83 Makoto Wada
84, 85 Kenji Sekido
87 Nobuki Sato
88 Cameron Gerlach
89 Nicola Amandonico

82

83

DESIGNER / GESTALTER / MAQUETTISTE:

82, 83 Yuji Tokoi/Koichi Yoshiizumi
84, 85 Kenji Sekido
86 Jeff A. Barnes
87 Junsei Kubota
88 Charles B. Clark

ART DIRECTOR / DIRECTEUR ARTISTIQUE:

82, 83 Kazumasa Nagai
84, 85 Hiroshi Tanaka
86 Jeff A. Barnes
87 Takumi Kato
88 Charles B. Clark
89 Allan Jungbeck

84

85

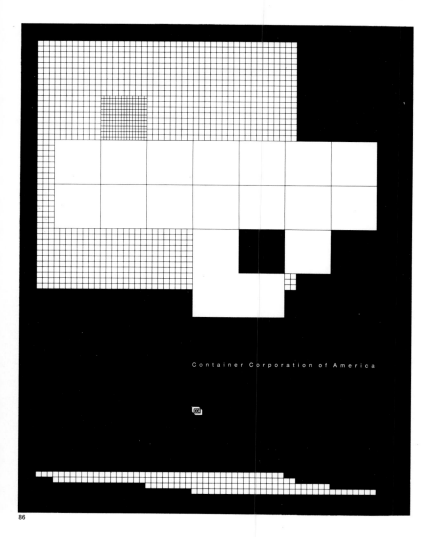

Container Corporation of America

86

AGENCY / AGENTUR / AGENCE – STUDIO:

82–85, 87 Nippon Design Center
86 Container Corporation of America
88 Webb & Athey, Inc.
89 Sören Blanking

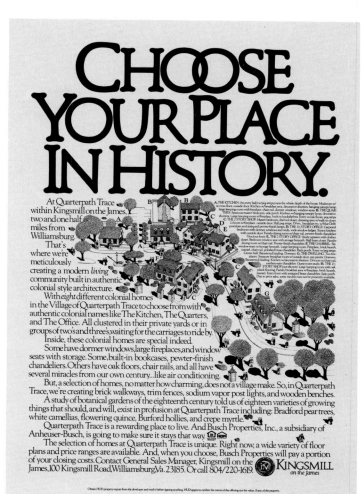

CHOOSE YOUR PLACE IN HISTORY.

88

87

MER VÄRME, MINDRE JOBB.

Emmaboda

89

90, 91 Full-colour newspaper advertisements from a campaign launched by a Tokyo department store, with suggestions for presents for "Father's Day" and "Wedding". (JPN)
92 Black-and-white newspaper advertisement from a long-standing series for *Kikkoman Shoyu*. (JPN)

90, 91 Mehrfarbige Zeitungsanzeigen aus der von einem tokyoter Warenhaus lancierten Werbekampagne, hier mit Geschenkvorschlägen zum «Vatertag» und zur «Hochzeit». (JPN)
92 Schwarzweisse Zeitungsanzeige aus einer langjährigen Serie für *Kikkoman Shoyu*. (JPN)

90, 91 Annonces de journaux (en couleurs) figurant dans la campagne publicitaire d'un grand magasin de Tokyo présentant des cadeaux pour «La fête des pères» et «Le mariage». (JPN)
92 Annonce de presse en noir et blanc d'une longue série pour *Kikkoman Shoyu*. (JPN)

90
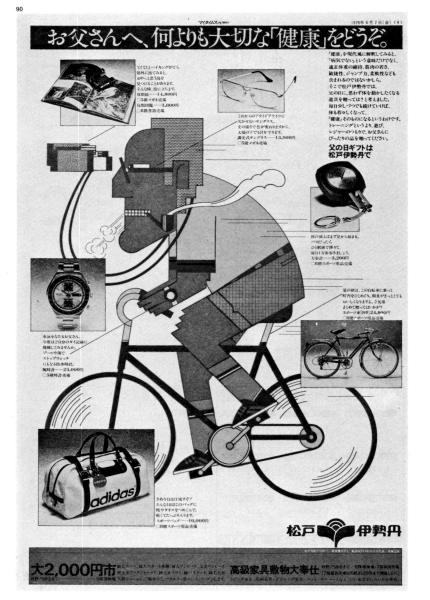

91

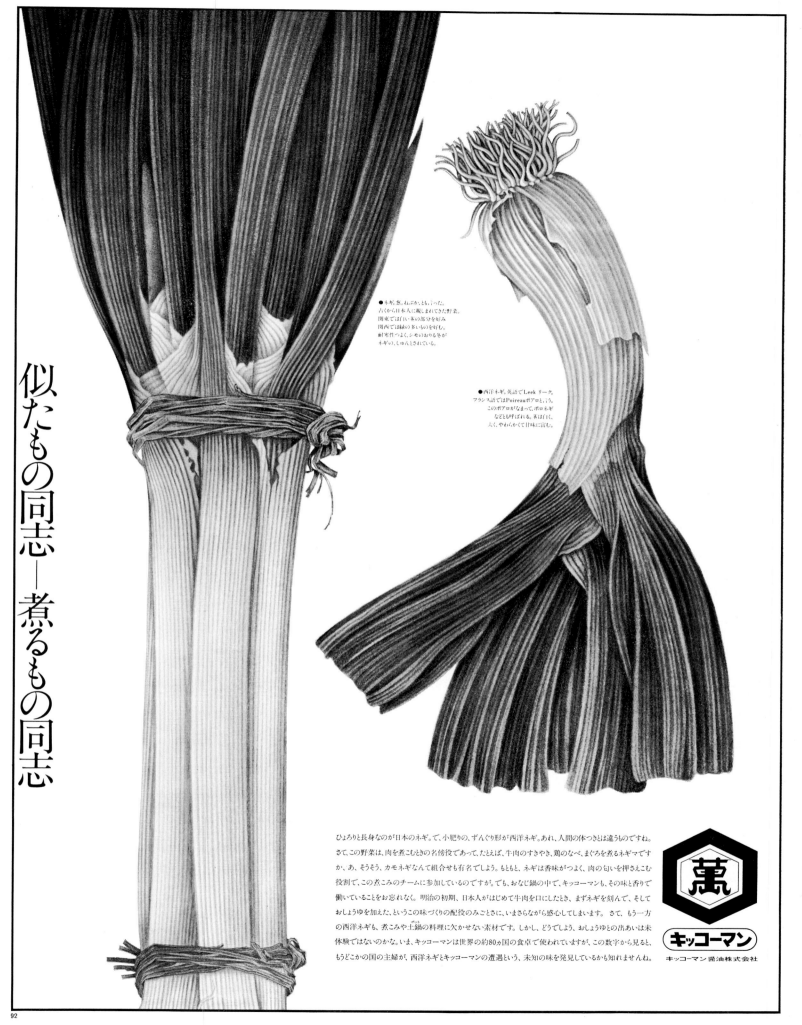

2

Booklets

Folders

Catalogues

Invitations

Programmes

Broschüren

Faltprospekte

Kataloge

Einladungen

Programme

Brochures

Dépliants

Catalogues

Invitations

Programmes

93, 94 Double spread and single page from a brochure for a medicine for the treatment of oedema and heart weakness resulting therefrom. Both illustrations portray Willem Einthoven, the inventor of the electrocardiograph. (USA)
95—98 Full-page black-and-white illustrations and complete double spread from a brochure for *Anafranil*, a sedative manufactured by *Geigy*. (GBR)

93, 94 Doppelseite und einzelne Seite aus einem Prospekt für ein Mittel zur Behandlung von Oedemen und dadurch verursachte Herzschwächen. In beiden Illustrationen sehen wir Willem Einthoven, den Erfinder des Elektrocardiographen. Grün auf Blaugrau, resp. Braun. (USA)
95—98 Ganzseitige Schwarzweiss-Illustrationen und vollständige Doppelseite aus einer Broschüre über die Behandlung von Angstzuständen mit *Anafranil*, einem Beruhigungsmittel von *Geigy*. (GBR)

95

96

93

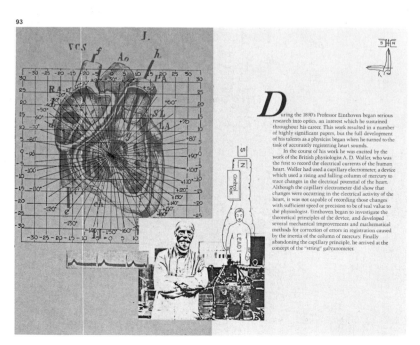

94

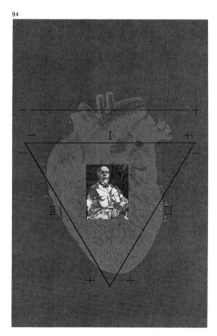

ARTIST / KÜNSTLER / ARTISTE:

93, 94 Jack Freas
95—98 Peter Till

DESIGNER / GESTALTER / MAQUETTISTE:

93, 94 Bruno Mease
95—98 Brian Stones

ART DIRECTOR / DIRECTEUR ARTISTIQUE:

93, 94 A. Neal Siegel
95—98 Brian Stones

AGENCY / AGENTUR / AGENCE – STUDIO:

93, 94 Smith Kline & French Labs.
95—98 Geigy Pharmaceuticals Studio

**Booklets / Prospekte
Brochures**

93, 94 Page double et page figurant dans un prospectus pour un produit pharmaceutique utilisé dans le traitement d'oedèmes et de troubles cardiaques qu'ils provoquent. Les deux illustrations présentent Willem Einthoven, l'inventeur de l'électrocardiographe. (USA)
95—98 Illustrations pleines pages (en noir et blanc) et page double complète d'une brochure sur le traitement d'états d'anxiété à l'aide d'Anafranil, un tranquillisant de Geigy. (GBR)

98

97

Booklets / Prospekte / Brochures

ARTIST / KÜNSTLER / ARTISTE:

101, 102 Dr. Bräuer/Medical Service
105 Eduardo A. Cánovas
106 Omar Tracogna

99

99, 100 Complete cover of a brochure for the broad-spectrum antibiotic *Bactrim*, and illustrations pertaining to it in pale violet, green and blue. (CAN)
101, 102 Illustration in actual size and complete front page of a folding brochure sent to doctors, dealing with a broad-spectrum antibiotic manufactured by *Hoechst* for the treatment of inflammation of the gall-bladder. (GER)
103, 104 Front pages of two press-release folders from *Ciba-Geigy*, dealing with the themes ''Telecommunication and Electricity'' and ''Energy''. The covers in various colours of the brochures inside them have the same design. Fig. 103: Rusty/yellow, 104: Brown/yellow. (USA)
105, 106 From a series of brochures of a pharmaceutical company, here for an antidepressant and a drug for the treatment of intestinal infections. (MEX)

99, 100 Vollständiger Umschlag einer Broschüre für das Breitspektrum-Antibiotikum *Bactrim* und dazugehörige Illustration in Lila, Grün und Blau. (CAN)
101, 102 Illustration in Originalgrösse und vollständige Vorderseite eines an Ärzte versandten Faltprospektes für ein Breitspektrum-Antibiotikum von *Hoechst* zur Behandlung von Entzündungen der Gallenblase. (GER)
103, 104 Vorderseiten von zwei Pressemappen von *Ciba-Geigy* zum Thema «Telekommunikation und Strom» und «Energie». Auf den verschiedenfarbigen Umschlägen der darin enthaltenen Broschüren wiederholt sich das Design. Abb. 103: Rostrot/Gelb, 104: Braun/Gelb. (USA)
105, 106 Aus einer Serie von Broschüren eines Arzneimittelkonzerns, hier für ein Psychopharmakum und ein Mittel gegen Darminfektionen. (MEX)

99, 100 Couverture complète d'une brochure sur *Bactrim*, un antibiotique à large spectre, et son illustration en lilas, vert et bleu. (CAN)
101, 102 Illustration (en grandeur nature) et recto d'un dépliant destiné au corps médical: publicité en faveur d'un antibiotique à large spectre produit par *Hoechst*. Il est utilisé surtout pour le traitement d'inflammations de la vésicule biliaire. (GER)
103, 104 Rectos de deux dossiers de presse publiés par *Ciba-Geigy*. Ils se réfèrent à la télécommunication et à l'énergie. Le même design se retrouve sur les couvertures des dépliants y contenus. Rouille et jaune, resp. brun et jaune. (USA)
105, 106 D'une série de brochures des *Laboratoires Bagó*, ici pour un produit pharmaceutique contre l'entérite et pour un psychotropique. (MEX)

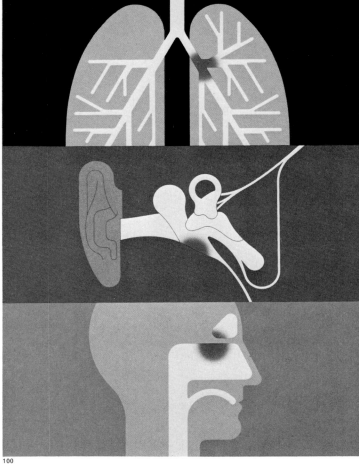
100

DESIGNER / GESTALTER / MAQUETTISTE:

99, 100 Rolf Harder
101, 102 Karl W. Henschel/Bengt Fosshag
103, 104 Sigrid Geissbühler
105, 106 Eduardo A. Cánovas

ART DIRECTOR / DIRECTEUR ARTISTIQUE:

99, 100 Rolf Harder/Karl Hardy
101,102 Karl W. Henschel/Bengt Fosshag
103, 104 Markus Low
105, 106 Eduardo A. Cánovas

103

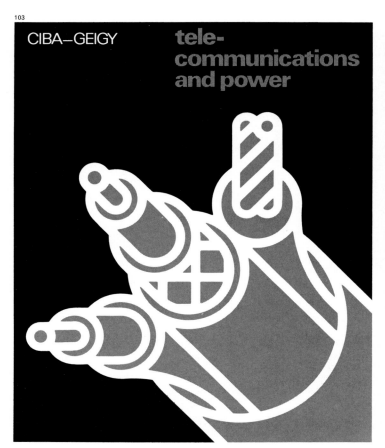

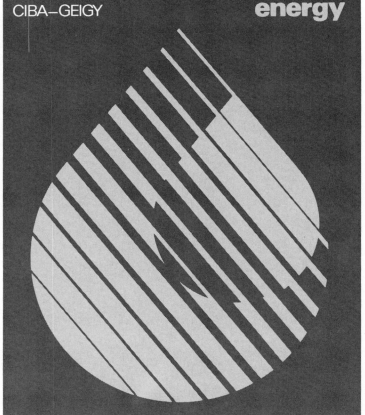
104

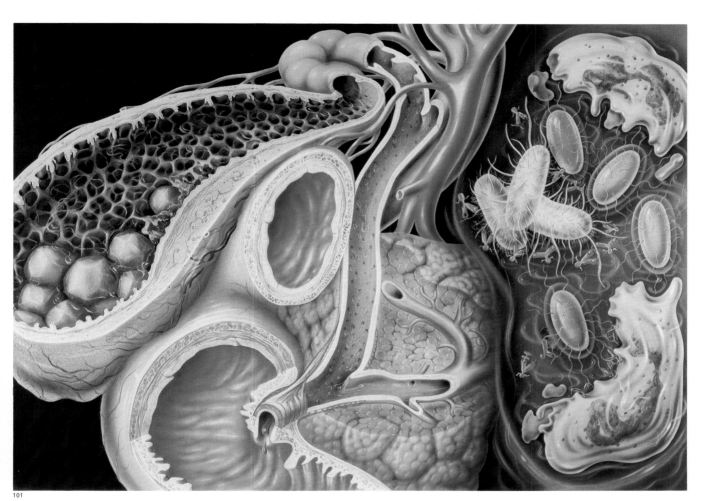

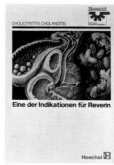

101

102

AGENCY / AGENTUR / AGENCE – STUDIO:

99, 100 Rolf Harder & Assoc.
101, 102 Studio Sign
103, 104 Ciba Geigy/Corporate Art Service
105, 106 Estudio Cánovas

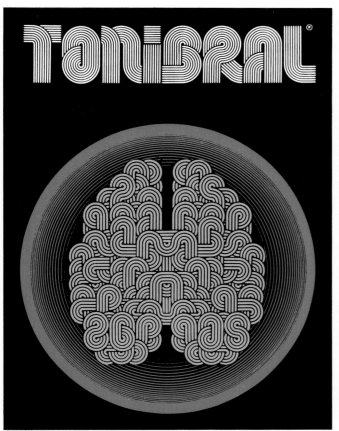

105

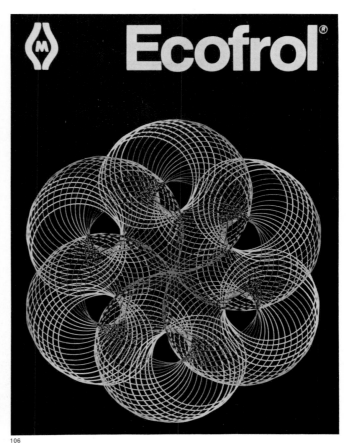

106

ARTIST / KÜNSTLER / ARTISTE:

107, 108 Lutz Reinhardt
109 Claude Luyet
110 D. Nicolaci
111 Seymour Mednick Studio

DESIGNER / GESTALTER / MAQUETTISTE:

107, 108 Lutz Reinhardt
109 Claude Luyet
110 M. Azzariti
111 Lou Gaal

ART DIRECTOR / DIRECTEUR ARTISTIQUE:

107, 108 Lutz Reinhardt
109 Carlo Bonaccorsi
110 G. Brughitta

AGENCY / AGENTUR / AGENCE – STUDIO:

107, 108 Atelier Reinhardt
109 Edelta SA
110 Selenia SpA/Ufficio Pubblicità
111 Mandala

DEGUSSA-MESSTECHNIK

Thermoelemente und Widerstandsthermometer
für Schiffsanlagen und erschwerte Einsatzbedingungen

Degussa ◆

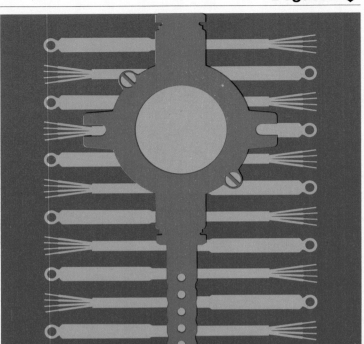

107

DEGUSSA-MESSTECHNIK

Einsteck-Widerstandsthermometer

Degussa ◆

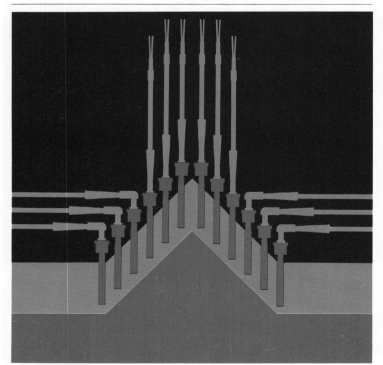

108

109

110

107, 108 Two title pages from a series of catalogues dealing with technical metal products from *Degussa.* (GER)
109 From a series of uniform folding brochures – all with three-dimensional animal motifs – for *Data General* computers. Cuttle-fish in blue, violet and pink.(SWI)
110 A page from the information brochure of a company in the space-travel industry, with illustrations depicting the company's participation, in percentages, in various space projects. Red, black and blue on grey paper. (ITA)
111 Cover illustration in actual size of a *Sperry-Univac* brochure. (USA)

107, 108 Zwei Titelblätter aus einer Serie von Katalogen für technische Metallerzeugnisse von *Degussa*. (GER)
109 Aus einer Serie einheitlich gestalteter Faltprospekte – alle mit dreidimensionalen Tiermotiven – für Computer von *Data General*. Tintenfisch in Blau, Lila und Rosa. (SWI)
110 Seite aus der Informationsbroschüre eines Unternehmens der Raumfahrtindustrie mit Illustrationen, die die prozentuale Beteiligung an verschiedenen Raumfahrtprojekten versinnbildlichen. Rot, schwarz und blau auf grauem Papier. (ITA)
111 Umschlagillustration in Originalgrösse einer Broschüre von *Sperry-Univac*. (USA)

107, 108 Deux couvertures de catalogues figurant dans une série consacrée aux différents produits de métallurgie de *Degussa*. (GER)
109 D'une série de dépliants de conception uniforme – tous avec des motifs d'animaux tridimensionnels – pour une marque d'ordinateurs. Seiche en bleu, lilas et rose. (SWI)
110 Page d'une brochure d'information de la Compagnia Industriale Aerospaziale. Les illustrations symbolisent la participation en pour-cent à divers projets aérospaciaux. Rouge, noir et bleu sur papier gris. (ITA)
111 Illustration de couverture (grandeur nature) d'une brochure de *Sperry-Univac*. (USA)

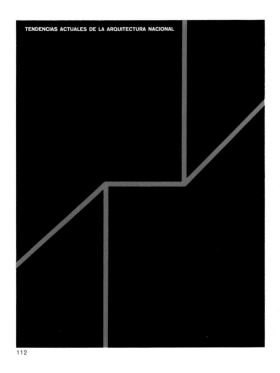

112

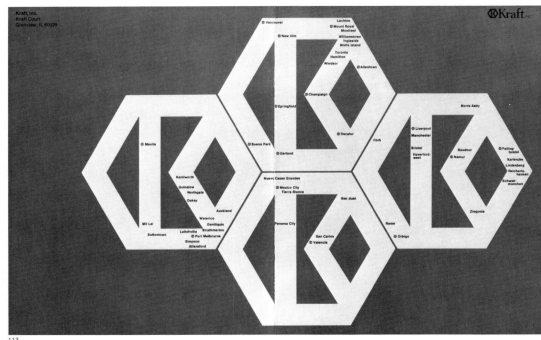

113

ARTIST / KÜNSTLER / ARTISTE:

112 Félix Beltrán
113 Elaine Kobold
116, 117 André François

DESIGNER / GESTALTER / MAQUETTISTE:

112 Félix Beltrán
113 Norman Perman
114 Tiit Telmet
115 Rinaldo Del Sordo/Giuseppe Berlinghieri
118 Russell Tatro
119 Danda Nenzi
120 Bobbi Adair

ART DIRECTOR / DIRECTEUR ARTISTIQUE:

112 Félix Beltrán
113 Norman Perman/Gerald Sweda
114 Gottschalk & Ash
115 Rinaldo Del Sordo/Giuseppe Berlinghieri
116, 117 M. Damiens
118 Frank Rupp
119 Gian Vittorio Plazzogna
120 John William Brown

AGENCY / AGENTUR / AGENCE – STUDIO:

112 Félix Beltrán
113 Norman Perman Inc.
114 Gottschalk & Ash Ltd.
115 Studio Giob
116, 117 Synergie
118 Pepsi-Cola Graphic Arts Dept.
119 Quadragono
120 TV Guide – Promotion Art Dept.

116

HABITAT SOLEIL

117

114

115

118

119

120

112 Cover of a brochure dealing with new trends and tendencies in Cuban architecture. (CUB)
113 Front and back cover of a brochure of the *Kraft* foodstuffs company. Four intertwined company symbols (in silver) as a cover design, with indications (in blue) of production locations. (USA)
114 Cover of a catalogue for *Flexijoint* pipe joints and couplings. Orange, grey and black and white. (CAN)
115 Cover of a folder dealing with components manufactured by *Fiat* for nuclear plants. Grey and dark blue. (ITA)
116, 117 Complete cover and illustration of a folder about new solar energy collectors from *Saint-Gobain*. (FRA)
118 Cover of a programme issued by the *Pepsi-Cola* Management Institute. Dun with dark brown design, white lettering. (USA)
119 Cover of a catalogue effected in yellow shades, for plastic dishes, utensils and food containers. (ITA)
120 Direct-mail folder of a TV magazine about the success of a *Del Monte* advertising campaign published in this periodical. (USA)

112 Umschlag einer Broschüre über neue Tendenzen in der kubanischen Architektur. (CUB)
113 Vorder- und Rückseite des Umschlags der Broschüre einer Nahrungsmittelfirma. Vier aneinandergefügte Firmensymbole (in Silber), mit Angaben der Produktionsstätten (in Blau). (USA)
114 Umschlag eines Katalogs für Rohrverbindungsstücke. Orange, Grau und Schwarzweiss. (CAN)
115 Umschlag eines Faltprospektes über Bestandteile, die *Fiat* für Kernkraftwerke herstellt. Grau und Dunkelblau. (ITA)
116, 117 Umschlag und Illustration eines Faltprospektes über neue Sonnen-Kollektoren von *Saint-Gobain*. (FRA)
118 Kursprogramm des *Pepsi-Cola*-Management-Instituts. Graubraun mit dunkelbraunem Design, weisse Schrift. (USA)
119 In Gelbtönen gehaltener Umschlag eines Katalogs für Plastik-Geschirr und Vorratsbehälter. (ITA)
120 Direktwerbung einer TV-Zeitschrift über den Erfolg einer *DelMonte*-Werbekampagne in diesem Magazin. (USA)

112 Couverture d'une brochure présentant les nouvelles tendances dans l'architecture cubaine. (CUB)
113 Recto et verso de la couverture d'une brochure publiée par une compagnie de produits alimentaires. Quatre marques de fabrique (en argent) avec indications des centres de production (en bleu). (USA)
114 Couverture d'un catalogue pour des raccords de tuyaux. Orange, gris et noir-blanc. (CAN)
115 Couverture d'un dépliant sur les pièces détachées que *Fiat* fabrique pour les centrales nucléaires. Gris, bleu foncé. (ITA)
116, 117 Couverture complète et illustration d'un dépliant sur les capteurs solaires de *Saint-Gobain*. (FRA)
118 Couverture du programme des cours de l'Institut de Management *Pepsi-Cola*. Design en brun foncé sur brun gris. (USA)
119 Couverture d'un catalogue présentant la gamme des services en plastique. Prédominance de tons jaunes. (ITA)
120 Publicité directe d'une revue TV sur le succès d'une campagne publicitaire qui a paru dans cette revue. (USA)

THE HARBOR

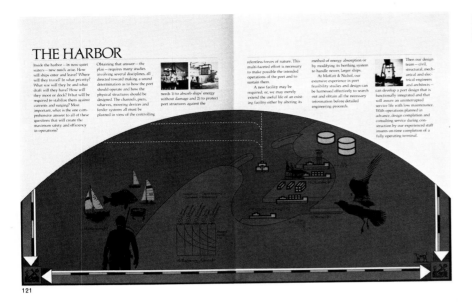

Inside the harbor — in now-quiet waters — new needs arise. How will ships enter and leave? Where will they travel? In what priority? What size will they be and what draft will they have? How will they moor or dock? What will be required to stabilize them against currents and surging? Most important, what is the one comprehensive answer to all of these questions that will create the maximum safety and efficiency in operations?

Obtaining that answer — the plan — requires many studies involving several disciplines, all directed toward making a sound determination as to how the port should operate and how the physical structures should be designed. The channels, piers, wharves, mooring devices and fender systems all must be planned in view of the controlling needs 1) to absorb ships' energy without damage and 2) to protect port structures against the relentless forces of nature. This multi-faceted effort is necessary to make possible the intended operations of the port and to sustain them.

A new facility may be required; or, we may merely extend the useful life of an existing facility either by altering its method of energy absorption or by modifying its berthing system to handle newer, larger ships.

At Moffatt & Nichol, our extensive experience in port feasibility studies and design can be harnessed effectively to search out and obtain all the necessary information before detailed engineering proceeds.

Then our design team — civil, structural, mechanical and electrical engineers and architects — can develop a port design that is functionally integrated and that will assure an uninterrupted service life with low maintenance. With operations planned in advance, design completion and consulting service during construction by our experienced staff insures on-time completion of a fully operating terminal.

121

ARTIST / KÜNSTLER / ARTISTE:

121 Douglas Reeder/Chikako Matsubayashi
122, 124, 125 Bengt Fosshag

DESIGNER / GESTALTER / MAQUETTISTE:

121 Don Weller/Chikako Matsubayashi
122, 124, 125 Karl W. Henschel/Bengt Fosshag
123 Stephen Cole
126 Harry O. Diamond
127 Joseph Boggs

ART DIRECTOR / DIRECTEUR ARTISTIQUE:

121 Don Weller
122, 124, 125 Karl W. Henschel/Bengt Fosshag
126 Harry O. Diamond
127 Joseph Boggs

AGENCY / AGENTUR / AGENCE – STUDIO:

121 The Weller Institute for the Cure of Design
122, 124, 125 Studio Sign
127 Joseph Boggs

122

126

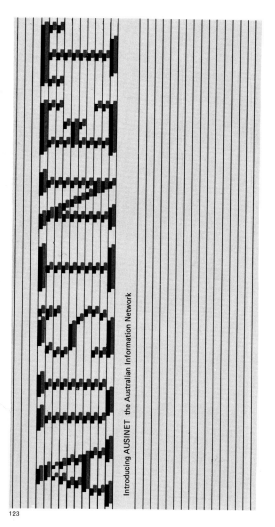

123

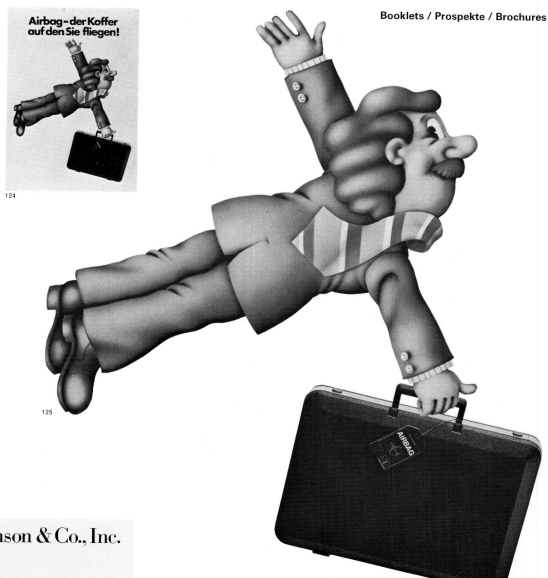

Airbag – der Koffer auf den Sie fliegen!

124

125

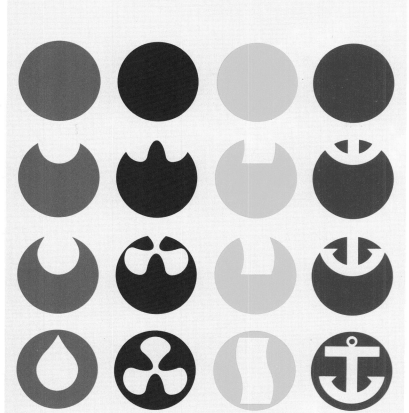

A. Johnson & Co., Inc.

127

121 Double spread from a brochure of a company specializing in the construction of ports and harbours. Dark blue sea, olive-green land. (USA)
122 Example from an information series by *Asche* pharmaceuticals, distributed for many years to doctors, dealing here with the pill. Full-colour illustration. (GER)
123 Front page of a folder issued by the Australian National Library about its new computer service. Red and black on light beige paper. (AUS)
124, 125 Complete front page and illustration (in actual size) of a small-format folder advertising *Airbag* cases. (GER)
126 Double spread from an *Exxon* brochure devoted to the detailed account of energy supply from the beginning until the present. Full colour on blue surface. (USA)
127 Cover of a brochure for A. Johnson & Co., Inc. The symbols pertain to the various branches of production. Red, blue, yellow and green. (USA)

121 Doppelseite aus der Broschüre eines Unternehmens, das sich auf den Bau von Hafenanlagen spezialisiert hat. Dunkelblaues Meer, olivgrünes Land. (USA)
122 Beispiel aus einer seit Jahren an Ärzte verteilten Informationsserie des Arzneimittelherstellers *Asche*, hier zum Thema Pille. Mehrfarbige Illustration. (GER)
123 Vorderseite eines Faltprospektes, der den neuen, von der australischen Nationalbibliothek eingeführten Computer-Dienst vorstellt. Rot und Schwarz auf hellbeigem Papier. (AUS)
124, 125 Vollständige Vorderseite und Illustration (in Originalgrösse) eines kleinformatigen Faltprospektes für *Airbag*-Koffer. (GER)
126 Doppelseite aus einer Broschüre von *Exxon,* die vollständig der Entwicklung der Energieversorgung, von den Anfängen bis heute, gewidmet ist. Mehrfarbig auf blauem Grund. (USA)
127 Umschlag der Broschüre eines diversifizierten Industriebetriebes. Die Symbole beziehen sich auf die Produktionszweige: Petrochemie (rot), Schiff- und Maschinenbau (blau), Metallverarbeitung (gelb) und Transport (Grün). (USA)

121 Page double tirée de la brochure d'une entreprise qui s'est spécialisée sur la construction d'installations portuaires. Mer en bleu foncé, paysage vert olive. (USA)
122 Exemple d'une série de dépliants d'information qu'une compagnie de produits pharmaceutiques adresse au corps médical. Sujet: la contraception. Illustration polychrome. (GER)
123 Recto d'un dépliant présentant le nouveau service électronique récemment établi par la Bibliothèque Nationale australienne. Rouge et noir sur papier beige. (AUS)
124, 125 Couverture complète et illustration (en grandeur originale) d'un petit dépliant pour les valises *Airbag*. (GER)
126 Page double d'une brochure d'*Exxon,* consacrée entièrement au développement de l'alimentation en énergie. Polychromie sur fond bleu. (USA)
127 Couverture de la brochure d'une compagnie industrielle largement diversifiée. Les symboles se réfèrent aux divers domaines de production: pétrochimie (rouge), construction navale et mécanique (bleu), métallurgie (jaune) et transport (vert). (USA)

128, 129 Front page and illustration (actual size) from a series of folders issued by the *Aargauer Tagblatt* (Aargau daily paper) as space promotion items. (SWI)
130 Title page of the concert programme of the Bavarian Radio. Illustrations in colour. (GER)
131 From an *Itel* prospectus concerning a 10-year jubilee cruise organized for employees. (USA)
132 Title page (brown shades) of a paper-mill's catalogue. (CSR)
133, 134 Front and back page of a concertina-type folder for a newly opened shopping-centre. Full-colour illustrations. (GBR)

128, 129 Vorderseite und Illustration (Originalgrösse) aus einer Serie von Faltprospekten, die das *Aargauer Tagblatt* als Anzeigenwerbung verschickt. (SWI)
130 Titelseite des Konzert-Programms des *Bayerischen Rundfunks*. Illustrationen in Farbe. (GER).
131 Aus dem Prospekt über die von *Itel* für die Angestellten organisierte Kreuzfahrt zum 10jährigen Jubiläum, hier mit Anspielungen auf Tennis und Spielkasinos. (USA)
132 Titelblatt (in Brauntönen) des Katalogs einer Papierfabrik. (CSR)
133, 134 Vorder- und Rückseite eines Leporello-Prospektes für ein neueröffnetes Einkaufszentrum. Mehrfarbige Illustrationen. (GBR)

128, 129 Recto et illustration d'un dépliant figurant dans une série promotionnelle distribuée par un quotidien du canton de l'Argovie. (SWI)
130 Couverture du programme des concerts présentés par la radiodiffusion bavaroise. Illustration en couleurs. (GER)
131 Page double d'une brochure consacrée à la croisière offerte par l'Itel Corp. à son personnel à l'occasion de son 10e anniversaire, ici avec référence au tennis et aux casinos. (USA)
132 Couverture d'un catalogue publié par une papeterie. Prédominance de tons bruns. (CSR)
133, 134 Recto et verso d'un dépliant en accordéon présentant un nouveau centre commercial. Illustrations en couleurs. (GBR)

128

130

129

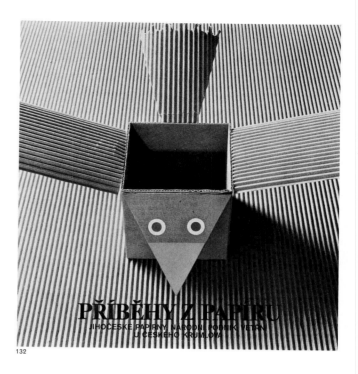

131

132

133

134

ART DIRECTOR / DIRECTEUR ARTISTIQUE:

128, 129 Edmond M. Seiler
131 John Casado
133, 134 Alan Fletcher

AGENCY / AGENTUR / AGENCE – STUDIO:

128, 129 Werbeabt. Aargauer Tagblatt AG
131 Casado Ltd.
133, 134 Pentagram

Booklets / Prospekte / Brochures

67

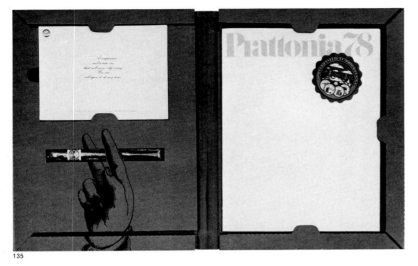

135

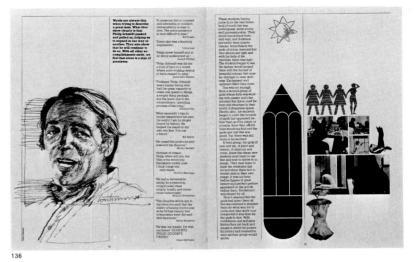

136

137

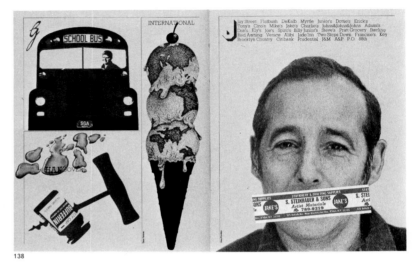

138

139

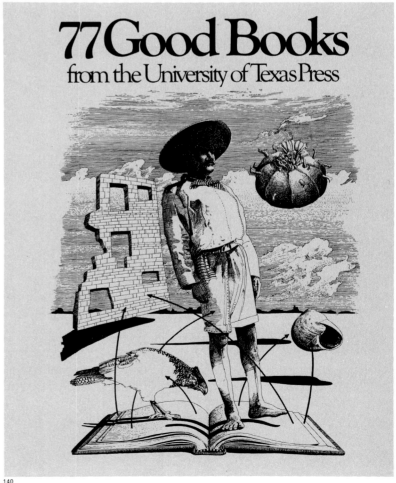

140

ARTIST / KÜNSTLER / ARTISTE:

136 Gerry Contreras
138 Diana Vasquez/Doug Wonders
139 Judy Pensky/Ozzie Simmonds
140–142 Ed Lindlof

DESIGNER / GESTALTER / MAQUETTISTE:

135–139 J. Michael McGinn/S. Gresh
140–142 Richard Hendel

ART DIRECTOR / DIRECTEUR ARTISTIQUE:

135–139 J. Michael McGinn/S. Gresh
140–142 Richard Hendel

AGENCY / AGENTUR / AGENCE – STUDIO:

140–142 Ed Lindlof

141

135—139 Examples from the annual report made up by students from the Pratt Institute in New York. Fig. 135: open package made of corrugated cardboard with a real cigar and report in silver-grey. Other images show double spreads from the front part of the report, where the different departments are presented, and the back part in which "Et-ceteras" are shown in alphabetical sequence in picture form. (USA)
140—142 Title page, illustration and double spread from a catalogue published by the University of Texas Press in which 77 books are given a short review. Black-and-white illustrations. (USA)

135—139 Beispiele aus dem von den Studenten des Pratt Institute in New York gestalteten jährlichen Bericht. Abb. 135: geöffnete Verpackung aus braunem Wellkarton mit echter Zigarre und Bericht in Silbergrau. Die übrigen Abbildungen zeigen Doppelseiten aus dem vorderen Teil des Berichtes, wo die verschiedenen Abteilungen vorgestellt werden, und dem hinteren Teil, in welchem «Et-ceteras» in alphabetischer Reihenfolge bildlich dargestellt werden. (USA)
140—142 Titelblatt, Illustration und Doppelseite aus einem auf Zeitungspapier gedruckten Katalog, in welchem 77 Bücher kurz besprochen werden. Schwarzweisse Illustrationen. (USA)

135—139 Exemples figurant dans le rapport que les étudiants de l'Institut Pratt de New York publient chaque année. Fig. 135: emballage en carton brun avec une vraie cigare et le rapport (à droite) en argent. Les autres illustrations présentent des pages doubles du rapport qui est consacré aux divers départements de l'institut (fig. 136, 137) et de la deuxième partie où sont présentés des «Et-ceteras» par ordre alphabétique. (USA)
140—142 Couverture, illustration et page double d'un catalogue contenant des comptes rendus de 77 livres. Catalogue imprimé sur le papier de journal. Illustrations en noir et blanc. (USA)

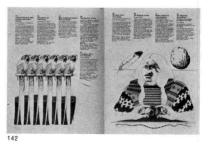

142

Booklets / Prospekte / Brochures

143

144

EMORY & HENRY COLLEGE 7879

145

146

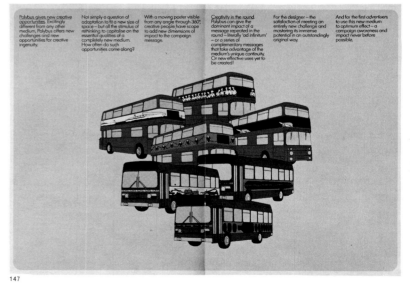

148

147

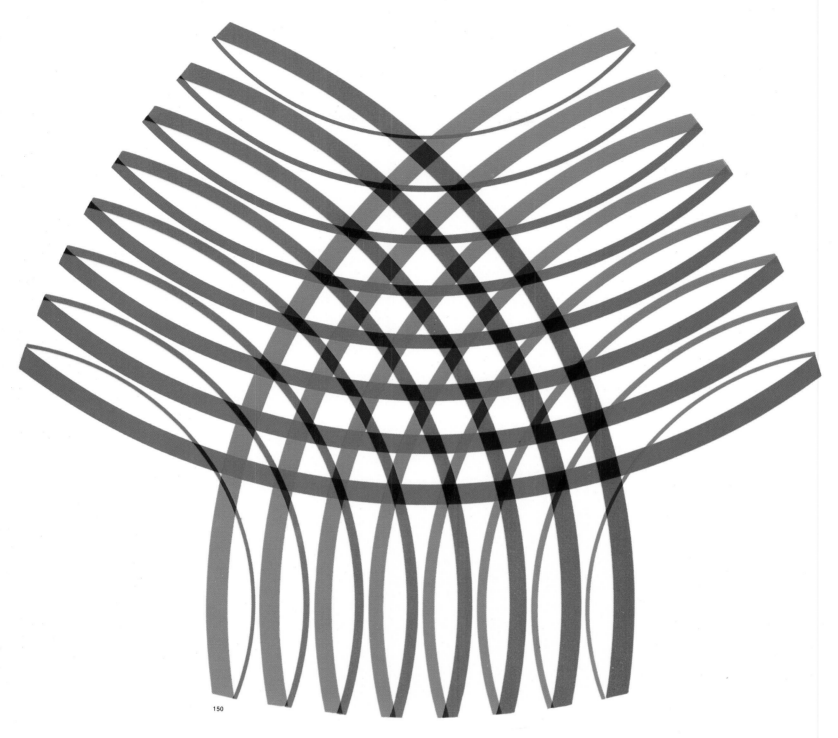

150

149

143, 144 Cover and double spread from a brochure by a diversified industrial concern showing contrasts between old and new. (USA)
145, 146 Cover and double spread from an Emory and Henry College prospectus. Lettering in ruby-red and black on beige paper. (USA)
147, 148 Double spreads from a brochure dealing with new advertising possibilities on buses. Fig. 148: Bus in blue and green on yellowish paper. (GBR)
149 Information folder issued by *Fortune* dealing with management and banking. (USA)
150, 151 Co-ordination of three computer systems for the German Post. (GER)

143, 144 Umschlag und Doppelseite aus der Broschüre eines diversifizierten Industriebetriebes mit Gegenüberstellung von alten Xylographien und Aufnahmen der entsprechenden modernen Produkte. (USA)
145, 146 Umschlag und Doppelseite aus einem Vorlesungsverzeichnis. (USA)
147, 148 Doppelseiten aus einer Broschüre über neue Werbemöglichkeiten an Autobussen. Abb. 148: Autobusse in Blau und Grün auf gelblichem Papier. (GBR)
149 Informationsmappe zum Thema Unternehmensführung und Bankwesen. (USA)
150, 151 Das Design symbolisiert die Koordination von drei EDV-Systemen durch die Deutsche Bundespost. (GER)

143, 144 Couverture et page double de la brochure d'une compagnie industrielle largement diversifiée. (USA)
145, 146 Couverture et page double du programme des cours d'une université. (USA)
147, 148 Pages doubles figurant dans une brochure sur la publicité d'autobus. Fig. 148: bus en bleu et vert sur papier jaunâtre. (GBR)
149 Couverture d'un dossier d'information sur l'administration et les banques, publié par le magazine économique *Fortune*. (USA)
150, 151 L'illustration de couverture symbolise la coordination de trois systèmes électroniques par les P & T allemandes. (GER)

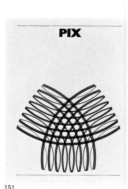

151

**Booklets / Prospekte
Brochures**

152

153

157

158

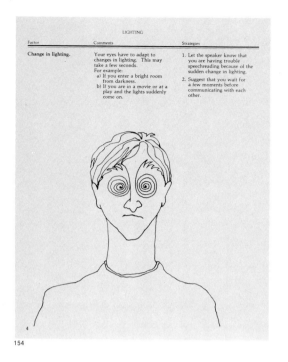

154

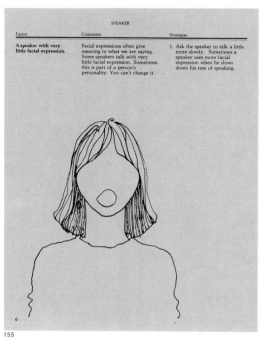

155

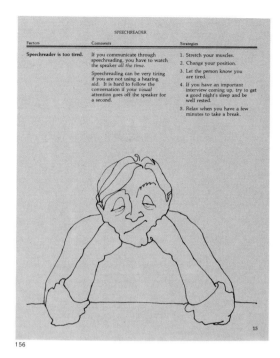

156

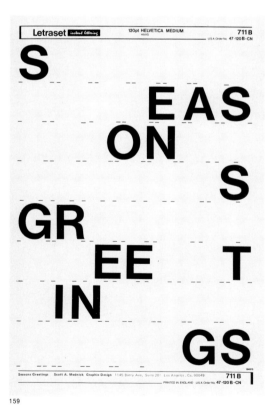

159

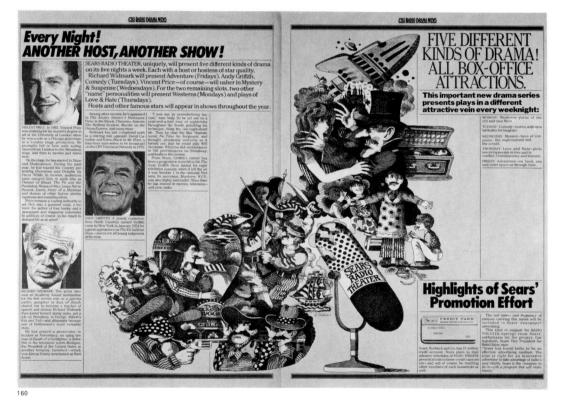

160

152 Cover of a *Haymarket* professional manual for school-leavers and college graduates. Bright pastel shades. (GBR)
153 Invitation to a matinée in honour of the 150th birthday of Henry Dunant, founder of the *Red Cross*. (SWI)
154–156 Three pages from a brochure by the National Technical Institute for the Deaf aimed at deaf students with tips for improving their ability to read. Black on beige paper. (USA)
157 Space-promotional folder distributed by *TV Guide*, a television periodical, to shopping-centres. (USA)
158 Postcard as season-ticket advertisement for the children's theatre in Bergisch Gladbach. Black and white, pink, green. (GER)
159 Christmas card from *Letraset*. Black and white. (USA)
160 Inside page from a large-format folder for radio advertising, coupled with a new dramatic series broadcast from a department store. (USA)

152 Umschlag eines *Haymarket*-Berufshandbuchs für Schul- und College-Abgänger. Helle Pastelltöne. (GBR)
153 Einladung zu einer Matinee anlässlich des 150. Geburtstages von Henry Dunant, dem Gründer des *Roten Kreuzes*. (SWI)
154–156 Drei Seiten aus einer Broschüre, die sich an taube Studenten wendet und Tips zur Verbesserung der Ablesefertigkeit enthält. Schwarz auf beigem Papier. (USA)
157 Faltprospekt, den eine TV-Zeitschrift als Anzeigenwerbung an Einkaufszentren verteilte. (USA)
158 Postkarte als Abonnentenwerbung des Kindertheaters der Stadt Bergisch Gladbach. Schwarzweiss, rosa und blaugrün. (GER)
159 Weihnachtskarte der Firma *Letraset*. Schwarzweiss. (USA)
160 Innenseite eines grossformatigen Faltprospektes für Radiowerbung im Anschluss an eine neue, von einem Warenhaus lancierte dramatische Sendereihe. (USA)

152 Couverture d'un guide d'orientation professionnelle *Haymarket*. Aplats pastels. (GBR)
153 Invitation à la matinée organisée lors du 150e anniversaire de Henri Dunant, fondateur de la *Croix-Rouge*. (SWI)
154–156 Trois pages d'une brochure destinée aux étudiants sourds: elle leur donne quelques propositions afin qu'il puissent communiquer plus facilement avec les autres. (USA)
157 Dépliant distribué dans un supermarché en tant que publicité promotionnelle d'une revue de TV. (USA)
158 Carte postale distribuée en faveur des abonnements d'un théâtre pour les enfants. Noir-blanc, rose et bleu vert. (GER)
159 Carte de Noël de *Letraset*. Noir et blanc. (USA)
160 Panneau intérieur d'un dépliant grand format pour la publicité à la radio à la suite d'une série d'émissions dramatiques diffusée sous le patronat d'un grand magasin. (USA)

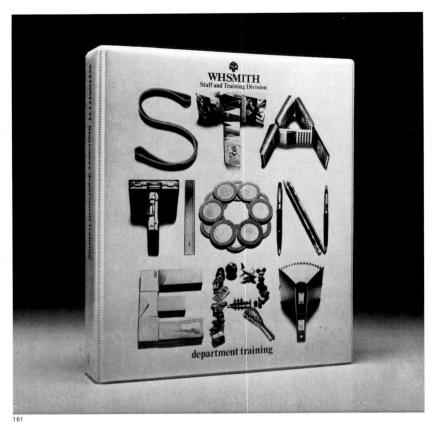

161

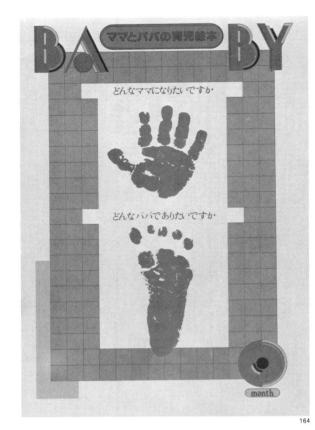

164

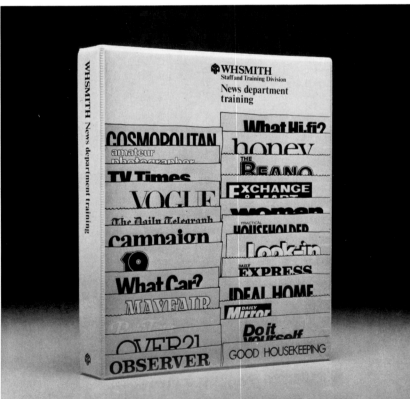

162

163

165

166

167

161, 162 Two manuals for the personnel training of the W.H. Smith department store, here for the stationery section and for the selling of newspapers and magazines. (GBR)
163 Cover of a brochure commemorating the 20th anniversary of Gulf and Western Industries, Inc. White with embossed northern hemisphere, red title, number "2" in black. (USA)
164—167 Cover and inside pages of a catalogue for baby articles, accessories, perambulators and furniture. Figs. 164 and 167 full colour. Figs. 165, 166: view with gatefold and complete spread in blue, white and silver. (JPN)

161, 162 Zwei Ringhefter für die Personalschulung eines Warenhauses, hier für die Papeteriewaren-Abteilung und für den Verkauf von Zeitungen und Zeitschriften. (GBR)
163 Umschlag einer Broschüre zum 20jährigen Bestehen eines diversifizierten Industrieunternehmens. Weiss mit blindgeprägter nördlicher Hemisphäre, Titel rot, «2» schwarz. (USA)
164—167 Umschlag und Innenseiten eines Katalogs für Baby-Artikel, Accessoires, Kinderwagen und -möbel. Abb. 164 und 167 mehrfarbig. Abb. 165, 166: Ansicht mit zurückgefalztem Ausleger und vollständig ausgelegte Seite in Blau, Weiss und Silber. (JPN)

161, 162 Couvertures de deux dossiers publiés par un grand magasin pour l'instruction du personnel, ici pour la vente d'articles de papeterie et de journaux et magazines. (GBR)
163 Couverture d'une brochure qui a paru à l'occasion du 20 anniversaire d'une compagnie industrielle. Blanc avec l'hémisphère boréal gaufré à sec, titre rouge, chiffre «2» en noir. (USA)
164—167 Couverture et pages intérieures figurant dans un catalogue pour des articles et accessoires de bébés, des voitures et meubles pour enfants. Figs. 164 et 167 en polychromie. Figs. 165 et 166: vue de la page avec partie repliée et page complètement dépliée en bleu, blanc et argent. (JPN)

ARTIST / KÜNSTLER / ARTISTE:

164—167 Kumiko Nagasaki

DESIGNER / GESTALTER / MAQUETTISTE:

161, 162 Ian James Wright
163 Sheldon Seidler/Irene Liberman
164—167 Kenzo Nakagawa/Hiro Nobuyama/
Satch Morikami/Tack Myoshi

ART DIRECTOR / DIRECTEUR ARTISTIQUE:

161, 162 Jan James Wright
163 Sheldon Seidler
164—167 Kenzo Nakagawa

AGENCY / AGENTUR / AGENCE – STUDIO:

161, 162 Guyatt/Jenkins
163 Sheldon Seidler Inc.
164—167 Nippon Design Center

Booklets / Prospekte / Brochures

III
L'IMPERATRICE

168

XX
IL GIUDIZIO

169

XII
L'APPESO

170

XIV
LA TEMPERANZA

171

XV
IL DIAVOLO

172

XVI
LA TORRE

173

VIII
LA GIUSTIZIA

174

XXI
IL MONDO

175

168–175 From a series of cards which resemble playing cards. They were distributed at a film festival instead of normal programmes and on the back of each is a short review of the films in question. (ITA)
176, 177 Recto and verso of the menu at the *O'Henry* restaurant in Zurich. Fig. 176: blue, white and red; Fig. 177: blue and white. (SWI)
178 Cover of a brochure in which the winners of the MVP awards offered by the Pepsi-Cola Company are presented. (USA)
179, 180 Invitation sent by *Lacoste* (open and folded) to prospective visitors to a stand at a sports clothes trade fair. (GER)

168–175 Aus einer Serie von Karten, deren Aufmachung an Spielkarten erinnert. Sie wurden anstelle von Programmheften an einem Filmfestival abgegeben und bringen auf der Rückseite, jeweils unter einem Begriff zusammengefasst, kurze Besprechungen der Filme. (ITA)
176, 177 Aussen- und Innenseite der Menukarte des Restaurants *O'Henry* in Zürich. Abb. 176: blau, weiss und rot; Abb. 177: blau und weiss. (SWI)
178 Umschlag einer Broschüre, in welcher die Gewinner des MVP-Award aufgeführt sind. (USA)
179, 180 Von *Lacoste* verschickte Einladung (geöffnet und zusammengelegt), ihren Stand an einer Sportbekleidungs-Messe zu besuchen. (GER)

168–175 D'une série de cartes dont la conception rapelle des cartes à jouer. Ces cartes ont été distribuées au lieu de programmes lors d'un festival du film à Rome. Les films résumés au verso des cartes ont été réunis sous divers aspects (justice, diable etc.). (ITA)
176, 177 Panneaux intérieurs et extérieurs du menu du restaurant *O'Henry* à Zurich. Fig. 176: bleu, blanc et rouge; fig. 177: bleu et blanc. (SWI)
178 Couverture d'une brochure dans laquelle figurent tous les lauréats d'un concours organisé par la Pepsi-Cola Co. (USA)
179, 180 Invitation (ouverte et pliée) de visiter le stand de *Lacoste*, fabricant de vêtements, à une foire de vêtements de sport. (GER)

Booklets / Prospekte / Brochures

176

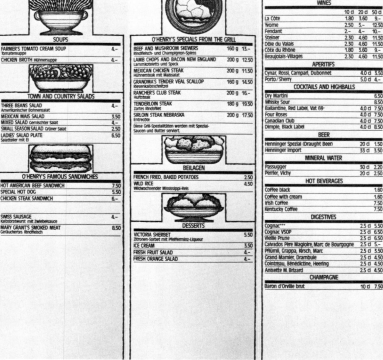

177

1978 MVP Awards

178

ARTIST / KÜNSTLER / ARTISTE:

168–175 Giuliano Vittori
179, 180 Dietrich Ebert

DESIGNER / GESTALTER / MAQUETTISTE:

168–175 Giuliano Vittori
176, 177 Lisbeth Wessbecher
178 Russell Tatro
179, 180 Dietrich Ebert

ART DIRECTOR / DIRECTEUR ARTISTIQUE:

176, 177 Lisbeth Wessbecher
178 Frank Rupp
179, 180 Dietrich Ebert

AGENCY / AGENTUR / AGENCE – STUDIO:

168–175 Giuliano Vittori
176, 177 Studio 3 Karpfen
178 Pepsi-Cola Graphic Arts Dept.
179, 180 Alain Fion

179

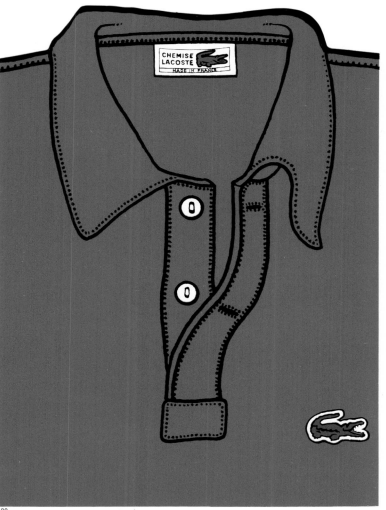

180

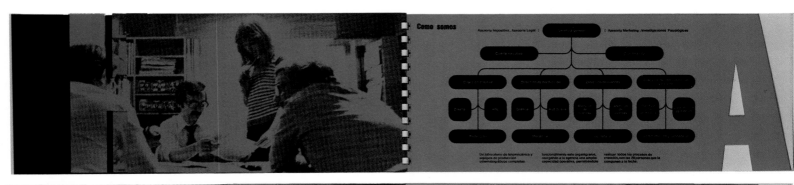

181

Booklets

Prospekte

Brochures

DESIGNER / GESTALTER / MAQUETTISTE:

181 Eduardo A. Cánovas
182 Saul Bass/Herb Yager/Vahe Fattal
185, 186 Rolf Müller/Veronika Wittermann
187 Eduard Prüssen
188 Zélio Alves Pinto

181 Three double spreads from a self-promotional brochure published by an advertising agency. (MEX)
182 Recto and verso of a gift catalogue distributed by *Goldwaters*, a department store, as a direct-mail item. (USA)
183, 184 From a catalogue designed by various illustrators. (NLD)
185, 186 Two double spreads from "Provocation of Reality", a book dedicated by the German Industrial and Commercial Chamber to its President, Otto Wolff von Amerongen, on the occasion of his 60th birthday. It is a historical sketch of 1918, the year of his birth. Blue-grey lettering. (GER)
187 A prospectus for Bergisch-Gladbach. Full colour. (GER)
188 Full-colour cover of a writing pad. (BRA)

181 Drei Doppelseiten aus der ringgehefteten Broschüre, die eine Werbeagentur als Eigenwerbung herausgab. (MEX)
182 Vorder- und Rückseite des von einem Warenhaus als Direktwerbung versandten Geschenkkatalogs. (USA)
183, 184 Seite und Doppelseite aus einem von verschiedenen Illustratoren gestalteteten Prospekt. Auf Umweltpapier. (NLD)
185, 186 Doppelseiten aus «Provokation der Realität», eine Schrift, die der Deutsche Industrie- und Handelstag seinem Präsidenten Otto Wolff von Amerongen zum 60. Geburtstag widmete. Es ist ein geschichtlicher Abriss über sein Geburtsjahr, 1918. (GER)
187 Werbeprospekt für Bergisch-Gladbach. Mehrfarbig. (GER)
188 Mehrfarbiges Deckblatt eines Schreibblocks. (BRA)

181 Trois pages doubles d'une brochure à reliure spirale, distribuée comme autopromotion d'une agence de publicité. (MEX)
182 Recto et verso d'un catalogue de cadeaux. (USA)
183, 184 Page et page double d'un catalogue réalisé par divers illustrateurs. Imprimé sur papier recyclé. (NLD)
185, 186 Pages doubles d'un livre (Provocation de la réalité) publié à l'occasion du 60e anniversaire de Otto Wolff von Amerongen, président de la Chambre de commerce et d'industrie. Il présente un aperçu historique de l'année 1918, année de naissance de Amerongen. Texte en bleu gris. (GER)
187 Publicité touristique pour Bergisch-Gladbach. (GER)
188 Couverture (en polychromie) d'un bloc-notes. (BRA)

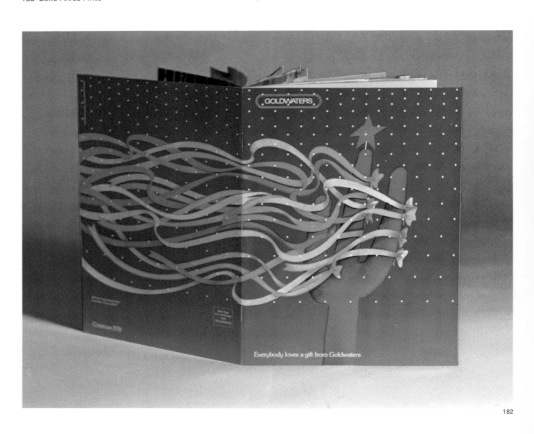

182

183

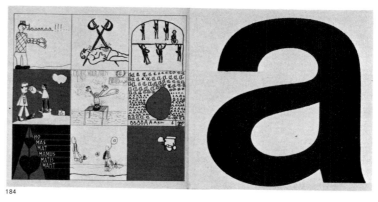

184

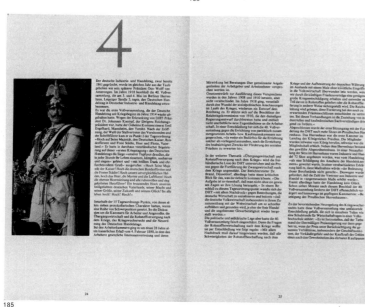

185

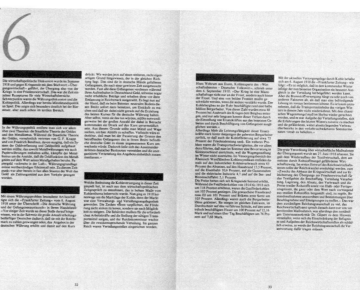

186

187

188

189

Berliner Sommerkirche '78

an der
Gedächtniskirche

Freitag, 30. Juni   16 – 22 Uhr
Sonnabend, 1. Juli   10 – 22 Uhr

feiern, erleben,
zuhören, sprechen,
fragen, ausruhen –

einfach mal
rankommen,
mitmachen

191

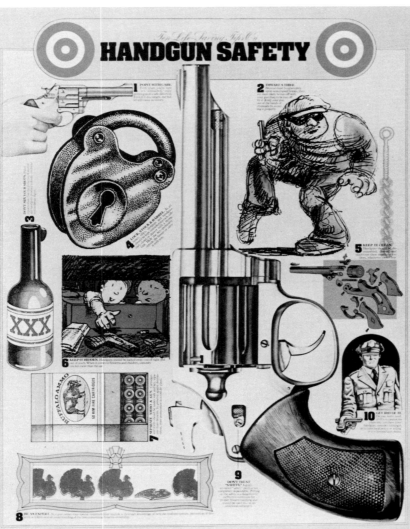

194

195

ARTIST / KÜNSTLER / ARTISTE:

189, 190 Maryann Neilson
192, 193 R. Henderson/R. Goode/T. Flett
194 Bill Mayer/Pamela Smith/Gail McCrory/Sandra Glass
195 Wilbur D. Davidson
196, 197 Steve Grohe/Bob O'Shaughnessy/David Niles/
John Gatie

DESIGNER / GESTALTER / MAQUETTISTE:

189, 190 Vicki Navratil/Jerry Cosgrove
191 Reinhart Braun
192, 193 Flett Henderson & Arnold Pty Ltd
194 Nancy Hoefig/Whole Hog Studios
195 Bob Warkulwiz
196, 197 Robert Cipriani

ART DIRECTOR / DIRECTEUR ARTISTIQUE:

189, 190 Jerry Cosgrove/Vicki Navratil
191 Reinhart Braun
192, 193 Flett Henderson & Arnold Pty Ltd
194 Carl T. Herrman
195 Bob Warkulwiz
196, 197 Robert Cipriani

Booklets
Prospekte
Brochures

FIVE FACES OF GLOPAQUE

POSTERS

192

193

196

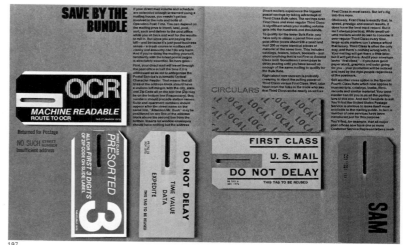

197

189, 190 Title page and inside page of a small-format prospectus with ideas for gifts and various suggestions for the Christmas season. It is part of an advertising campaign launched by a department store. (USA)
191 Title page of a folder with the programme for a religious event in Berlin. Light and dark green, white lettering. (GER)
192, 193 Title page and inside page of a paper-mill's advertising brochure. The five inside pages illustrate the utilization of the paper. In brilliant colours. (AUS)
194 Instruction leaflet issued by a municipal government authority with ten safety rules for the handling of small firearms. (USA)
195 Cover of a brochure in which an insurance company introduces a new fire accident insurance policy. Dark brown cross on a light brown surface. (USA)
196, 197 A paper-mill's prospectus. Two full-colour double spreads. (USA)

189, 190 Titelblatt und Innenseite eines kleinformatigen Prospektes mit Geschenkideen und verschiedenen Vorschlägen für die Weihnachtstage. Er ist Teil der von einem Warenhaus lancierten Werbekampagne und wurde an Kunden verteilt. (USA)
191 Titelblatt eines Faltprospektes mit dem Programm einer kirchlichen Veranstaltung in Berlin. Hell- und Dunkelgrün, weisse Schrift. (GER)
192, 193 Titelseite und Innenseite der Werbebroschüre einer Papierfabrik. Die fünf Innenseiten illustrieren den Verwendungszweck des Papiers – hier Plakate. In bunten Farben. (AUS)
194 Von Stadtverwaltungen herausgegebenes Merkblatt mit zehn Sicherheitsbestimmungen für die Handhabung von Handfeuerwaffen. (USA)
195 Umschlag einer Broschüre, mit welcher eine Versicherungsgesellschaft eine neue Feuerversicherung vorstellt. Dunkelbraunes Kreuz auf hellbraunem Grund. (USA)
196, 197 Zwei mehrfarbige Doppelseiten aus dem Prospekt einer Papierfabrik. (USA)

189, 190 Couverture et page intérieure d'un petit prospectus contenant des propositions pour les jours de fête et présentant une série de cadeaux. Ce prospectus fait partie d'une campagne publicitaire lancée par un grand magasin. (USA)
191 Couverture d'un dépliant contenant le programme d'une manifestation religieuse à Berlin. Vert clair et foncé, texte blanc. (GER)
192, 193 Couverture et page intérieure d'une brochure publicitaire d'une papeterie. Les illustrations des cinq pages intérieures se réfèrent à l'usage du papier – ici pour affiches. (AUS)
194 Avertissement des autorités municipales sur les dangers qu'il y a à manier les armes à feu et des dispositions de sécurité qu'il faut observer. (USA)
195 Couverture d'une brochure par laquelle une compagnie d'assurance lance sa nouvelle assurance incendie. Croix en brun foncé sur fond brun clair. (USA)
196, 197 Pages doubles tirées du prospectus d'une papeterie. (USA)

AGENCY / AGENTUR / AGENCE – STUDIO:

189, 190 Cosgrove Associates, Inc.
191 Reinhart Braun
192, 193 K.M. Campbell Pty Ltd
194 Super Creato
195 Carlyle & Warkulwiz, Inc.
196, 197 Gunn Assoc.

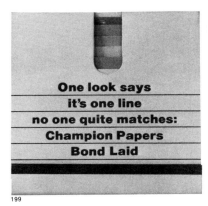

ARTIST / KÜNSTLER / ARTISTE:

198 David Barnett/Charles Goslin
199, 200 Miho
201, 202 Walter Tafelmaier
203 Herman Vahramian
204–206 Bodo Rieger/Olaf Leu

ART DIRECTOR / DIRECTEUR ARTISTIQUE:

198 Stuart Silver
199, 200 Miho
201, 202 Walter Tafelmaier
203 Herman Vahramian

AGENCY / AGENTUR / AGENCE – STUDIO:

198 Goslin/Barnett Inc.
204–206 Zanders Werbeabt.

Booklets / Prospekte / Brochures

205

198 Cover of a prospectus for a Tutankh-amen exhibition in New York at the Metropolitan Museum of Art. Ruby-red and black on grey paper. (USA)
199, 200 Matchbox containing paper specimens from *Champion Paper.* Red text. (USA)
201, 202 From a series of individually produced programme leaflets for Musica Viva concerts organized by the *Bayerische Rundfunk* (Bavarian Radio). Fig. 201: Brown and white on black; Fig. 202: Grey, black and white on grey. (GER)
203 Cover of a four-language brochure with musical examples and texts pertaining to contemporary Armenian music. Black and white, green circle. (ITA)
204—206 Two complete pages and illustration shown here in actual size from a spirally bound catalogue for the *Zanders* paper company, published under the motto *"Zanders paper carries Zanders."* (GER)

198 Umschlag des Prospektes für die Ausstellung «Die Schätze des Tutenchamun» im Metropolitan Museum of Art. Weinrot und Schwarz auf grauem Papier. (USA)
199, 200 Als Streichholzbriefchen aufgemachte Papierkollektion von *Champion Paper.* Rote Schrift. (USA)
201, 202 Aus einer Serie von einheitlich gestalteten Programmheften für Musica Viva Konzerte, die vom *Bayerischen Rundfunk* organisiert werden. Abb. 201: Braun und Weiss auf Schwarz; Abb. 202: Grau, Schwarz und Weiss auf Grau. (GER).
203 Umschlag einer Broschüre (in vier Sprachen) mit Musikbeispielen und Texten zu zeitgenössischer armenischer Musik. Schwarzweiss, grüner Kreis. (ITA)
204—206 Zwei vollständige Seiten und Illustration in Originalgrösse aus einem ringgehefteten Katalog der Papierfabrik *Zanders,* der unter dem Motto «*Zanders* Papier transportiert *Zanders*» herauskam. (GER)

198 Couverture du prospectus annonçant l'exposition «Les trésors du Tout Ankh Amon» au Metropolitan Museum of Art de New York. Rouge foncé et noir sur papier gris. (USA)
199, 200 Collection de papiers de *Champion Papers,* rappelant une pochette d'alumettes. Texte rouge. (USA)
201, 202 D'une série de programmes de conception uniforme pour les concerts Musica Viva, organisés par la radiodiffusion bavaroise, *Bayerischer Rundfunk.* Fig. 201: brun et blanc sur fond noir; fig. 202: gris, noir et blanc sur fond gris. (GER)
203 Couverture d'une brochure consacrée à la musique contemporaine arménienne. Noir et blanc, cercle vert. (ITA)
204—206 Deux pages complètes et illustration (en grandeur originale) figurant dans un catalogue à reliure spirale d'une papeterie. Il est intitulé: «papier *Zanders* transporte *Zanders*». (GER)

Papier transportiert
Schrift Bilder Farben

Papier transportiert
Information, die man sehen kann

204

206

ARTIST / KÜNSTLER / ARTISTE:

207 Wayne McLoughlin
208, 209 Don Weller

DESIGNER / GESTALTER / MAQUETTISTE:

207 Peter Coutroulis
208, 109 Mark Wallin
210, 211 Julien van der Wal

ART DIRECTOR / DIRECTEUR ARTISTIQUE:

207 Peter Coutroulis
208, 209 Lawrence Bender
210, 211 Julien van der Wal

AGENCY / AGENTUR / AGENCE – STUDIO:

207 Lerman & Van Leeuwen, Inc.
208, 209 Lawrence Bender & Associates
210, 211 Julien van der Wal

209

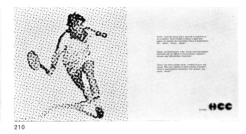

210

208

207

211

207 «Werbung sollte nie langweilig sein.» Aus der Broschüre einer Werbeagentur. (USA)
208, 209 Illustration und vollständige Doppelseite aus einem Prospekt, der ein neues System für Programmierer, das Wartepausen ausschliesst, vorstellt. Matte Farben. (USA)
210, 211 Doppelseite und Illustration (in Originalgrösse) aus einem kleinformatigen Prospekt, in welchem die von *Henri-Charles Colsenet* für verschiedene Sportarten entworfene Bekleidung gezeigt wird. (SWI)

207 From an advertising agency's self-promotional brochure. (USA)
208, 209 Illustration and complete double spread from a prospectus introducing a new programming system to cut out time-wasting interludes. Mat colours. (USA)
210, 211 Double spread and illustration, shown here in actual size, from a small-format prospectus in which clothing designed by *Henri-Charles Colsenet* for various sporting activities is shown. (SWI)

207 «Il n'a jamais été question de faire de la publicité une source d'ennui.» Pour une agence. (USA)
208, 209 Illustration et page double complète figurant dans un prospectus en faveur d'un nouveau système pour la programmation éliminant les périodes d'attente. Tons atténués. (USA)
210, 211 Page double et illustration (en grandeur originale) d'un prospectus de prestige. Il s'agit d'une représentation des divers départements du sportswear créé par *Henri-Charles Colsenet,* sans qu'un modèle spécifique soit reproduit. (SWI)

Booklets / Prospekte / Brochures

212

213

214

**Booklets / Prospekte
Brochures**

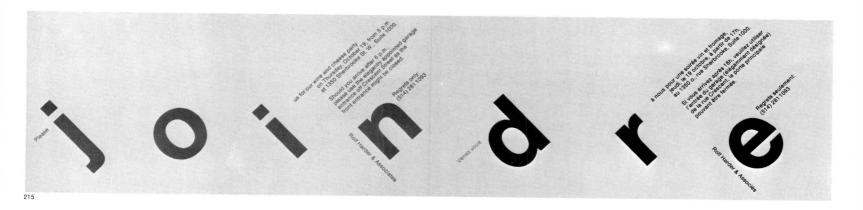

215

216

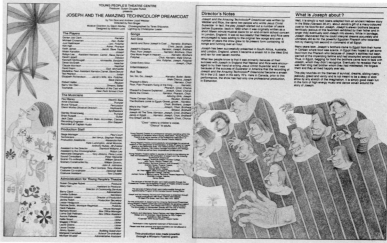

217

212, 213 Notification (actual size) of removal by a printing firm. (NLD)
214 Inside of a Christmas card sent by a record company. Dark shades. (USA)
215 Bilingual invitation to a wine and cheese party at the design studio Rolf Harder & Assoc., with a play on English and French words. (CAN)
216, 217 Recto and verso of a programme for a play. Grey shades. (CAN)
218 Exhibition of the 50 best record sleeves designed under the art direction of John Berg at CBS. Steely blue and black, gold lettering. (FRA)

212, 213 Umzugsanzeige (Originalgrösse) einer Druckerei, mit transparentem Aufleger. (NLD)
214 Innenseite der Weihnachtskarte einer Schallplattenfirma. Dunkle Farbtöne. (USA)
215 Zweisprachige Einladung zu einer Wein- und Käseparty des Design-Studios Rolf Harder & Assoc. Gelungene Lösung durch Kombination des englischen «join» und französischen «joindre». (CAN)
216, 217 Vorder- und Innenseite des Programms für ein Theaterstück. Grautöne. (CAN)
218 Ausstellung über die 50 besten, unter der künstlerischen Leitung von John Berg bei CBS erschienenen Schallplattenhüllen. Stahlblau und Schwarz, goldene Schrift. (FRA)

212, 213 Changement d'adresse (en grandeur originale) d'une imprimerie. (NLD)
214 Carte de Noël d'un producteur de disques. Tons foncés. (USA)
215 Invitation bilingue pour une soirée vin et fromage organisée par le studio Rolf Harder & Assoc. Combinaison du mot anglais «join» et du mot français «joindre». (CAN)
216, 217 Recto et panneau intérieur du programme pour une représentation de théâtre. (CAN)
218 Pour une exposition présentant un choix des 50 meilleures couvertures de disques illustrées par divers artistes et produites par CBS sous la direction artistique de John Berg. (FRA)

ARTIST / KÜNSTLER / ARTISTE:

212, 213 Angela Devens-deVrede
214 Stanislaw Zagorski
216, 217 Blair Drawson
218 John Berg

DESIGNER / GESTALTER / MAQUETTISTE:

212, 213 Baer Cornet
214 P. Corriston
215 Rolf Harder
216, 217 David Wyman
218 Nick Fasciano

ART DIRECTOR / DIRECTEUR ARTISTIQUE:

212,213 Baer Cornet
214 P. Corriston
215 Rolf Harder
216, 217 David Wyman
218 John Berg

AGENCY / AGENTUR / AGENCE – STUDIO:

215 Rolf Harder & Assoc.
216, 217 Fifty Fingers Studio
218 CBS

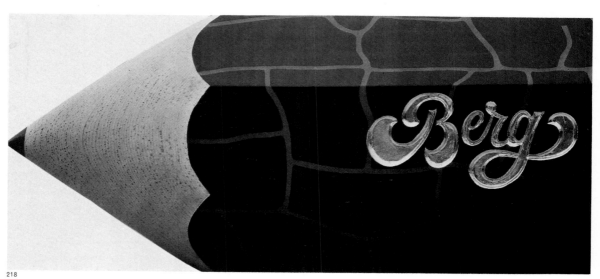

218

219 Cover of a jubilee brochure by the German Confederation of Interior Decorators. (GER)
220, 221 Title pages of an investment consulting agency's brochure. Orange and green. (USA)
222 Invitation to the Hamburg Press Ball. Door can be opened. Blue and grey shades. (GER)
223, 224 Emblem and cover of a self-promotional brochure "Alternative B" by the Peter Berger advertising agency. Perforated white and red cover, black paper underneath. (SWI)
225 A genuine 100-Belgian-franc note that the two designers sent as an advertising gift in the interests of self promotion. In the text (silver on black cardboard) they point out that the note is guaranteed as being genuine and that they as designers also have to work within the law for violation of the law, is rewarded with hard labour. (BEL)

219 Umschlag einer Jubiläumsbroschüre des Bundes Deutscher Innenarchitekten. (GER)
220, 221 Titelseiten der Broschüren von zwei Anlageberatungsfirmen, hier über Investitionen auf dem amerikanischen Markt und die Einrichtung von Pensionsversicherungen. Orange und Grün. (USA)
222 Einladung zum Hamburger Presseball. Tür kann geöffnet werden. Blau- und Grautöne. (GER)
223, 224 Signet und Umschlag der Eigenwerbebroschüre «Alternative B» der Werbeagentur Peter Berger. Der Umschlag in Weiss und Rot ist perforiert und mit einem schwarzen Blatt unterlegt. (SWI)
225 Echter belgischer 100-Franc-Schein, den die beiden Entwerfer als Eigenwerbung und Werbegeschenk verschickten. Im Text (Silber auf schwarzem Karton) weisen sie darauf hin, dass der Geldschein garantiert echt sei, da auch sie sich als Entwerfer an die Gesetze zu halten hätten, denn Zuwiderhandeln werde mit Zwangsarbeit bestraft. (BEL)

219 Couverture d'une brochure publiée par un groupement d'architectes-décorateurs. (GER)
220, 221 Couvertures de brochures publiées par deux conseillers financiers, se référant ici aux investissements dans le marché américain et aux assurances-retraite. Orange et vert. (USA)
222 Invitation pour le bal de la presse à Hambourg. La porte se laisse ouvrir. Bleu et gris. (GER)
223, 224 Marque et couverture d'une brochure autopromotionnelle de l'agence de publicité Peter Berger, intitulée «Alternative B». Couverture perforée, lignes rouges. (SWI)
225 Autopromotion et cadeau publicitaire des deux auteurs de ce «vrai» billet de banque de 100 francs belges. Dans le texte (argent sur carton noir) ils soulignent que ce billet est bel et bien revêtu de toutes les garanties fiduciaires accordées par la Banque nationale car eux aussi, bien qu'étant les auteurs, seraient punis des travaux forcés en cas de contrefaçon. (BEL)

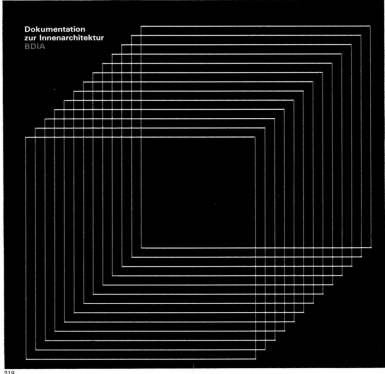

219

222

ARTIST / KÜNSTLER:

222 Rudolf Wernitz

DESIGNER / GESTALTER:

219 Judith Kleint
220, 221 Joseph Moore
222 Rudolf Wernitz
223, 224 Milo Schraner
225 Manfred Hürrig

ART DIRECTOR:

219 Judith Kleint
220, 221 Joseph Moore
222 Rudolf Wernitz
223, 224 Ernst Schadegg
225 Manfred Hürrig/
Yvon Adam

AGENCY / AGENTUR:

220, 221 Logowitz + Moore
Design Associates
223, 224 Peter Berger AG

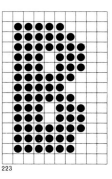

223

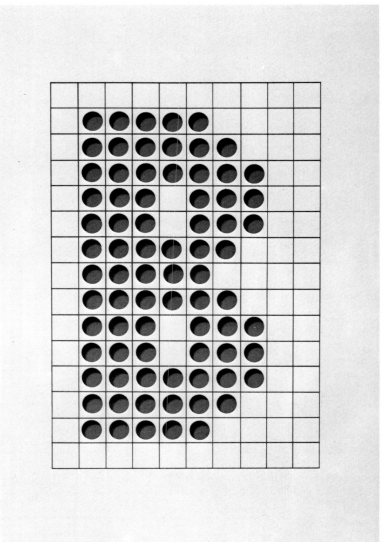

224

A Technical
Case for Equities

220

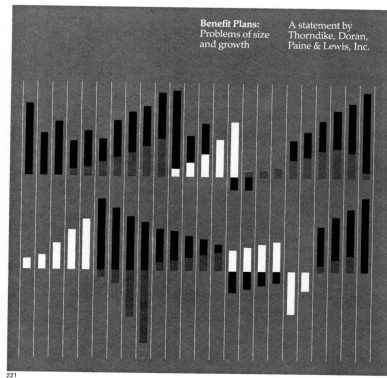

Benefit Plans:
Problems of size
and growth

A statement by
Thorndike, Doran,
Paine & Lewis, Inc.

221

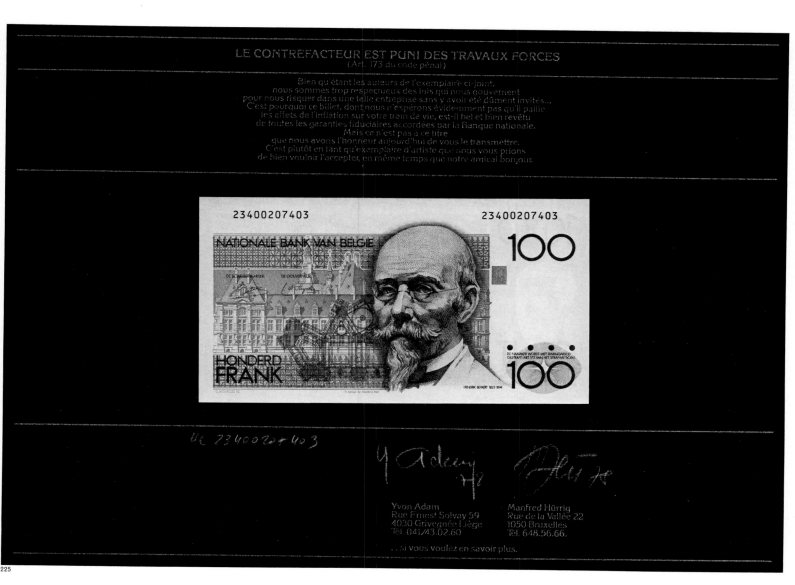

225

226

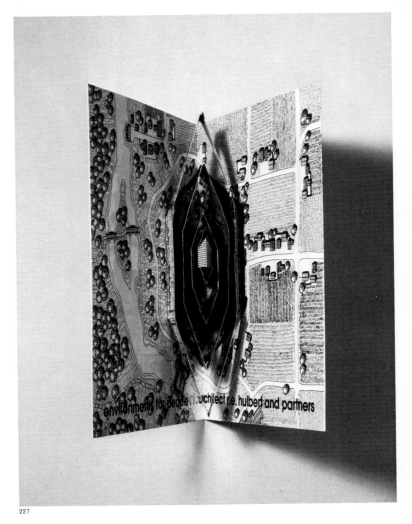

227

ARTIST / KÜNSTLER / ARTISTE:

227, 228 Eugene V. Radvenis
230–232 Luigi Morisetti

DESIGNER / GESTALTER / MAQUETTISTE:

226 Ann Ames
227, 228 Eugene V. Radvenis
229 Kristian Roth
230–232 Luigi Morisetti

229

226 Cover page of a self-promotional brochure by an international consultancy agency. Blue and white with a red label. (CAN)
227, 228 View of a half open and fully open advertising folder with a three-dimensional old town, published by a team of architects. Brown and white. (CAN)
229 Cover of a presentation folder by a team of landscape gardeners and planners. Various shades of green, yellow tree. (GER)
230–232 Black-and-white pages of an advertising agency's "hand"-book, with illustrated plays on words at hand. (ITA)

226 Umschlagseite der Eigenwerbebroschüre einer international tätigen Beraterfirma. Blau und weiss mit rotem Etikett. (CAN)
227, 228 Ansicht einer halb- und vollständig geöffneten Werbemappe mit dreidimensionaler Altstadt, herausgegeben von einem Architektenteam, das eine lebensgerechte Umwelt für den Menschen schaffen will. Braun und weiss. (CAN)
229 Umschlag der Präsentationsmappe eines Gartenarchitekten-Teams. Verschiedene Grünschattierungen, gelber Baum. (GER)
230–232 Aus dem «Hand»-Buch einer Werbeagentur, mit illustrierten Wortspielen zu Hand: manomorta = Tote Hand, manicotto = Muff, manometro = Druckmesser. Schwarzweiss. (ITA)

226 Couverture de la brochure autopromotionnelle d'un bureau de conseillers financiers travaillant dans le monde entier. Bleu et blanc, étiquette rouge. (CAN)
227, 228 Dossier publicitaire publié par un groupement d'architectes qui cherchent à humaniser notre espace vital. Une ancienne ville s'élève en ouvrant le dossier. (CAN)
229 Couverture d'un dossier de présentation d'un groupement d'architectes paysagistes. Divers tons verts, arbre jaune. (GER)
230–232 Pages noir-blanc du manuel d'une agence publicitaire avec des jeux de mots illustrés sur le sujet de la main: manomorta = main morte, manicotto = manchon, manometro = manomètre. (ITA)

ART DIRECTOR / DIRECTEUR ARTISTIQUE:

226 Robert Burns
227, 228 David Clifford

Booklets / Prospekte / Brochures

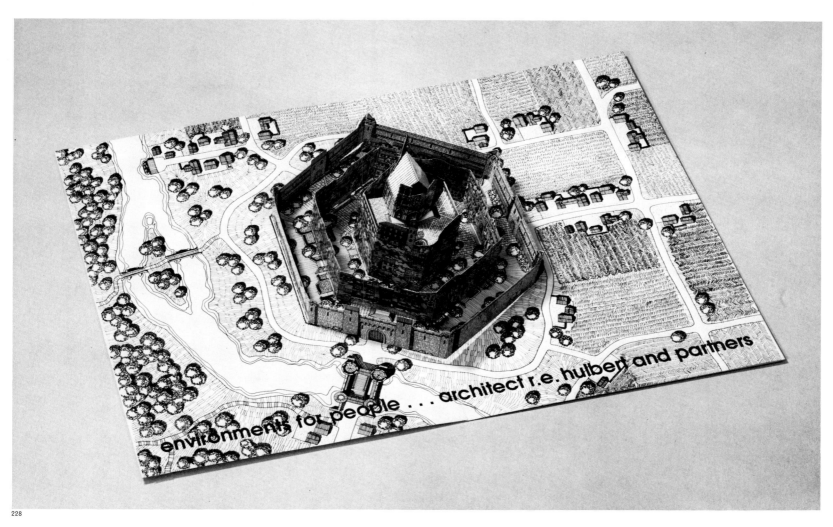

228

AGENCY / AGENTUR / AGENCE – STUDIO:

226 Burns, Cooper, Hynes Ltd.
227, 228 Image Makers
230–232 MAC S.p.A.

230

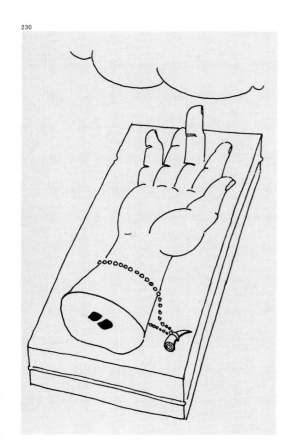

231

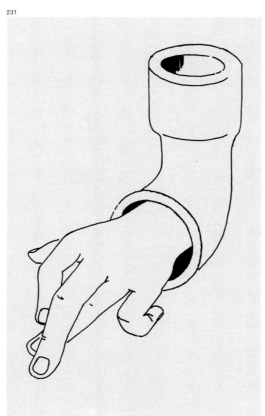

232

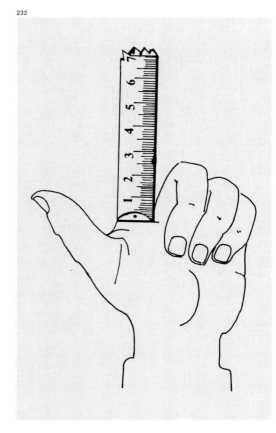

233

234

236

237

233 Page from a University of Texas brochure. Beige paper. (USA)
234 Folder published by *The New York Times* as space promotion for the weekly feature "Living." House made out of newspaper collage. (USA)
235 Concertina-type folder, sent as direct mail by a Tokyo department store for Kyoto kimonos. Full-colour illustrations. (JPN)
236 Thank-you card for the Curt Visel publishing company. Black and white. (GER)
237, 238 Double spreads from a *Reuters* brochure. Fig. 237: the passing on of information; Fig. 238: exchange of information. Full colour. (GBR)

233 Seite aus einer Broschüre der University of Texas. Beiges Papier. (USA)
234 «Schau, wer bei uns zu Hause war!» Faltprospekt der *New York Times*, die Inserenten für die wöchentliche Beilage über «Wohnen» sucht. Haus aus Zeitungspapier-Collage. (USA)
235 Leporello, der als Direktwerbung eines Tokioter Warenhauses für Kyoto-Kimonos versandt wurde. Mehrfarbige Illustrationen. (JPN)
236 Dankeskarte des Verlags Curt Visel. Schwarzweiss. (GER)
237, 238 Doppelseiten aus einer Broschüre von *Reuters*: Abb. 237 zeigt die Weitergabe der Informationen, Abb. 238 den Informationsaustausch zwischen den Hauptzentren. Mehrfarbig. (GBR)

233 Page d'une brochure publiée par l'Université du Texas. Papier beige. (USA)
234 «Regarde voir qui était chez nous!» Dépliant promotionnel du *New York Times* en faveur du supplément hebdomadaire «Habitation». Collage en papier de journal. (USA)
235 Dépliant en accordéon publié par un grand magasin de Tokyo. Publicité directe pour les kimonos Kyoto. Illustration en couleurs. (JPN)
236 Carte de remerciement d'une maison d'édition. Noir et blanc. (GER)
237, 238 Pages doubles d'une brochure de *Reuters*; fig. 237: diffusion des informations, fig. 238: échange des informations entre les centres principaux. En polychromie. (GBR)

ART DIRECTOR / DIRECTEUR ARTISTIQUE:

233 Richard Hendel
234 Andrew Kner
235 Kenzo Nakagawa
237, 238 Mervyn Kurlansky

ARTIST / KÜNSTLER / ARTISTE:

233 Ed Lindlof
234 Isadore Seltzer
235 Mamoru Sugiyama
236 Eduard Prüssen
237, 238 Wolf Spoerl

DESIGNER / GESTALTER / MAQUETTISTE:

233 Richard Hendel
234 Andrew Kner
235 Kenzo Nakagawa/Hiro Nobuyama
236 Eduard Prüssen
237,238 Mervyn Kurlansky/Lora Starling

**Booklets
Prospekte
Brochures**

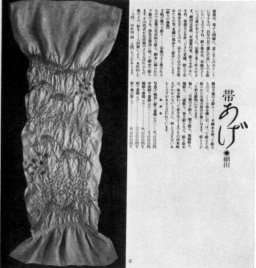

235

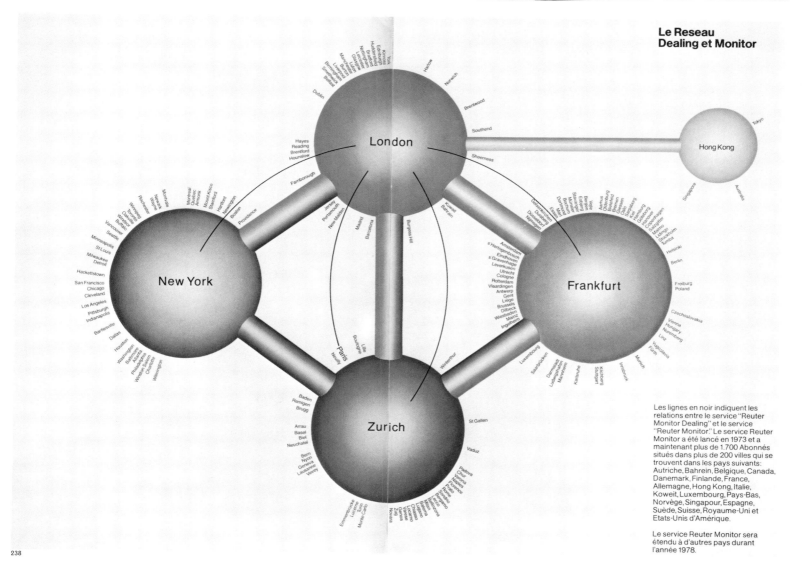

238

**Le Reseau
Dealing et Monitor**

Les lignes en noir indiquent les relations entre le service "Reuter Monitor Dealing" et le service "Reuter Monitor." Le service Reuter Monitor a été lancé en 1973 et a maintenant plus de 1.700 Abonnés situés dans plus de 200 villes qui se trouvent dans les pays suivants: Autriche, Bahrein, Belgique, Canada, Danemark, Finlande, France, Allemagne, Hong Kong, Italie, Koweit, Luxembourg, Pays-Bas, Norvège, Singapour, Espagne, Suède, Suisse, Royaume-Uni et Etats-Unis d'Amérique.

Le service Reuter Monitor sera étendu à d'autres pays durant l'année 1978.

AGENCY / AGENTUR / AGENCE – STUDIO:

233 Ed Lindlof
235 Nippon Design Center
237, 238 Pentagram

MODA NUOVA U.S.A.

239

La moda nuova U.S.A. è arrivata! Ti aspetta qui alla mostra-mercato ABBIGLIAMENTO U.S.A. all'United States Trade Center, in Via Gattamelata, 5 - Milano

240

E' la moda spiritosa e un po' selvaggia – come gli abiti dei cow boys, per intenderci – e tanto, tanto pratica!

241

Arriva la moda giovane «made in U.S.A.»! Moda nuova. Sportiva ma anche tanto elegante! Vieni a vederla subito alla mostra-mercato ABBIGLIAMENTO U.S.A.

242

239–242 Pages from a direct-mail brochure of an American shopping-centre in Milan. (ITA)
243 "Do you have a friend? The book you are giving him for Christmas comes from *Mondadori*." An advertising campaign launched at Christmastime by the *Mondadori* publishing firm. (ITA)
244 Inside page of a folder for the magazine *Money*. Three-dimensional house, lettering in lime-green on black. (USA)
245 Title-page of a brochure published by the periodical *Redbook* with various suggestions and tips for recipes to be enjoyed during the Christmas season. Full colour. (USA)
246 Page from a prospectus of a textile manufacturer. Orange and olive-green with white on a yellow surface. (USA)

239–242 Seiten aus einer Direkt-Werbebroschüre eines amerikanischen Einkaufszentrums in Mailand. (ITA)
243 «Hast Du einen Freund? Sein Buch zu Weihnachten kommt von *Mondadori*.» Aus einer zu Weihnachten vom Verlagshaus *Mondadori* lancierten Werbekampagne. (ITA)
244 Innenseite eines Faltprospektes für die Zeitschrift *Money*. Dreidimensionales Haus, Schrift in Lindengrün auf Schwarz. (USA)
245 Titelblatt einer Broschüre der Zeitschrift *Redbook* mit Rezeptvorschlägen für die Weihnachtsfesttage. Mehrfarbig. (USA)
246 Seite aus dem Prospekt eines Textilfabrikanten. Orange und Olivgrün mit Weiss auf gelbem Grund. (USA)

239–242 Pages d'une brochure publié par un centre commercial américain à Milan. Elément de publicité directe. (ITA)
243 «T'as un ami? Son livre de Noël est de *Mondadori*.» Elément d'une campagne publicitaire lancée avant les Fêtes par la maison d'édition *Mondadori*. (ITA)
244 Panneau intérieur d'un dépliant pour le magazine *Money*. Maison tridimensionnelle, texte en vert clair sur fond noir. (USA)
245 Couverture d'une brochure de la revue *Redbook* contenant une série de recettes pour la fête de Noël. En polychromie. (USA)
246 Page d'un prospectus publié par un fabricant de textiles. Blanc, orange et olive sur fond en jaune foncé. (USA)

ARTIST / KÜNSTLER / ARTISTE:

239–242 Monica Mayer
243 Ferenc Pintér
245 Nancy Stahl
246 Gene Wilkes

DESIGNER / GESTALTER / MAQUETTISTE:

239–242 Simona Fausti
244 Pierre Asselin
245 Sandra Lee Spaeth
246 Larry Smith

ART DIRECTOR / DIRECTEUR ARTISTIQUE:

239–242 Simona Fausti
243 Arturo Martinez
244 Pierre Asselin
245 Sandra Lee Spaeth
246 Larry Smith

AGENCY / AGENTUR / AGENCE – STUDIO:

239–242 Compton Dupuy Italia
243 Direzione propaganda Mondadori
244 ABCO Graphique Corp.
246 Luckie & Forney

244

243

245

246

Booklets / Prospekte
Brochures

95

3

Magazine Covers

Magazine Illustrations

Newspaper Illustrations

Trade Magazines

House Organs

Book Covers

Annual Reports

Zeitschriften-Umschläge

Zeitschriften-Illustrationen

Zeitungs-Illustrationen

Fachzeitschriften

Hauszeitschriften

Buchumschläge

Jahresberichte

Couvertures de périodiques

Illustrations de périodiques

Illustrations de journaux

Revues professionnelles

Journaux d'entreprises

Couvertures de livres

Rapports annuels

247

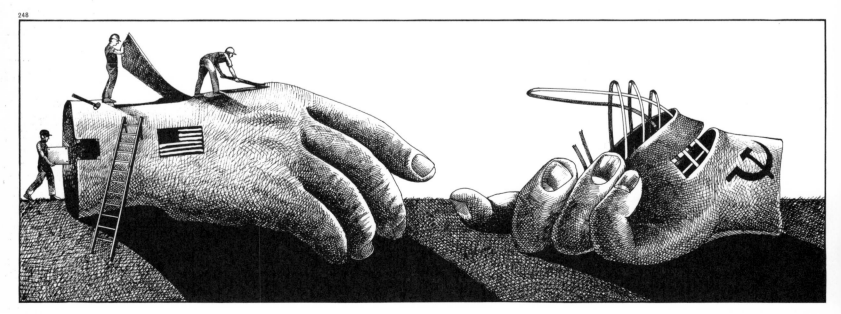

248

249

251

250

247 Illustration for an article about forced committal into a psychiatric clinic and the laws pertaining to this. From the *New York Times*. (USA)
248 Illustration from the Sunday edition of *Newsday* concerning the paucity of efforts by Russia to establish better relations with America. (USA)
249 Colour illustration accompanying a poem by Henri Dès. From *la Suisse*. (SWI)
250 Black-and-white illustration from the political weekly *Movimento*. (BRA)
251 Caricature of Jimmy Carter in conjunction with an article about his difficulties in the White House. From *U.S. News and World Report*. (USA)

247 Illustration zu einem Artikel über Zwangseinlieferungen in psychiatrische Anstalten und die entsprechende Gesetzeslage. Aus der *New York Times*. (USA)
248 Illustration aus der Sonntagsausgabe von *Newsday*. Es geht um mangelnde Bemühungen der UdSSR um freundschaftliche Beziehungen mit den USA. (USA)
249 Farbige Illustration zu einem Gedicht von Henri Dès auf der Titelseite der Weihnachtsausgabe der Zeitung *La Suisse*. (SWI)
250 Schwarzweiss-Illustration aus dem politischen Wochenmagazin *Movimento*. (BRA)
251 Karikatur Jimmy Carters zu einem Artikel über seine Schwierigkeiten im Weissen Haus. Aus *U.S. News and World Report*. (USA)

247 Illustration accompagnant un article sur l'hospitalisation forcée dans une clinique psychiatrique et les lois s'y référant. Elément du *New York Times*. (USA)
248 Illustration de l'édition dominicale de *Newsday*. L'article traite de l'URSS qui ne s'efforce guère à améliorer les relations avec les Etats-Unis. (USA)
249 Illustration (en polychromie) figurant sur la première page de l'édition de Noël du quotidien *La Suisse*. Elle accompagne un poème de Henri Dès. (SWI)
250 Illustration noir-blanc d'un hebdomadaire politique. (BRA)
251 Caricature de Jimmy Carter tirée d'un article sur les difficultés qui se présentent dans la Maison Blanche. Elément de *U.S. News and World Report*. (USA)

ARTIST / KÜNSTLER / ARTISTE:

252, 253, 256 Kent Barton
254, 255 Staffan Schultz
257 Sue Coe

ART DIRECTOR:

252, 253, 256 Kent Barton
257 Pamela Vassil

PUBLISHER / VERLEGER / EDITEUR:

252, 253, 256 The Miami Herald
254, 255 Dagens Nyheter
257 The New York Times

254

252

252, 253, 256 Illustrations from *The Miami Herald*. The themes deal with the influence of Z. Brzezinski (department for national security affairs) on U.S. politics, China's sudden leap into the outside world, and the situation in Italy after Moro's assassination. (USA)
254, 255 Illustrations from the weekly column in the newspaper *Dagens Nyheter* on Swedish affairs. (SWE)
257 Illustration from the *New York Times*. Should doctors lie to critically ill patients? (USA)

252, 253, 256 Illustrationen aus der Zeitung *The Miami Herald*. Die Themen sind hier der Einfluss von Z. Brzezinski (Departement für nationale Sicherheit) auf die U.S. Politik, Chinas «grosser Sprung nach draussen» und die Situation in Italien nach Moros Tod. (USA)
254, 255 Illustrationen aus der wöchentlich in der Zeitung *Dagens Nyheter* erscheinenden Kolumne über Geschehnisse in Schweden. (SWE)
257 Illustration aus der *New York Times* zu der Frage, ob Ärzte schwerkranke Patienten belügen sollen. (USA)

252, 253, 256 Illustrations d'un quotidien. Elles se réfèrent à l'influence de Z. Brzezinski (Département pour la sécurité nationale) sur la politique américaine, sur le «grand pas» en avant que la Chine a fait quant aux relations extérieures et la situation en Italie après l'assassinat de Aldo Moro. (USA)
254, 255 Illustrations qui ont paru dans une rubrique hebdomadaire sur divers événements en Suède. (SWE)
257 Illustration du *New York Times*. Article sur le dilemma du médecin face au patient grièvement malade: faut-il dire la vérité ou des mensonges? (USA)

253

255

256

257

Newspaper Illustrations
Zeitungs-Illustrationen
Illustrations de journaux

258 From the *New York Times*. Carter's efforts to cut back on inflation. (USA)
259 Illustration from a *New York Times* article on Peking's rediscovery of overseas Chinese. (USA)
260 Illustration to an article in the *New York Times* about exile in Siberia. (USA)
261 Illustration from *Newsday* pertaining to acne. (USA)
262 Illustration from the political weekly *Movimento*. Black and white. (BRA)
263 From an article in *The Miami Herald*. "Courage Is Legal Madness in Russia." (USA)

258 Aus der *New York Times*. Das Thema: Carters Bestreben, die Inflation «zurückzuschneiden». (USA)
259 «Peking entdeckt die Ausland-Chinesen.» Illustration zu einem Artikel in der *New York Times*. (USA)
260 Illustration zu einem Artikel über die Verbannungen nach Sibirien. Aus der *New York Times*. (USA)
261 Illustration aus *Newsday* zum Thema Akne und dem Problem, das es für junge Mädchen darstellt. (USA)
262 Illustration aus dem politischen Wochenmagazin *Movimento*. Schwarzweiss. (BRA)
263 «Mut ist in Russland geistige Verwirrung.» Aus einem Artikel in der Zeitung *The Miami Herald*. (USA)

258 Illustration du *New York Times* sur les efforts de Jimmy Carter de «freiner» l'inflation. (USA)
259 «Pékin découvre les Chinois vivant à l'étranger.» Illustration figurant dans le *New York Times*. (USA)
260 Illustration accompagnant un article sur la relégation de personnes en Sibérie. Du *New York Times*. (USA)
261 Illustration de journal abordant le problème de l'acne qui se pose particulièrement aux jeunes filles. (USA)
262 Illustration tirée de *Movimento*, un hebdomadaire politique. En noir et blanc. (BRA)
263 «En URSS, courage signifie égarement d'esprit.» D'un article publié dans un quotidien américain. (USA)

ARTIST / KÜNSTLER / ARTISTE:

258, 260 Eugene Mihaesco
259 Marguerita
261 Gary Viskupic
262 Rubem Campos Grilo
263 Kent Barton

ART DIRECTOR / DIRECTEUR ARTISTIQUE:

258–260 Eric Seidman
261 Paul Back
263 Kent Barton

PUBLISHER / VERLEGER / EDITEUR:

258–260 The New York Times
261 Newsday Inc.
262 Movimento
263 The Miami Herald

258

259

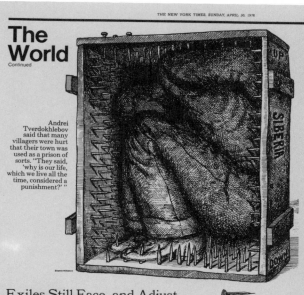

The World
Continued

Andrei Tverdokhlebov said that many villagers were hurt that their town was used as a prison of sorts. "They said, 'why is our life, which we live all the time, considered a punishment?'"

Exiles Still Face, and Adjust To Siberia's Inhumanity to Man

By DAVID K. SHIPLER

In Czarist Times, They Went on Foot

Some Natives Think They Are Spies

A Few Do Not Want to Leave

David K. Shipler is Moscow bureau chief of The New York Times.

Mondale Comes Calling

In Indonesia, Everybody That Counts Is a General

By HENRY KAMM

JAKARTA, Indonesia —

Henry Kamm covers Southeast Asia for The New York Times.

260

262

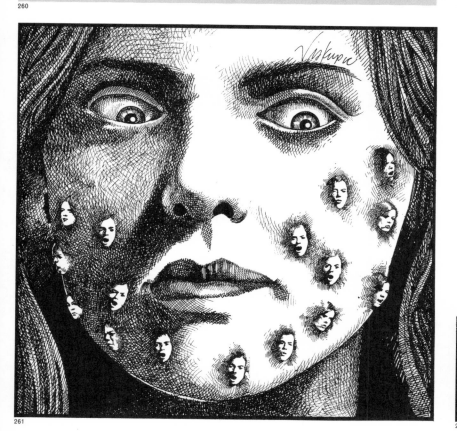

261

263

264

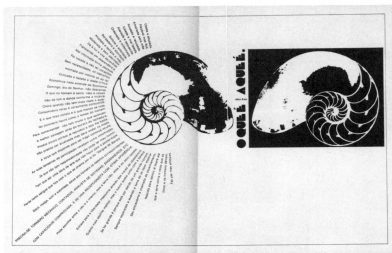

265

266

267

ARTIST / KÜNSTLER / ARTISTE:

264–268 Miran
269 Caribé
270 Eugene Mihaesco
271 George Stavrinos
271a Gary Viskupic

DESIGNER / GESTALTER / MAQUETTISTE:

264–269 Miran
270 Nancy Kent
271 Ruth Ansel

ART DIRECTOR / DIRECTEUR ARTISTIQUE:

264–269 Oswaldo Miranda
270 Nancy Kent
271 Ruth Ansel
271a Paul Back

AGENCY / AGENTUR / AGENCE – STUDIO:

271 Push Pin Studios, Inc.

PUBLISHER / VERLEGER / EDITEUR:

264–269 Diario do Parana
270, 271 The New York Times
271a Newsday Inc.

Newspaper Illustrations
Zeitungs-Illustrationen
Illustrations de journaux

270

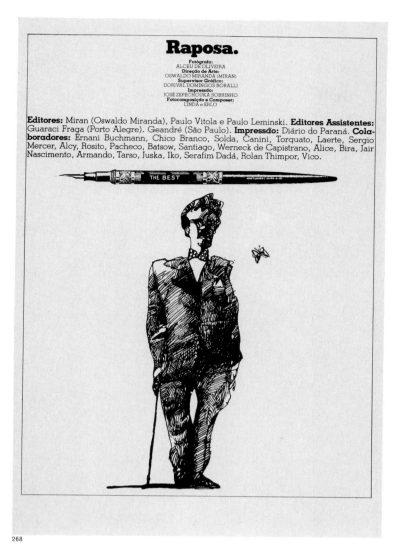
268

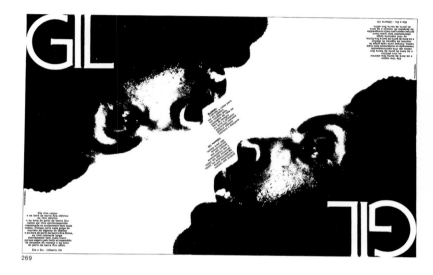
269

264—269 Five double spreads and a single page (Fig. 268) from *Raposa* (the fox), a fortnightly supplement to the newspaper *Diario do Parana,* with satirical texts and illustrations (all black and white). Fig. 268 is the copyright page. (BRA)
270 Black-and-white illustration for an article in the *New York Times* on the situation in Nicaragua in fall 1978. (USA)
271 Page from the fashion section of the *New York Times.* (USA)
271a Illustration to an article in *Newsday* about pollution of the seas with oil. (USA)

264—269 Fünf Doppelseiten und eine einzelne Seite (Abb. 268) aus *Raposa* (der Fuchs), einer zweiwöchentlich erscheinenden Beilage der Zeitung *Diario do Parana,* mit satirischen Texten und Illustrationen (alle schwarzweiss). Abb. 268 zeigt die Seite mit dem Impressum. (BRA)
270 Schwarzweiss-Illustration aus der *New York Times* zu einem Artikel über die Situation in Nicaragua (Herbst 1978). (USA)
271 Seite aus dem Mode-Sektor der *New York Times.* Hier geht es um die neuen Spangen für ordentliche Frisuren, passend zur neuen Mode. (USA)
271a Illustration aus der Zeitung *Newsday* zu einem Artikel über die Gefahr der Verseuchung der Meere durch auslaufendes Öl. (USA)

264—269 Cinq pages doubles et page (fig. 268) figurant dans *Raposa* (renard), un supplément qui paraît toutes les deux semaines dans le quotidien *Diario do Parana,* avec des textes et illustrations satiriques (toutes en noir-blanc). Fig. 268: illustration accompagnant la mention des responsables de l'édition et du contenu. (BRA)
270 Illustration en noir et blanc du *New York Times* figurant dans un article sur la situation au Nicaragua en automne 1978. (USA)
271 Page du supplément modes du *New York Times.* On y présente les nouvelles barrettes. (USA)
271a Illustration de *Newsday,* accompagnant un article sur la pollution de la mer par le pétrole. En noir et blanc. (USA)

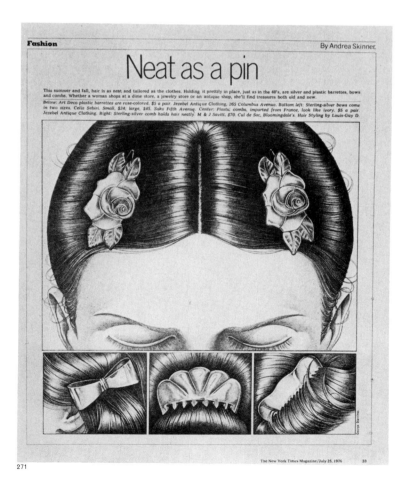
271

271a

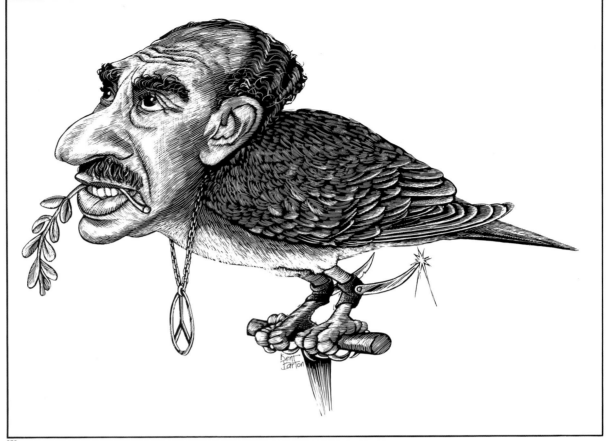

272

273

Newspaper Illustrations
Zeitungs-Illustrationen
Illustrations de journaux

272 Illustration to an article about peace negotiations between Israel and Egypt and the role of the USA. From *The Miami Herald*. (USA)
273 Illustration to an article in the *New York Times* about wars in Africa. (USA)
274 Full-page illustration to the weekly supplement *Calendar* of *The Boston Globe* newspaper, dealing with loud music and hearing. (USA)
275 Page from the newspaper *O Jornal Da Tarde* syndicating a report from *U.S. News & World Report* about possibilities in life after 40. (BRA)
276 Illustration to a discussion in the *Los Angeles Times* about the Californian death penalty. (USA)

272 Illustration zu einem Artikel über die Friedensverhandlungen zwischen Israel und Ägypten und die Rolle der USA. Aus dem Sektor «Standpunkt» der Zeitung *The Miami Herald*. (USA)
273 «Schmutzige kleine Kriege können plötzlich ausarten.» Illustration zu einem Artikel über die Kriege in Afrika und ihre Ursachen. Aus der *New York Times*. (USA)
274 Ganzseitige Illustration aus der wöchentlichen Beilage *Calendar* der Zeitung *The Boston Globe*. Thema sind die Auswirkungen lauter Musik auf das Gehör. (USA)
275 Seite aus der Zeitung *O Jornal Da Tarde* mit einem von *U.S. News & World Report* übernommenen Bericht über das Leben nach 40 und seine Möglichkeiten. (BRA)
276 Illustration zu einer Diskussion über die Abstimmungs-Frage in Kalifornien, ob das Gesetz über die Anwendung der Todesstrafe einer neuen Definition bedarf. Aus *Los Angeles Times*. (USA)

272 Illustration figurant dans un article sur les négociations de la paix entre Israël et l'Egypte et le rôle qu'ont joué les Etats-Unis. (USA)
273 «Des petites guerres sales peuvent éclater d'un coup.» Illustration d'un article sur les guerres en Afrique et leurs causes. Elément du *New York Times*. (USA)
274 Illustration pleine page du supplément hebdomadaire *Calendar* publié dans le *Boston Globe*. Sujet: la musique forte et les effets qu'elle a sur l'ouïe. (USA)
275 Page du quotidien *O Jornal Da Tarde* présentant un article reproduit d'un magazine américain. Il traite de la vie à l'âge de quarante et les possibilités qu'elle offre. (BRA)
276 Illustration accompagnant une discussion publiée dans le *Los Angeles Times* à l'occasion de la votation en Californie sur la loi de la peine capitale et la nouvelle interprétation de cette loi. (USA)

274

275

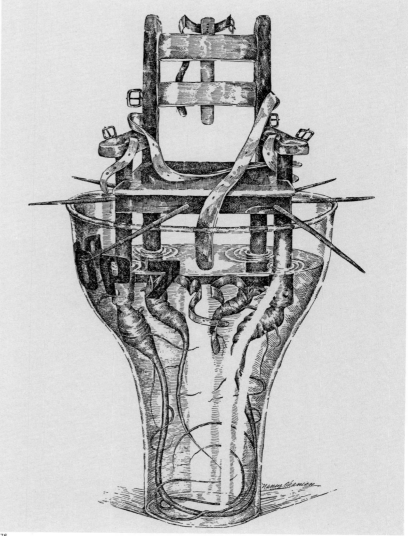

276

277

278

ARTIST / KÜNSTLER / ARTISTE:

277 Richard Hess
278 John Holmes
279 Gabriel Pascalini
280 Peter Brookes
281, 282 Ralph Steadman

279

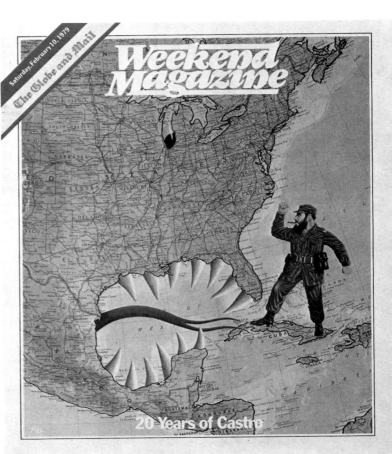

280

Magazine Covers

DESIGNER / GESTALTER / MAQUETTISTE:
277–282 Derek Ungless

ART DIRECTOR / DIRECTEUR ARTISTIQUE:
277–282 Robert Priest

PUBLISHER / VERLEGER / EDITEUR:
277–282 Montreal Standard Publishing Ltd.

277–282 Five covers of the newspaper-like *Weekend Magazine* and detail of one of them. Fig. 277 for an autumn number, in warm shades; Fig. 278 on the subject of ten years of women's liberation, in blue shades; Fig. 279 for a summer issue with red flowers and a white dress; Fig. 280 on the twenty-year rule of Fidel Castro, with a coloured map and red tongue; Figs. 281 and 282 on the controversial subject of seal hunting. (CAN)

277–282 Fünf Umschläge und Detail einer Illustration des in Zeitungsform erscheinenden *Weekend Magazine*. Abb. 277 für eine Herbstausgabe, in warmen Tönen; Abb. 278 zum Thema der Frauenemanzipation, in Blautönen; Abb. 279 für eine Sommerausgabe, mit roten Blumen und weissem Kleid; Abb. 280 zum Thema «Zwanzig Jahre Fidel Castro», mit farbiger Landkarte und roter Zunge; Abb. 281 und 282 zum Thema Robbenjagd. (CAN)

277–282 Cinq couvertures et détail d'une illustration du *Weekend Magazine* publié sous forme d'un quotidien. Fig. 277: pour le numéro d'automne, coloris chauds; fig. 278: sur l'émancipation des femmes, tons bleus; fig. 279: pour le numéro d'été, avec des fleurs rouges et une robe blanche; fig. 280: sur le 20ᵉ anniversaire de la prise de pouvoir par Fidel Castro, avec carte couleur et langue rouge; fig. 281 et 282: sur le sujet de la chasse aux phoques. (CAN)

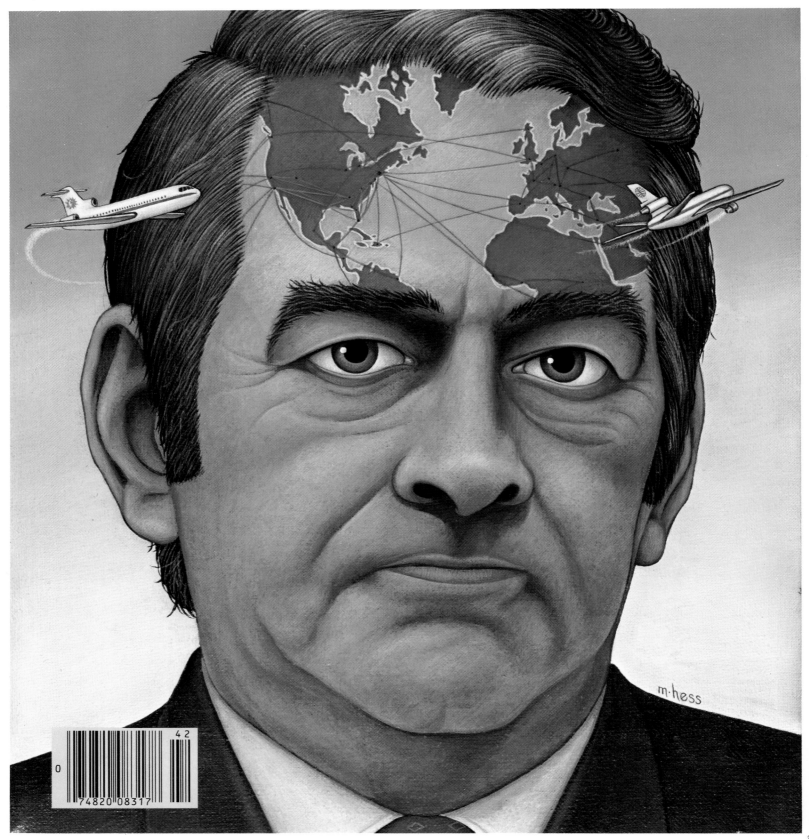

283

283, 284 Detail from an illustration and complete cover of *Forbes* magazine. Development of the *Pan Am* company. (USA)
285, 286 Colour covers of the building trade journal *Seko.* (JPN)
287 Cover of the magazine *Il Mondo.* "Does the Super Monetary Serpent Suit Italy?" Serpent mostly in green, blue and yellow. (ITA)
288 Colour cover of *Publishers Weekly,* dealing here with the announcement of new books in the spring. (USA)

283, 284 Detail der Illustration und kompletter Umschlag der Zeitschrift *Forbes.* Thema ist die Entwicklung der Fluggesellschaft *Pan Am.* (USA)
285, 286 Farbige Umschläge der Bau-Fachzeitschrift *Seko.* (JPN)
287 Umschlag des Magazins *Il Mondo.* «Passt Italien die Super-(Währungs)-Schlange?» Farben der Schlange vorwiegend Grün, Blau und Gelb. (ITA)
288 Farbiger Umschlag von *Publishers Weekly,* hier mit den Buchankündigungen für das Frühjahr. (USA)

283, 284 Détail de l'illustration et couverture complète du magazine *Forbes.* Elle se réfère au développement de la compagnie aérienne *PanAm.* (USA)
285, 286 Couvertures d'un magazine professionnel. En polychromie. (JPN)
287 «Le super-sepent, convient-il à l'Italie?» Couverture du magazine *Il Mondo.* Serpent en vert, bleu et jaune prédominant. (ITA)
288 Couverture polychrome de *Publishers Weekly,* ici présentant les nouvelles publications de printemps. (USA)

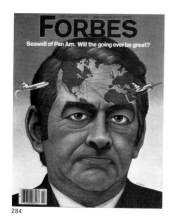

284

285

286

ARTIST / KÜNSTLER / ARTISTE:

283, 284 Mark Hess
287 Pietro Bestetti
288 Marguerita

DESIGNER / GESTALTER / MAQUETTISTE:

283, 284 Mark Hess
285, 286 Takenobu Igarashi

ART DIRECTOR / DIRECTEUR ARTISTIQUE:

283, 284 Peter Palazzo
285, 286 Takenobu Igarashi

AGENCY / AGENTUR / AGENCE – STUDIO:

285, 286 Takenobu Igarashi Design

PUBLISHER / VERLEGER / EDITEUR:

283, 284 Forbes Inc.
285, 286 Shokokusha Publishing Co., Inc.
287 Corriere della Sera
288 R.R. Bowker Company

287

288

289

290

Magazine Covers
Zeitschriften-Umschläge
Couvertures de périodiques

291

292

293

294

289 Full-colour cover of the magazine *Le Monde de la Musique*, published by the *Le Monde* newspaper. (FRA)
290 Cover of *Harrowsmith*, special magazine for those whose hobby is gardening. Green peas on a brown background. (USA)
291, 292 Covers of *Time* in full colour. Portrayed here are "The Man of the Year" and one of the numerous Russian dissenters facing trial in Russia. (USA)
293 Cover of the magazine *Poland*, which appears in six languages. Green latch. (POL)
294 Complete cover-page of the magazine *Poland*. (POL)
295–297 Covers of the literary magazine *The New Yorker*, Fig. 295: Wood colours with reddish-brown text, Fig. 296: Black and white with blue window and red-blue airmail envelope and stamp, Fig. 297: Colourful umbrellas on a yellowish background with blue lettering. (USA)

289 Farbiger Umschlag des Magazins *Le Monde de la Musique*, das von der Zeitung *Le Monde* herausgegeben wird. (FRA)
290 Umschlag von *Harrowsmith*, Fachzeitschrift für Hobbygärtner. Grüne Erbsen auf braunem Hintergrund. (USA)
291, 292 Farbige Umschläge des Magazins *Time*. Hier der «Mann des Jahres», Ten Hsiao-P'ing, und der Prozess von Anatoli Schtscharansky. (USA)
293 Umschlag der Zeitschrift *Polen*, die in sechs Sprachen erscheint. Grüne Klinke auf Fassung in Magenta-Rot. (POL)
294 Komplette Umschlagseite der Zeitschrift *Polen*. (POL)
295–297 Umschläge der Zeitschrift *The New Yorker*. Abb. 295 in Holzfarben mit rotbrauner Schrift, Abb. 296 schwarzweiss mit blauem Fenster und rot-blauem Luftpostcouvert und Briefmarke, Abb. 297 bunte Regenschirme auf gelblichem Hintergrund, blaue Schrift. (USA)

289 Couverture du magazine *Le Monde de la Musique*, publié par le quotidien *Le Monde*. En polychromie. (FRA)
290 Couverture d'une revue professionnelle s'adressant aux jardiniers de dimanche. Pois verts sur fond brun. (USA)
291, 292 Couvertures polychromes du magazine d'information *Time*, se référant à Ten Hsiao-Ping et aux procès des nombreux dissidents soviétiques. (USA)
293 Couverture du magazine *Pologne*, publié en six langues. Poignée en vert sur porte en magenta. (POL)
294 Couverture complète du magazine *Pologne*. (POL)
295–297 Couvertures du magazine *The New Yorker*. Fig. 295: typo rouge brun sur fond brun; fig. 296: illustration en noir et blanc avec fenêtre bleue et lettre aéropostale et timbre-poste en rouge et bleu; fig. 297: parapluies en couleurs vives sur fond jaunâtre, typo bleue. (USA)

295

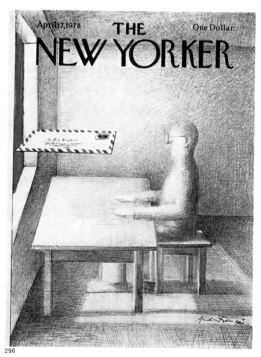

296

297

Télérama

1500

AH ! QUE C'ÉTAIT BEAU LE CINÉMA DU SAMEDI SOIR

298

Télérama

299

TODAY'S TEENS
*They have no respect for their elders, they dress like bums,
and their music... it's just noise.*

NATIONAL LAMPOON

August 1978   The Humo $1.50

McAfee

300

informations
et expressions culturelles

arts plastiques
littératures / poésies
musiques / spectacles
artisanats / sciences
alternatives

paraît le 1er et le 15

15/31 mai 1977

canal

4
numéro

5F

Peinture, quotidien et politique, débat avec Félix Guattari
Entretien avec Bernard Noël

Vostell / Baruchello / Dotremont / Art-Language
Jean Frémont / Rafael Alberti /

301

298, 299 Covers of the magazine *Télérama*. Fig. 298: "Those were wonderful times, when one used to go to the cinema on Saturdays", Fig. 299: New Year 1979, white flower with colourful orange, reddish-brown headline. (FRA)
300 Full-colour cover of the humour magazine *National Lampoon*, dealing here with the modern teenager. (USA)
301 Cover of the cultural periodical *Canal*, large format, in black and white. (FRA)
302 Full-colour draft for a *Spiegel* cover, dealing with the theme of solar energy. (GER)
303, 304 "The Price of a Frenchman." Detail and complete cover of the periodical *Le Nouvel Observateur*. (FRA)

298, 299 Umschläge des Magazins *Télérama*. Abb. 298: «Wie schön waren die Zeiten, als man samstags noch ins Kino ging», Abb. 299: Zum Jahresanfang 1979. Weisse Blume mit farbiger Orange, rotbrauner Titel. (FRA)
300 Farbiger Umschlag des Humor-Magazins *National Lampoon*. Thema: die heutigen Teenager. (USA)
301 Umschlag der Kultur-Zeitschrift *Canal*, grossformatig, in Schwarzweiss. (FRA)
302 Farbiger Entwurf für einen *Spiegel*-Umschlag, zum Thema Sonnenenergie. (GER)
303, 304 «Der Preis eines Franzosen.» Detail und kompletter Umschlag des Magazins *Le Nouvel Observateur*. (FRA)

298, 299 Couvertures du magazine *Télérama*, l'hebdomadaire d'opinion sur la télévision, le cinéma, la radio, les disques. Fig. 298: prédominance de tons bruns; fig. 299: numéro de Nouvel An. (FRA)
300 Couverture (polychrome) du magazine satirique *National Lampoon*. Sujet: les teenagers d'aujourd'hui. (USA)
301 Couverture d'un magazine culturel. Illustration en noir et blanc. (FRA)
302 Projet de couverture pour le magazine d'information *Der Spiegel*, se référant à l'énergie solaire. (GER)
303, 304 Détail et couverture complète du magazine d'information *Le Nouvel Observateur*. (FRA)

303

304

302

ARTIST / KÜNSTLER / ARTISTE:

298, 299 Etienne Delessert
300 Mara McAfee
301 Roman Cieslewicz
302 Ute Osterwalder
303, 304 André François

ART DIRECTOR / DIRECTEUR ARTISTIQUE:

298, 299 Pierre Bérard
300 Peter Kleinman
301 Alain Macaire
302 Eberhard Wachsmuth
303, 304 Robert Delpire

PUBLISHER / VERLEGER / EDITEUR:

298, 299 Télérama
300 21st Century Communications, Inc.
301 Canal
302 Spiegel-Verlag
303, 304 Nouvel Observateur

Magazine Covers

306

Magazine Covers

307

308

ARTIST / KÜNSTLER / ARTISTE:

305, 306 Patrice Ricord
307, 311 René Fehr
308, 309, 312 Barth
310 Fredy Sigg

ART DIRECTOR / DIRECTEUR ARTISTIQUE:

305, 306 Michael Rand
307–312 Franz Mächler

PUBLISHER / VERLEGER / EDITEUR:

305, 306 Sunday Times Magazine
307–312 Nebelspalter-Verlag

309

310

305, 306 Portrait and complete cover for an edition of the *Sunday Times Magazine* with an article about Valéry Giscard d'Estaing, the French President. (GBR)
307–312 Full-colour covers of the satirical magazine *Nebelspalter*, relating to the following: the "Click War" (Fig. 307), emancipation (Fig. 308), solar energy (Fig. 309), "The rich live more dangerously" with a suggestion for a camouflage outfit to be worn on the way to work (Fig. 310), mushrooms – with notification of a "mushroom party" in the magazine (Fig. 311) and pocket calculators and their consequences (Fig. 312). (SWI)

305, 306 Portrait und kompletter Umschlag für eine Nummer des *Sunday Times Magazine* mit einem Artikel über den französischen Staatspräsidenten Valéry Giscard d'Estaing. (GBR)
307–312 Mehrfarbige Umschläge der wöchentlich erscheinenden satirischen Zeitschrift *Nebelspalter*. Die Themen sind hier der «Klick-Krieg» (Abb. 307), die Emanzipation (Abb. 308), Sonnenenergie (Abb. 309), «Reiche leben gefährlicher» mit dem entsprechenden Vorschlag für einen Tarnanzug, der auf dem Weg zur Arbeit zu tragen ist (Abb. 31), Pilze, mit Hinweis auf eine «Pilzparty» in der Zeitschrift (Abb. 311) und Taschenrechner und ihre Folgen (Abb. 312). (SWI)

305, 306 Portrait et couverture complète d'un numéro du supplément hebdomadaire du *Sunday Times* avec un article sur le président de la République, Valéry Giscard d'Estaing. (GBR)
307–312 Couvertures (en polychromie) de l'hebdomadaire humoristique *Nebelspalter*. Elles se réfèrent à «La guerre clic» (fig. 307), à l'émancipation (fig. 308), à l'énergie solaire (fig. 309), «la vie des riches est plus dangereuse» avec des propositions concernant un vêtement de camouflage qu'ils portent en allant au travail (fig. 310), référence à la fête aux champignons (fig. 311) et aux calculatrices de poche et leurs conséquences (fig. 312). (SWI)

311

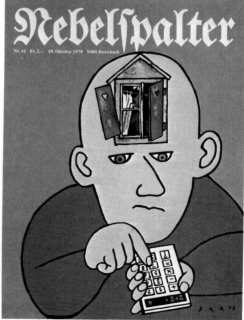

312

Magazine Illustrations

313

314

315

316

317

318

AGENCY / AGENTUR / AGENCE – STUDIO:

318 Eichinger Inc.

PUBLISHER / VERLEGER / EDITEUR:

313, 314 Penthouse International
315, 316 The Boston Globe
317 Promesses
318 Continental Group

313, 314 Lettering of the title and full-page illustration in full colour pertaining to a serial in *Penthouse*. The same lettering is used for all further instalments. Further illustrations from this serial are shown in Figs. 320 and 323. (USA)
315, 316 Full-page illustration in colour from the *Boston Sunday Globe*, with articles about Christmas (Fig. 315) and "moral education" in schools. (USA)
317 Black-and-white illustration from *Quart de Siècle*, a special edition from *Promesses*. (FRA)
318 Black-and-white illustration of the cover of *Insight*. A family consulting service provided by a bottle stopper manufacturer for his employees. (USA)

313, 314 Schriftzug des Titels und ganzseitige Illustration in Farbe zu einer Fortsetzungsgeschichte in *Penthouse*. Der Schriftzug wird für alle Folgen verwendet. Weitere Illustrationen daraus in Abb. 320 und Abb. 323. (USA)
315, 316 Ganzseitige Illustration in Farbe aus der Zeitung *Boston Sunday Globe*, mit Artikeln über Weihnachten (Abb. 315) und über ein neues Unterrichtsfach: Moral-Erziehung. (USA)
317 Schwarzweiss-Illustration aus *Quart de Siècle*, Sonderausgabe von *Promesses*. (FRA)
318 Schwarzweiss-Illustration des Umschlags von *Insight*. Das Thema: Familienberatungs-Dienst bei einem Flaschenverschluss-Hersteller für seine Angestellten. (USA)

313, 314 Conception calligraphique du titre et illustration pleine page (en polychromie) accompagnant une série d'articles dans *Penthouse*. La même conception typographique a été utilisée pour la série entière. Voir aussi les figs. 320 et 323. (USA)
315, 316 Illustrations pleines pages (en couleurs) du journal *Boston Sunday Globe*, se référant à un article sur la fête de Noël et à une nouvelle matière: éducation morale. (USA)
317 Illustration d'un numéro de *Quart de Siècle*, numéro spécial de *Promesses*. (FRA)
318 Illustration noir-blanc figurant sur la couverture de *Insight*. Sujet: service de planning familial dont profitent les employés d'un producteur de bouchons de cannettes. (USA)

319

320

Magazine Illustrations
Zeitschriften-Illustrationen
Illustrations de périodiques

319 Full-page illustration in full colour to a report in *Penthouse*. (USA)
320 Full-page introductory illustration to a serial feature published in *Penthouse*. In full colour. See also Figs. 313, 314 and 323. (USA)
321 Illustration to an article in *Penthouse*. Various brown shades, bright green garment with black. (USA)
322 Illustration in actual size to a story published in *Penthouse*. (USA)

319 Ganzseitige Illustration in Farbe zu einem Bericht in *Penthouse*: «Das Sex-Roulette». (USA)
320 Einleitende Illustration, ganzseitig, zu einer Fortsetzungsgeschichte («Tagebuch einer Jungfrau») in *Penthouse*. In Farbe. Siehe auch Abb. 313, 314 und 323. (USA)
321 «Der olympische Alptraum.» Illustration zu einem Artikel über die Gefahren eines übertriebenen athletischen Trainings für Kinder in *Penthouse*. Verschiedene Brauntöne, leuchtend grünes Trikot mit Schwarz. (USA)
322 Illustration in Originalgrösse zu einer Geschichte in *Penthouse*: «September Song». (USA)

319 «La sex-roulette.» Illustration pleine page accompagnant un rapport dans le magazine *Penthouse*. En polychromie. (USA)
320 Illustration pleine page, introduisant une histoire à suivre, publiée dans le magazine *Penthouse* («Journal d'une vierge»). En polychromie. Voir aussi les figs. 313, 314 et 323. (USA)
321 «Le cauchemar olympique.» Illustration figurant dans un article sur les dangers que l'entraînement athlétique forcé présente pour les enfants. Elément du magazine *Penthouse*. Divers tons bruns, tricot en vert et noir. (USA)
322 «Chanson de septembre.» Illustration (grandeur originale) de *Penthouse*. (USA)

ARTIST / KÜNSTLER / ARTISTE:

319 Ignazio Gomez
320 Robert Giusti
321 Alex Gnidziejko
322 Richard Waldrep

ART DIRECTOR / DIRECTEUR ARTISTIQUE:

319–322 Joe Brooks

PUBLISHER / VERLEGER / EDITEUR:

319–322 Penthouse International

321

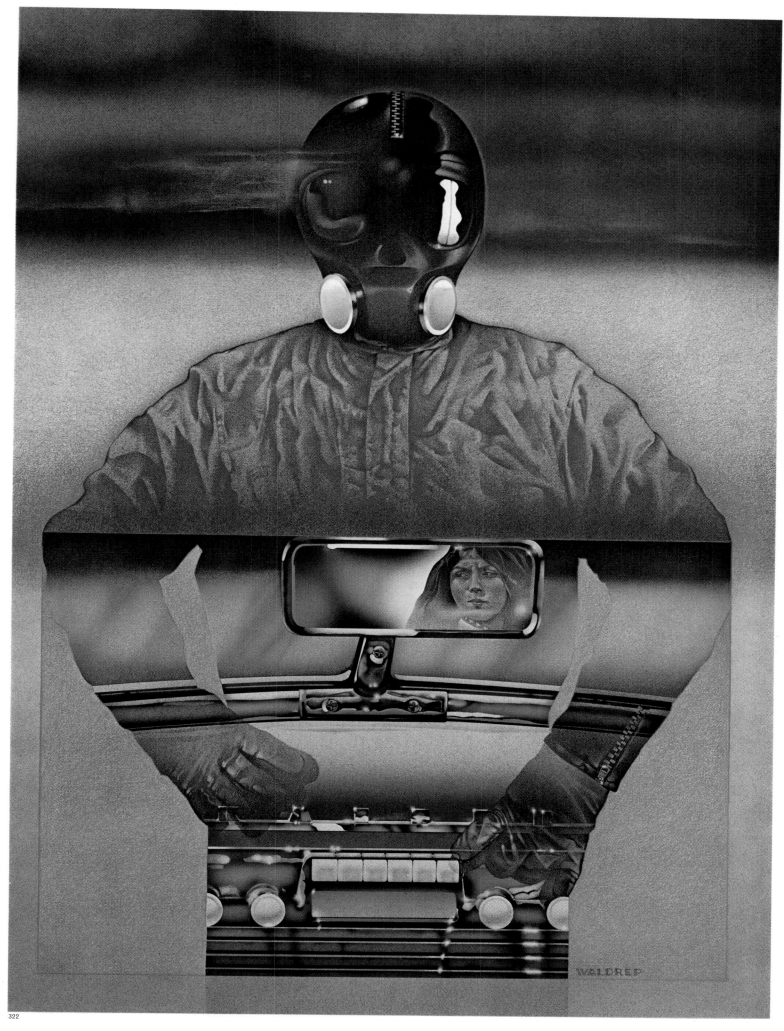

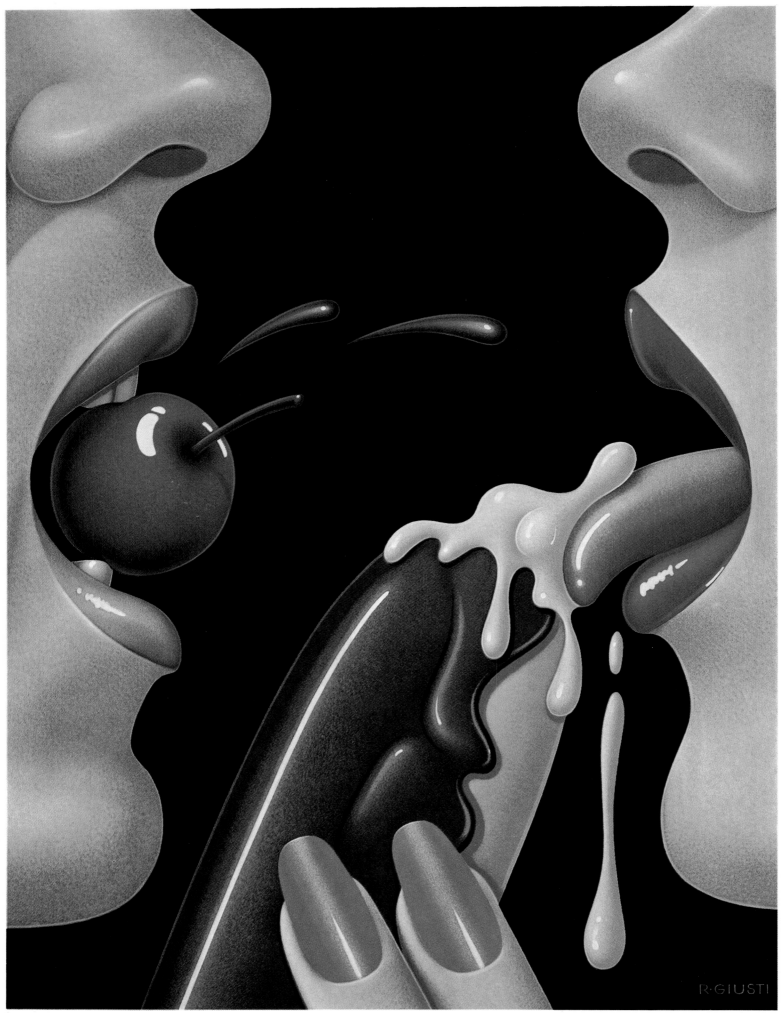

323

324

323 Illustration in actual size to an instalment of a serial published in *Penthouse*. See also Figs. 313, 314 and 320. (USA)
324 Introductory illustration in colour to an article in *Penthouse* pertaining to the reports of police brutality in Philadelphia. (USA)
325 Full-colour illustration of the introductory double spread to an article about the murder of Orlando Letelier. The current military régime in Chile is accused in this article of having assassinated its most vehement critic in the streets of Washington, D.C., with apparent impunity. From *Penthouse*. (USA)

323 Illustration in Originalgrösse zu einer Folge der in *Penthouse* veröffentlichten Geschichte «Tagebuch einer Jungfrau». Siehe auch Abb. 313, 314 und 320. (USA)
324 Einleitende Illustration in Farbe zu einem Artikel in *Penthouse* über Polizei-Brutalität in Philadelphia. (USA)
325 Farbige Illustration der einleitenden Doppelseite zu einem Artikel über die Ermordung von Orlando Letelier. Das gegenwärtige Militär-Regime in Chile wird beschuldigt, ihren schärfsten Kritiker in den Strassen von Washington, D.C., (ungestraft) ermordet zu haben. Aus *Penthouse*. (USA)

323 Illustration (en grandeur originale) accompagnant une série de récits du magazine *Penthouse*, intitulée «Journal d'une vierge». Voir aussi les illustrations 313, 314 et 320. (USA)
324 Illustration (en polychromie) introduisant un article sur la situation à Philadelphie: «Vivre dans l'angoisse» (face à la police). (USA)
325 Illustration couleur introduisant un rapport sur l'assassinat d'Orlando Letelier. On accuse le gouvernement militaire, actuellement au pouvoir au Chili, d'avoir fait liquider dans les rues de Washington l'un des critiques les plus acharnés du régime (sans punition des coupables). Elément de *Penthouse*. (USA)

ARTIST / KÜNSTLER / ARTISTE:

323 Robert Giusti
324 Jose Cruz
325 Kip Lott

ART DIRECTOR / DIRECTEUR ARTISTIQUE:

323–325 Joe Brooks

PUBLISHER / VERLEGER / EDITEUR:

323–325 Penthouse International

325

Magazine Illustrations
Zeitschriften-Illustrationen
Illustrations de périodiques

326

327

328

329

326, 327 Double spreads from the magazine *Grazia*. Fig. 326, with white/brown car on a brownish background, is the beginning of a story by Tennessee Williams, Fig. 327 introduces a story by John O'Hara. Mostly mustard brown, white and blue shades. (ITA)
328 Illustration from *Pardon* magazine. Grades of white, grey and brown. (GER)
329 Full-page illustration to a story in the periodical *Seventeen*. Subdued brown, yellow, green, blue and violet shades. (USA)
330 Page in full colour from *Weekend Magazine,* illustrating an article about mercenaries and the methods used to hire them. (CAN)

326, 327 Pages doubles du magazine de modes *Grazia*. La fig. 326 (voiture en brun et blanc sur fond brun) introduit une nouvelle de Tennessee Williams, la fig. 327 une nouvelle de John O'Hara. Prédominance de tons brun moutarde, blancs et bleus. (ITA)
328 Illustration tirée du magazine *Pardon*. Tons blancs, gris et bruns. (GER)
329 Illustration pleine page accompagnant un récit qui a paru dans le magazine *Seventeen*. Divers tons bruns, jaunes, verts, bleus et lilas. (USA)
330 Page (en couleurs) de *Weekend Magazine*. Elle accompagne un article sur la situation des mercenaires et les méthodes d'enrôlement. (CAN)

326, 327 Doppelseiten aus der Zeitschrift *Grazia*. Abb. 326, mit weiss/braunem Auto auf braunem Hintergrund, ist der Anfang einer Erzählung von Tennessee Williams, Abb. 327 leitet eine Erzählung von John O'Hara ein. Vorwiegend Senfbraun, Weiss und Blautöne. (ITA)
328 Illustration aus der Zeitschrift *Pardon*. Abstufungen von Weiss, Grau und Braun. (GER)
329 Ganzseitige Illustration zu einer Geschichte in der Zeitschrift *Seventeen*. Mit Schwarz gebrochene Braun-, Gelb-, Grün-, Blau- und Violett-Töne. (USA)
330 Farbige Seite aus *Weekend Magazine*. Sie illustriert einen Artikel über die Situation der Söldner und die Anheuerungsmethoden. (CAN)

ARTIST / KÜNSTLER / ARTISTE:

326, 327 Adelchi Galloni
328 Hans Arnold
329 Teresa Fasolino
330 Sue Coe

DESIGNER / GESTALTER / MAQUETTISTE:

330 Derek Ungless

ART DIRECTOR / DIRECTEUR ARTISTIQUE:

326, 327 Adelchi Galloni
328 Gerhard Kromschröder
329 Tamara Schneider
330 Robert Priest

PUBLISHER / VERLEGER / EDITEUR:

326, 327 Arnoldo Mandadori
328 Pardon Verlagsgesellschaft mbH
329 Seventeen Magazine
330 Montreal Standard Publishing Ltd.

330

331

Magazine Illustrations
Zeitschriften-Illustrationen
Illustrations de périodiques

331 Full-colour illustration to a short story in *Weekend Magazine* which appears in newspaper form. The story deals with a youngster who, by means of a clever trick with a coin, finally makes contact with his teacher. (CAN)
332 Double spread with full-colour illustrations from *Weekend Magazine*, pertaining to an article in which food is talked of in terms of a status symbol. (CAN)
333 A further illustration in full colour from *Weekend Magazine* relating to an article about the role of sneakers in the world of pop culture. (CAN)
334 Full-page illustration to an article about a football star. Brown face between colourful oranges and white paper. From *Weekend Magazine*. (CAN)
335 Full-colour illustration to an article about skiing in *Weekend Magazine*. (CAN)

332

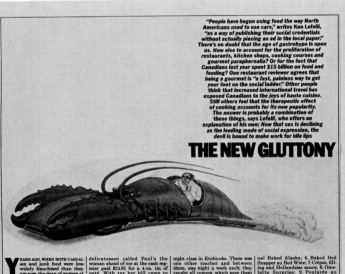

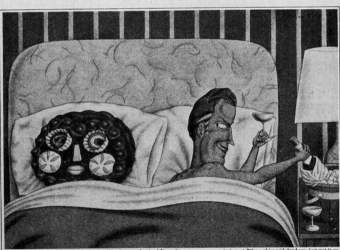

"People have begun using food the way North Americans used to use cars," writes Ken Lefolii, *"as a way of publishing their social credentials without actually placing an ad in the local paper."* There's no doubt that the age of gastrophy is upon us. How else to account for the proliferation of restaurants, kitchen shops, cooking courses and gourmet paraphernalia? Or for the fact that Canadians last year spent $15 billion on food and feeding? One restaurant reviewer agrees that being a gourmet is *"a fast, painless way to get your foot on the social ladder."* Other people think that increased international travel has exposed Canadians to the joys of haute cuisine. Still others feel that the therapeutic effect of cooking accounts for its new popularity. The answer is probably a combination of these things, says Lefolii, who offers an explanation of his own: Now that sex is declining as the leading mode of social expression, the devil is bound to make work for idle lips

THE NEW GLUTTONY

YEARS AGO, WHEN BOTH CASUAL sex and junk food were less widely franchised than they are now, the dean of women at an eastern university was reported to have issued a warning that began. "There is too much kissing going on right under my nose." We now know that kissing wasn't the half of it, having seen sex rise, peak and begin to decline as the leading mode of social expression. Today celibates are coming shyly out of the closet. Last May the Associated Press put on the wire a major survey of people who are withdrawing from participation in sexual activity. But we also know, or should have been able to guess, that the devil will find work for idle lips. Since kissing became passé I have been examining the evidence that these days what there is too much of going on under just about everybody's nose is eating.

The evidence is cast iron. We are now spending $15 billion a year on food and feeding. Since only a small part of this treasure goes into nourishment, the rest evidently goes into style, or what we might call gastrohype. The last time I was in a delicatessen called Paul's the woman ahead of me at the cash register paid $24.95 for a 4-oz. tin of paté. With tax her bill came to $26.50, so I told her in a spirit of neighborliness that spot silver was selling in the commodities markets that day for almost a dollar an ounce less than she was paying for liver paste. She said, "Really?" and turned her back. Meanwhile a marketing analyst named Mel Moyer at York University in Toronto has calculated that if present trends continue Canadians will soon be spending half their food money on eating outside their homes, and I have calculated that if everybody now enrolled in cooking classes goes home and cooks, there will be nobody on the streets after 6 p.m.

WE START THEM RIGHT AT the beginning," says Louise Dodson. "What knife to use for cutting up a tomato, how to cut it up without squirting juice all over yourself. But basically what I give them is just straight gourmet cooking." In 10 lessons the Wednesday gourmet class covers this written curriculum: 1. Puff pastries as Wines; 2. Montgomery's Meat Loaf with red salad; 3. Veal Cordon Bleu; 4. Beef Wellington; 5. Parsley rice, stuffed tomatoes, and individual Baked Alaska; 6. Baked Red Snapper au Red Wine; 7. Crêpes, filling and Hollandaise sauce, 8. Omelette Surprise; 9. Poularde au Champagne; and 10. Tournedos Grand Poivre Bouquetière.

Louise Dodson is a can-do woman; if she were a professional athlete, sports writers would say she had plenty smarts. So she tells her students that though they work only with the best ingredients in class, they can often get the same results at home by spending less. The Beef Wellington at Lesson 4 tastes no better made from filet than it does from a cut near the short ribs.

"They make it with filet anyway," she says. "They don't seem to care what things cost. When they're doing a salad they'll go for the Caesar every time. And they want to cook with liqueurs or wine. The countreau they burn up! I get the idea they don't think it's really gourmet unless there's wine in it."

Since nothing else her students say or do or wear or drive suggests they're all rich, Louise Dodson has come to believe that they're using food the way suburban North

HENCE THE RISE OF A CLASS of food merchant who caters to the demand. For instance, I have a Granny Smith habit, that started with a couple of apples a week and grew until now my main-

Americans once used cars, as a means of publishing their social credentials without actually placing an ad in the local paper. I've been able to forget a circulation manager who once gave me a ride in his new Buick, a four-holer, and, taking his eyes off the road to shoot me a significant look, said, "Let's face it, I'm buying prestige." He gave the impression that he had gone through the dealer's showroom like Commodore Vanderbilt through the boatyard, never asking the price of anything at home by spending less. The impression Louise Dodson's students want to give at table. "I'll teach them a seven-course menu. Then they'll invite their friends over for a dinner that takes three hours to eat. And not for one minute do they want anybody to get the idea that they're serving anything but the very best."

tenance dose is two a day (and I've been known to do three). This spring I could get them at a Loblaw store for 69 cents a pound, or at a Ziggy's store for 99 cents a pound. Same apples, same food chain—Ziggy's is the name Loblaw's puts on stores where the produce is less memorable than the prices. So successful was this tactic proven that new Ziggy's stores are opening while Loblaws' close. Dominion has its own high ticket stores, called Bittner's. In less time than it takes to munch a Granny Smith I can walk from (a) the Ziggy's where I began my researches into competitive overpricing to (b) a Bittner's where peameal bacon costs half a dollar a slice to (c) a high-cal boutique called Treats that sells big chocolate chip cookies for $3.50 each and often has customers lined up.

Treats is across the street from Creed's, where for many years well-heeled Toronto women went for clothes whose labels proclaimed their prices. These days much of the traffic through Creed's front door wheels sharply right and fetches up at Creed's own food boutique, where they carry asparagus at $15 each. This shop is actually a concession conceived and operated by two partners named Myra Sable and Carol Rosenfeld, who are doing more for mango chutney and sweet mustard than Simon and Garfunkel did for parsley, sage, rosemary and thyme. First, they keep a lot of women gainfully employed at home in their kitchens, putting up chutney and mustard and other things under the Sable and Rosenfeld label. They then sell these confections in their own shops, other specialty stores across Canada, in New York, Paris, London. Here, among customers who seek out such sophisticated provisioners, you would expect to find knowledgable shoppers with informed tastes.

"I can't really tell you that's so," says Carol Rosenfeld, her animated features sagging for an instant. "Around here it's show and tell."

A few yards away an elderly customer was discussing a purchase with the cashier.

"When do I put it on, dear?" she asked.

"It's, you know, mustard," the cashier said, "and you just put it on when you'd normally put mustard on."

YOU WILL HAVE NOTICED BY now that there is clearly a pricing mechanism at work in the food market these days that economic theory, whether in the tradition of Adam Smith in Karl Marx, has utterly failed to account for. What is pushing many of these prices up is neither the impersonal play of the marketplace nor the exploitative greed of the merchants, but the demands of the customers, who insist on paying more for food than it's worth. Only an economist would try to woo customers away from Creed's by offering asparagus at $14.50 a bottle; any good food merchant would know that his only chance was to put the stuff in a smaller bottle and charge $20. This is the mechanism that I earlier described as competitive overpricing, and though academics have been slow to grasp it, restaurant keepers have not.

For $4.50 we get five skinny little slices of dried-out Parma ham like

126

333

ARTIST / KÜNSTLER / ARTISTE:

331 Russel Mills
332 Blair Drawson
333 Milton Glaser
334 Peter Swan
335 Sue Coe

DESIGNER / GESTALTER / MAQUETTISTE:
331–335 Derek Ungless

ART DIRECTOR / DIRECTEUR ARTISTIQUE:
331–335 Robert Priest

PUBLISHER / VERLEGER / EDITEUR:
331–335 Montreal Standard Publishing Ltd.

331 Farbige Illustration zu einer Kurzgeschichte aus *Weekend Magazine,* das in Zeitungsform erscheint. Die Geschichte handelt von einem Jungen, der durch ein kleines Kunststück mit einer Münze Zugang zu seinem Lehrer findet. (CAN)
332 Doppelseite mit farbigen Illustrationen aus *Weekend Magazine.* «Die neue Gefrässigkeit» ist das Thema des Artikels, in dem von Nahrungsmitteln als Statussymbol gesprochen wird. (CAN)
333 Eine weitere Illustration, farbig, aus *Weekend Magazine,* hier zu einem Artikel über die Rolle von Turnschuhen in der Pop-Kultur. (CAN)
334 Ganzseitige Illustration zu einem Artikel über einen «Football»-Star. Braunes Gesicht zwischen farbigen Orangen und weissem Papier. Aus *Weekend Magazine.* (CAN)
335 Farbige Illustration zu einem Artikel über das Skilaufen. Aus *Weekend Magazine.* (CAN)

331 Illustration en couleurs accompagnant un récit qui a paru dans *Weekend Magazine.* On y raconte l'histoire d'un petit garçon, dont les relations avec son professeur s'améliorent grâce à un tour de passe-passe qu'il présente avec une pièce de monnaie. (CAN)
332 Page double avec des illustrations en couleurs, tirée de *Weekend Magazine.* L'article, intitulé «La nouvelle voracité», traite des denrés alimentaires en tant que symbole social. (CAN)
333 Illustration (en polychromie) de *Weekend Magazine,* figurant dans un article sur le rôle que jouent les chaussures de gymnastique dans la scène du pop. (CAN)
334 Illustration pleine page accompagnant un rapport sur un star de «Football». Visage brun, oranges polychromes sur papier blanc. Elément de *Weekend Magazine.* (CAN)
335 Illustration (en polychromie) de *Weekend Magazine.* Sujet: le ski. (CAN)

334

335

336

337

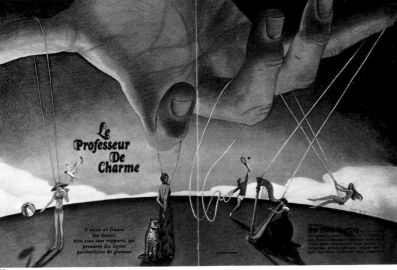
338

339

Magazine Illustrations

LE CADEAU *pour les cinq ans de play-boy, l'histoire vraie d'un trio amoureux...* D'ANNIVERSAIRE

ILLUSTRATION ALAIN GAUTHIER

nouvelle
Par ROBERT SABATIER de l'Académie Goncourt

ELLE SE PRENOMMAIT Beth. Sa bouche était couleur de lilas et une poussière de soleil constellait son nez. La vieille Angleterre avait façonné son éclat: les filles et les gazons sont ce que le temps réussit le mieux outre-Manche. Ses minces poignets, ses longues cuisses duvetées auraient suffi à m'affoler; je ne parle pas de l'ourlet de ses oreilles ou du pointu de sa langue passant rapidement sur ses lèvres. Je ne lui dis jamais mon adoration, car

340

ARTIST / KÜNSTLER / ARTISTE:

336 Eraldo Carugati
337 Tom Gala
338 Cathy Deeter
339, 340 Alain Gauthier
341 Dieter Ziegenfeuter

DESIGNER / GESTALTER / MAQUETTISTE:

336 Kerig Pope
337 Len Willis

ART DIRECTOR / DIRECTEUR ARTISTIQUE:

336, 337 Arthur Paul
338–340 Régis Pagniez
341 Rainer Wörtmann

PUBLISHER / VERLEGER / EDITEUR:

336, 337 Playboy Enterprises, Inc.
338–340 Publications Filipacchi
341 Heinrich Bauer Verlag

336 Portrait pleine page de Sirhan, l'assassin de Robert Kennedy. Cet article de *Playboy* se fonde sur les dépositions d'un camarade de Sirhan, détenu dans la même cellule. (USA)
337 Page double (en couleurs) d'un article de *Playboy* sur le parachutisme. (USA)
338 Page double introduisant un article dans l'édition française du *Playboy*. En couleurs. (FRA)
339 Page double introduisant une histoire sur une petite fille moderne dans l'édition française du *Playboy*. Fille blanche sur fond sombre, magasin bleu. (FRA)
340 Page double introduisant une histoire vraie d'un trio amoureux; c'était le cadeau pour les cinq ans de l'édition française du *Playboy*. Tons bleus et lilas atténué. (FRA)
341 Illustration d'un article sur le rôle que l'Allemagne a joué en Afrique. (GER)

341

345

342, 345 Critical illustrations from a feature on American television quiz shows with prize-money. Fig. 342: a red "sun", yellow and red sky above sparkling blue water. From the graphic design magazine *Idea*. (JPN)
343 Double spread from the youth magazine *Bananas*. Mostly in brown, yellow and green. (USA)
344 Full-page illustration to a story entitled "How one can get rid of an old uncle". Countryside in brown shades, white clouds and blue sky with the tree in dark brown. Published in the German edition of *Playboy*. (GER)

342, 345 ‚Kritische Illustrationen von amerikanischen Fernseh-Quiz-Sendungen, bei denen Geld zu gewinnen ist. Abb. 342 mit roter «Sonne», gelbem und rotem Himmel über blauem Wasser. Aus dem Graphik-Magazin *Idea*. (JPN)
343 Doppelseite aus der Jugend-Zeitschrift *Bananas*. Hier geht es um den Modespass mit Schals, Bändern, Gürteln und anderen Extras. Vorwiegend Braun, Gelb und Grün. (USA)
344 Ganzseitige Illustration zu einer Geschichte mit dem Titel: «Wie man einen alten Onkel los wird». Landschaft in Brauntönen, weisse Wolken und blauer Himmel, Baum in Dunkelbraun. Aus der deutschen Ausgabe des *Playboy*. (GER)

342, 345 Illustrations critiques sur un jeu de la TV américaine avec des prix en argent comptant. Fig. 342: «soleil» rouge, ciel jaune et rouge, mer bleue. Eléments publiés dans le magazine d'arts graphiques *Idea*. (JPN)
343 Page double d'un magazine pour les jeunes. On y montre que la mode est un jeu amusant avec des foulards, rubans, ceintures et accessoires. En brun, jaune et vert. (USA)
344 Illustration pleine page accompagnant une histoire intitulée «Comment se débarasser d'un vieil oncle». Paysage en tons bruns, nuages blanches, ciel bleu, arbre en brun foncé. Elément de l'édition allemande du *Playboy*. (GER)

ARTIST / KÜNSTLER / ARTISTE:

342, 345 Sue Coe
343 Teresa Anderko
344 Wurlitzer Studios

DESIGNER / GESTALTER / MAQUETTISTE:

343 Bob Feldgus
344 George Guther

ART DIRECTOR / DIRECTEUR ARTISTIQUE:

343 Bob Feldgus
344 Rainer Wörtmann

PUBLISHER / VERLEGER / EDITEUR:

342, 345 Seibundo-Shinkosha Publishing Co.
343 Scholastic Book Services
344 Heinrich Bauer Verlag

Magazine Illustrations
Zeitschriften-Illustrationen
Illustrations de périodiques

346

347

346 Illustration pleine page figurant dans un article de *Psychology Today*. On y aborde le sujet des camarades invisibles (ici la souris) avec qui la plupart des enfants joue. (USA)
347 Illustration en noir et blanc de *Psychology Today*. Elle se réfère aux chefs de file modernes tels qu'ils sont représentés dans les livres: le joueur et le narcisse. (USA)
348, 349 Illustrations pleines pages en couleurs de *Psychology Today*. Sujets des articles: les prédispositions criminelles et les possibilités d'influencer le cours des rêves. (USA)

346 Full-page illustration to an article in *Psychology Today*. (USA)
347 Black-and-white illustration from *Psychology Today*, dealing with the kind of leadership which the modern corporation fosters. Here the "gamesman" and "narcissus". (USA)
348, 349 Full-page illustrations in colour from *Psychology Today,* pertaining to the criminal mind and the possibility of an influence on dreams. (USA)

346 Ganzseitige Illustration zu einem Artikel in *Psychology Today*. Thema sind die unsichtbaren Spielgefährten, hier die Maus, die bei der Hälfte aller Kinder auftauchen. (USA)
347 Schwarzweiss-Illustration aus *Psychology Today*. Es geht um die in verschiedenen Büchern als typisch dargestellten Führungskräfte unserer Zeit, den Spieler und den Narziss. (USA)
348, 349 Ganzseitige Illustrationen in Farbe aus *Psychology Today*. Themen der Artikel sind kriminelle Veranlagungen und die Möglichkeit einer Einflussnahme auf Träume. (USA)

ARTIST / KÜNSTLER / ARTISTE:

346 Marvin Mattelson
347 Robert Pryor
348 Rich Grote
349 Paul Giovanopoulos

DESIGNER / GESTALTER / MAQUETTISTE:

346, 347 Rom Lulevitch
348, 349 Carveth Kramer

ART DIRECTOR / DIRECTEUR ARTISTIQUE:

346–349 Carveth Kramer

PUBLISHER / VERLEGER / EDITEUR:

346–349 Ziff-Davis Publishing

Magazine Illustrations

348

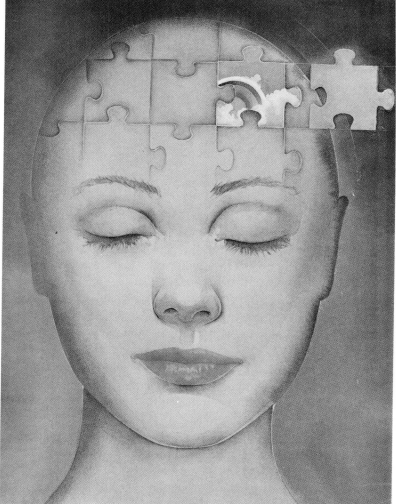

349

350 Introductory illustration to an article published in *Psychology Today*, in which certain aspects of the creative process and personal communication are compared. (USA)
351 Cover illustration from *TriQuarterly*, dealing with men and women. (USA)
352 Black-and-white illustration from the magazine *The Nation* concerning an article about activities of business groups against unions. (USA)
353 Illustration in blue and white to an article published in *Psychology Today* about the political journalists acting as "psycho-analysts" of presidential candidates. (USA)
354 Full-colour illustration to an article in *Psychology Today* on the theme of abrasive personalities in business and the resulting problems. (USA)
355 Full-page illustration to an article about the overwhelming popularity of beef in America. From *Psychology Today*. (USA)

350 Einleitende Illustration zu einem Artikel, in dem Vergleiche zwischen einem kreativen Prozess, wie dem des Malens, und der persönlichen Kommunikation gezogen werden im Hinblick auf die blockierende Wirkung einer zu starken Selbstkontrolle. Aus *Psychology Today*. (USA)
351 Umschlag-Illustration des Magazins *TriQuarterly* zum Thema Männer und Frauen. (USA)
352 Schwarzweiss-Illustration aus der Zeitschrift *The Nation* zu einem Artikel über die Aktivitäten grosser Unternehmensgruppen gegen die Gewerkschaften. (USA)
353 «Die Psychoanalytiker der (Präsidentschafts-)Kandidaten.» Illustration in Blauweiss zu einem Artikel in *Psychology Today*. (USA)
354 Farbige Illustration zu einem Artikel über den Typ eines taktlosen Menschen im Geschäftsleben und die daraus resultierenden Probleme. Aus *Psychology Today*. (USA)
355 Ganzseitige Illustration zu einem Artikel über die Favoritenstellung von Rindfleisch in den USA. Aus der Rubrik «Nahrung und Bewusstsein» in *Psychology Today*. (USA)

350 Illustration introduisant un article de *Psychology Today*. On y met en comparaison le processus créatif, la peinture p.ex., avec la communication personnelle sous l'aspect d'un auto-contrôle prononcé qui a un effet inhibitif. (USA)
351 Illustration de couverture d'un magazine. Sujet: l'homme et la femme. (USA)
352 Illustration en noir et blanc du magazine *The Nation*. Elle figure dans un article sur les activités des entreprises multinationales face aux syndicats. (USA)
353 «Les psychanalistes des candidats (à la présidence)». Illustration en blanc et bleu accompagnant un article du magazine *Psychology Today*. (USA)
354 Illustration (en polychromie) pour un article sur les hommes d'affaires qui manquent de tact et les problèmes qui en résultent. Elément de *Psychology Today*. (USA)
355 Illustration pleine page de la rubrique «Nourriture et conscience» de *Psychology Today*. On y aborde le problème de la viande de bœuf, la viande préférée aux Etats-Unis. (USA)

351

352

355

Magazine Illustrations
Zeitschriften-Illustrationen
Illustrations de périodiques

135

357

ARTIST / KÜNSTLER / ARTISTE:

356, 357 Monica Schultz
358 Roman Cieslewicz

ART DIRECTOR / DIRECTEUR ARTISTIQUE:

356, 357 Rolf Vestberg
358 Antoine Kieffer

PUBLISHER / VERLEGER / EDITEUR:

356, 357 Femina
358 Elle/France Editions et Publications

Magazine Illustrations
Zeitschriften-Illustrationen
Illustrations de périodiques

358

356, 357 Introductory double spread and detail of illustration to a short story in *Femina*. Green, blue-grey and orange. (SWE)
358 Full-page illustration in black and white from *Elle*, the women's periodical, pertaining to an invitation to readers to participate in a creativity competition in which works of weaving and embroidery can be sent in as well as entries for the painting and photographic section. (FRA)

356, 357 Einleitende Doppelseite und Detail der Illustration zu einer Kurzgeschichte in *Femina*. Grün, Blaugrau und Orange. (SWE)
358 Ganzseitige Illustration in Schwarzweiss aus der Frauenzeitschrift *Elle*. Es geht um eine Einladung an die Leserinnen zur Teilnahme an einem Kreativitäts-Wettbewerb, zu dem Stick- und Webarbeiten sowie auch Photos und Bilder eingereicht werden können. (FRA)

356, 357 Page double introduisant un conte dans le magazine *Femina* et détail de l'illustration. Vert, bleu gris et orange. (SWE)
358 Illustration pleine page (en noir et blanc) figurant dans le magazine féminin *Elle*. On invite les lectrices à participer dans un concours de créativité pour lequel sont acceptés des broderies, des tissages, des photos et des peintures. (FRA)

Magazine Illustrations

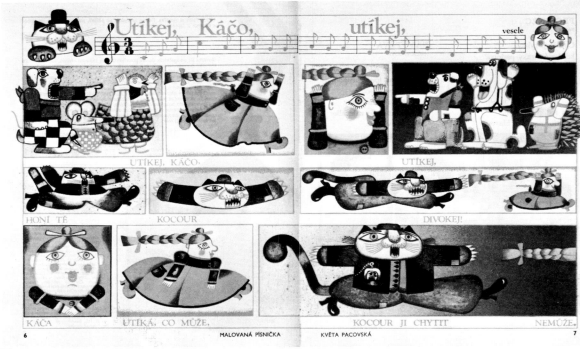

359

359 Double spread from a children's magazine. Mostly shades of red, orange and brown. (CSR)
360 Illustration for an article in the *New York Times* on the leading position of Japan in the world of audio equipment. (USA)
361 Full-page illustration from *Harrowsmith*, specialized magazine for hobby gardeners. (CAN)
362, 363 Illustrations from the monthly children's reading-book *J'aime lire.* (FRA)
364 A vision of horseracing from the magazine *Sports Illustrated*. Here roses draped around the winner, evoking for the artist "the ghosts of many notables of past eras. But few people saw them, absorbed as they were in watching the ceremony". (USA)

359 Doppelseite aus einer Kinderzeitschrift. Vorwiegend Rot-, Orange- und Brauntöne. (CSR)
360 «Wie lange noch kann Japan die Welt der Audio-Geräte regieren?» Illustration zu einem Artikel in der *New York Times*. (USA)
361 Ganzseitige Illustration aus *Harrowsmith*, Fachzeitschrift für Hobby-Gärtner. (CAN)
362, 363 Illustrationen aus dem monatlich erscheinenden Kinder-Lesebuch *J'aime lire.* (FRA)
364 Aus *Sports Illustrated,* eine Vision zu Pferderennen. Hier der Sieger, geschmückt mit Rosen, die «den Geist vieler Persönlichkeiten vergangener Zeiten heraufbeschwören. Aber nur wenige sahen sie, da sie in die Betrachtung der Siegerehrung versunken waren». (USA)

360   361

138

362

363

359 Page double d'un magazine pour enfants. Prédominance de tons rouges, orange et bruns. (CSR)
360 «Combien de temps la prédominance japonaise durera-t-elle encore dans le domaine des appareils audio-visuels?» Illustration d'un article paru dans le *New York Times*. (USA)
361 Illustration pleine page d'un magazine professionnel des jardiniers de dimanche. (CAN)
362, 363 Illustrations de *J'aime Lire*, un recueil de lectures mensuelles pour enfants. (FRA)
364 Voici la vision d'une course de chevaux, publiée dans *Sports Illustrated*. Pour l'artiste, cet événement évoque «les esprits de nombreuses personnalités d'antan. Mais ce n'étaient que quelques-uns qui les ont vus, parce qu'ils étaient absorbés par la remise des prix». (USA)

364

365

366

367

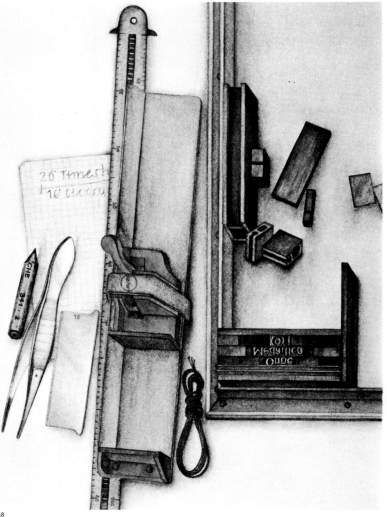

368

ARTIST / KÜNSTLER / ARTISTE:

365 Cathy Hull
366 John O'Leary
367 Oscar de Mejo
368 Dora Wespi
369 Jacqui Morgan
370 Hedda Johnson

DESIGNER / GESTALTER / MAQUETTISTE:

365 Nancy Kent
366 Vincent Winter
367 Richard Gangel
370 Herb Lubalin

ART DIRECTOR / DIRECTEUR ARTISTIQUE:

365 Nancy Kent
366 Robert Black
367 Richard Gangel
368 Albert Kaelin
369 Joe Connolly
370 Herb Lubalin

AGENCY / AGENTUR / AGENCE – STUDIO:

370 LSC&P Design Group

PUBLISHER / VERLEGER / EDITEUR:

365 The New York Times
366 Straight Arrow Publishers
367 Sports Illustrated
368 Tages-Anzeiger AG
369 Genesis Magazine
370 International Typeface Corp.

365 Illustration from the *New York Times*. (USA)
366 Portrait of a famous billiard player in *Rolling Stone* magazine. Face in yellow, blue and red. (USA)
367 From a feature in *Sports Illustrated* on horse racing. See also Fig. 364. (USA)
368 Colour spread from the *Tages-Anzeiger Magazin*, pertaining to an article on the development of printing. (SWI)
369 Page from *Genesis* magazine with a report on the supposedly highest paid baseball player in America. (USA)
370 Double spread out of *U&lc*, the printed organ of the International Typeface Corporation. Animal names for cars. (USA)

365 Illustration aus der *New York Times*: «Denker denken über das Lehren des Denkens – indem sie Computer benutzen um Gedanken vorzutäuschen.» (USA)
366 Portrait eines berühmten Billard-Spielers aus *Rolling Stone*. Gesicht in Gelb, Blau und Rot. (USA)
367 Aus einer Reihe von «Visionen» zu Pferderennen. Siehe auch Abb. 364. Aus *Sports Illustrated*. (USA)
368 Farbige Seite aus dem *Tages-Anzeiger Magazin*. Aus einem Artikel über die Entwicklung des Druckens, hier das Handwerkszeug des Handsetzers. (SWI)
369 Seite aus der Zeitschrift *Genesis* mit Bericht über den angeblich bestbezahlten Baseball-Spieler der USA. (USA)
370 Doppelseite aus *U&lc*, Zeitschrift einer Typographen-Vereinigung. Hier die Tiernamen für Autos. (USA)

365 Illustration du *New York Times*: «Les penseurs méditent sur l'enseignement de la méditation – en utilisant des ordinateurs pour simuler des pensées.» (USA)
366 Portrait d'un joueur de billard bien connu. Visage en jaune, bleu et rouge. (USA)
367 D'une série de visions de courses de chevaux. Voir aussi la fig. 364. De *Sports Illustrated*. (USA)
368 Page du magazine hebdomadaire d'un quotidien. Elle accompagne un article sur le développement de l'impression. On y montre les outils du compositeur à main. (SWI)
369 Page du magazine *Genesis* avec un rapport sur le joueur de baseball le mieux payé aux Etats-Unis. (USA)
370 Page double du magazine d'une association de typographes. Sujet: noms d'animaux donnés aux voitures. (USA)

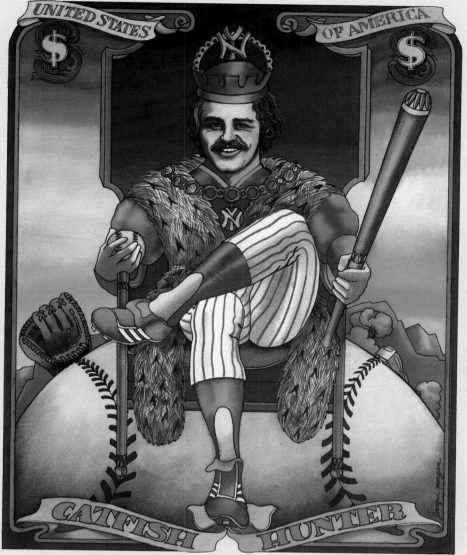

369

370

374

371

372

371 Colour portrait of the young mayor of Cleveland, shown in *Ohio Magazine*. (USA)
372 Double spread with colour illustration for ironical suggestions for gifts. Published in *Bananas*. (USA)
373 Illustration from *Kontakt* with tips for preparing tea when a gale force 10 is blowing. (GER)
374, 375 Two double spreads from the literary magazine *The New Yorker*. Fig. 375: beginning of the series "Screen", Fig. 374: the end. (USA)
376, 377 Double spreads from an article about the maltreatment of women which appeared in the *Civil Rights Digest*, published by the Human Rights Committee. (USA)

371 Farbiges Portrait des jungen Bürgermeisters von Cleveland aus *Ohio Magazine*. (USA)
372 Doppelseite mit farbigen Illustrationen zu ironischen Geschenkvorschlägen. Aus *Bananas*. (USA)
373 Illustration aus *Kontakt* mit Tips für die Tee-Zubereitung bei Windstärke zehn. (GER)
374, 375 Zwei Doppelseiten aus der Zeitschrift *The New Yorker*. Abb. 375 zeigt den Anfang der Folge mit dem Titel «Bildschirm», Abb. 374 das Ende. (USA)
376, 377 Doppelseiten aus einem Artikel über die Misshandlung von Frauen, erschienen in dem von der amerikanischen Menschenrechtskommission herausgegebenen Zeitschrift *Civil Rights Digest*. (USA)

371 Portrait (en couleurs) du jeune maire de Cleveland. Elément du *Ohio Magazine*. (USA)
372 Page double avec des illustrations en couleurs présentant des cadeaux «ironiques». De *Bananas*. (USA)
373 Illustration du magazine *Kontakt*: propositions pour préparer du thé par un vent qui souffle à une intensité de 10. Reproduction en grandeur originale. (GER)
374, 375 Pages doubles du magazine littéraire *The New Yorker*. Fig. 375 montre le début de l'histoire intitulée «Ecran», la fig. 376 la fin. (USA)
376, 377 Début et illustration double page d'un article sur les femmes battues dans le *Civil Rights Digest*, publié par la commission américaine des droits civiques. (USA)

373

Magazine Illustrations
Zeitschriften-Illustrationen
Illustrations de périodiques

378

379

ARTIST / KÜNSTLER / ARTISTE:

378, 380 Tullio Pericoli
379 Peter Brookes
381 John Holmes
382 Reagan Wilson

378 Colour illustration to an article in the magazine *Espresso* about the consequences of Moro's death in relation to individual Italians and especially the mentally ill. (ITA)
379 Colour illustration to an article in the *Sunday Times Magazine* about animals in danger of becoming extinct due to the fashion industry. (GBR)
380 Portrait of the philosopher Herbert Marcuse in conjunction with an interview with him in *Espresso* about the emancipation of women. In colour. (ITA)
381 From the *Sunday Times Magazine* on a father's role in pre-school education. (GBR)
382 Colour page from *Body Forum Magazine*. (USA)

378 Farbige Illustration zu einem Artikel in der Zeitschrift *Espresso* über die Auswirkungen von Moros Tod auf den einzelnen Italiener und speziell auf psychisch Kranke. (ITA)
379 Farbige Illustration aus einem Artikel im *Sunday Times Magazine* über die durch die Mode-Industrie gefährdeten Tiere. (GBR)
380 Portrait des Philosophen Herbert Marcuse aus einem Interview mit ihm in *Espresso*. Thema ist die Emanzipation der Frau. In Farbe. (ITA)
381 Aus *Sunday Times Magazine:* Die Rolle des Vaters in der Vorschulerziehung. (GBR)
382 Farbige Seite aus dem Gesundheits- und Schönheitsmagazin *Body Forum Magazine*. (USA)

378 Illustration polychrome accompagnant un article du magazine d'information *Espresso*. On y discute les conséquences qu'a eu la mort de Moro sur l'Italien et les malades mentaux. (ITA)
379 Illustration polychrome d'un numéro du *Sunday Times Magazine*. L'article traite des animaux menacés par les besoins de la mode. (GBR)
380 Portrait du philosophe allemand Herbert Marcuse, figurant dans un interview avec lui dans le magazine d'information *Espresso*. On y discute l'emancipation de la femme. (ITA)
381 *Sunday Times Magazine:* le rôle du père dans l'éducation avant l'entrée en maternelle. (GBR)
382 Page (en couleurs) tirée d'un magazine de santé et de beauté. (USA)

DESIGNER / GESTALTER / MAQUETTISTE:

382 Art Jones

ART DIRECTOR / DIRECTEUR ARTISTIQUE:

378, 380 Elio Aloisio
379, 381 Michael Rand
382 Art Jones

PUBLISHER / VERLEGER / EDITEUR:

378, 380 L'Espresso
379, 381 Sunday Times Magazine
382 Body Forum Magazine

Magazine Illustrations

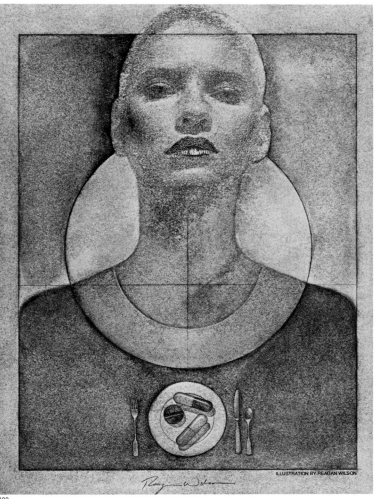

383

383 Illustration to a story in serial form published in the magazine *Stern*. (GER)
384 Double spread in *Family Health* magazine. The feature is about so-called "surgery by substitutes" in American hospitals. (USA)
385 Illustration from *Marie-Claire*: women's possibilities of defence. (FRA)
386 Eugene Mihaesco's rendering of a redesigned New York City incorporating suggestions from several architects, artists and culture raters who were asked for their ideas on this subject. From *Art News*. (USA)

383 Illustration zu einem Fortsetzungsroman im *Stern*. Hier ein Amtsdiener. (GER)
384 Doppelseite in Blau und Weiss aus *Family Health*. Der Titel «Ghost Surgery» (Geister-Chirurgie) bezieht sich auf Berichte, denen zufolge Chirurgen sich ohne Wissen der Patienten durch Assistenten oder zu «kaufende», wenig erfahrene Chirurgen vertreten lassen. (USA)
385 Illustration aus *Marie-Claire*: Die Verteidigungsmöglichkeiten der Frauen. (FRA)
386 Illustration aus *Art News* zu einem Bericht über Änderungsvorschläge von zweiundzwanzig Architekten, Künstlern und Kulturbeauftragten für die Stadt New York. (USA)

383 Illustration en noir et blanc introduisant un roman à suivre dans le magazine *Stern*. (GER)
384 Page double de *Family Health*. L'article, intitulé «La chirurgie des fantômes», discute des investigations selon lesquelles les chirurgiens se sont fait remplacer par des assistants ou des chirurgiens peu expérimentés qu'ils ont «achetés», sans informer le patient. (USA)
385 Illustration de *Marie-Claire* accompagnant un article intitulé: «Se défendre avec ses talons ou son fusil de chasse». En noir et blanc. (FRA)
386 Illustration de *Art News*: rapport sur les propositions que vingt-deux architectes, artistes et créateurs culturels ont fait en vue de modifications de la ville de New York. (USA)

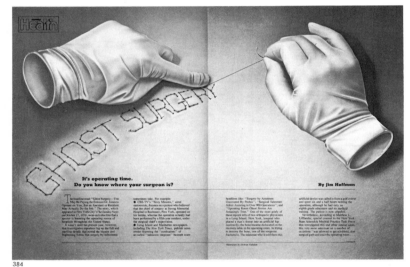

384

ARTIST / KÜNSTLER / ARTISTE:

383 Dietrich Lange
384 Dickran Palulian
385 Cyril Arnstam
386 Eugene Mihaesco

DESIGNER / GESTALTER / MAQUETTISTE:

384 Lester Goodman

ART DIRECTOR / DIRECTEUR ARTISTIQUE:

384 Lester Goodman
385 Dominique Pennors
386 Mary Mullin

PUBLISHER / VERLEGER / EDITEUR:

383 Gruner & Jahr AG & Co
384 Family Media Inc.
385 Marie-Claire
386 Art News

Magazine Illustrations

385

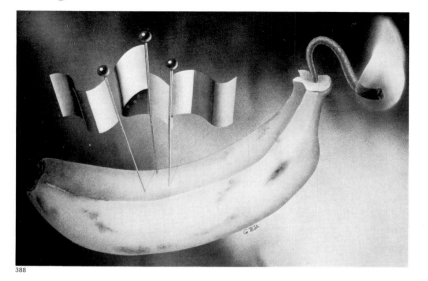

388

389

387 Page from an article published in *Esquire* magazine. (USA)
388 Illustration to an article in *Lui* pertaining to the tense situation on the Canary Islands. Yellow banana with white-blue-yellow banners on blue. (SPA)
389 Colour illustration to a short story in *Femina*. (SWE)
390 Colour illustration for an article in *Creative Living* magazine. (USA)
391 Full-page black-and-white illustration from *Technology Review*. (USA)

387 Seite aus einem Artikel in der Zeitschrift *Esquire*. (USA)
388 Illustration zu einem Artikel über die gespannte Lage auf den Kanarischen Inseln, in *Lui*. Gelbe Banane mit weiss-blau-gelben Fähnchen auf Blau. (SPA)
389 Farbige Illustration zu einer Kurzgeschichte in *Femina*. (SWE)
390 Farbige Illustration zu einem Artikel über das Thema Kommunikation in der Zeitschrift *Creative Living*. (USA)
391 Ganzseitige Schwarzweiss-Illustration aus *Technology Review*. (USA)

387 Page d'un article qui a paru dans le magazine *Esquire*. (USA)
388 Illustration pour un article sur la situation tendue sur les îles Canaries. Banane jaune, drapeau blanc-bleu-jaune sur fond bleu. (SPA)
389 Illustration (en polychromie) du magazine *Femina*. (SWE)
390 Illustration polychrome accompagnant un article sur la communication. Il a paru dans le magazine *Creative Living*. (USA)
391 Illustration pleine page en noir et blanc. (USA)

390

391

ARTIST / KÜNSTLER / ARTISTE:

392 Don Punchatz
393 Fred Nelson
394 Rubem Campos Grilo
395 Mark Hess
396 Jean Michel Folon

DESIGNER / GESTALTER / MAQUETTISTE:

392 James Kiehle
393 George Kenton
395 Mark Hess

ART DIRECTOR / DIRECTEUR ARTISTIQUE:

392, 393, 395 Michael Brock

PUBLISHER / VERLEGER / EDITEUR:

392, 393, 395 Playboy Publications Inc.
394 VERSUS
396 New York Magazine

392 Double spread from *Oui* entitled "The three most important things in life" (sex, violence and work). Monkeys' fur in shades of blue, green and brown. (USA)
393 Double spread from the magazine *Oui* with an article about all the peculiar objects and parts of insects and small animals found in canned food and drinks and which are now produced for the record. Red soup in a white soup-plate and animal in brown shades. (USA)
394 Illustration from *Versus*, a monthly magazine ranging over culture and politics. The article deals with "gloomy political prospects". (BRA)
395 Full-page illustration in colour from the magazine *Oui*. (USA)
396 Full-page illustration from the periodical *New York* pertaining to an article about loneliness in New York. Gradations of colour from yellow through orange to red, some blue. (USA)

392 Doppelseite aus *Oui* zu «Memoiren» unter dem Titel «Die drei wichtigsten Dinge im Leben» (Sex, Gewalttätigkeit und Arbeit). Fell der Affen in Blau-, Grün- und Brauntönen. (USA)
393 Doppelseite aus der Zeitschrift *Oui* mit einem Artikel über Feststellungen von Rattenhaaren, Fliegen- und Käferbestandteilen etc. in konservierten Nahrungsmitteln und Getränken. Rote Suppe in weisser Suppentasse und Tier in Brauntönen. (USA)
394 Illustration aus *Versus*, einem monatlich erscheinenden Magazin für Kultur und Politik. Es geht um «trübe politische Aussichten». (BRA)
395 Ganzseitige Illustration aus der Zeitschrift *Oui*. In Farbe. (USA)
396 Ganzseitige Illustration aus der Zeitschrift *New York* zu einem Artikel über Einsamkeit in New York. Farbabstufungen von Gelb über Orange bis Rot und Blau. (USA)

392 Page double de *Oui* pour un article intitulé «Les trois choses les plus importantes de la vie» (sex, violence et travail). Poile des singes en bleu, vert et brun. (USA)
393 Page double du magazine *Oui* figurant dans un article sur le traitement «hygiénique» des boissons et aliments en conserve et des poils de rats, des parties de mouches et de bestioles qu'on y trouve. Potage rouge dans une tasse blanche, bête en tons bruns. (USA)
394 Illustration de *Versus*, magazine hebdomadaire de politique et de culture. On y discute les perspectives politiques assez sombres. (BRA)
395 Illustration pleine page du magazine *Oui*. En polychromie. (USA)
396 Illustration pleine page du magazine *New York*. Elle accompagne un article sur la solitude à New York. Couleurs passant du jaune et orange au rouge, tons bleus. (USA)

Magazine Illustrations

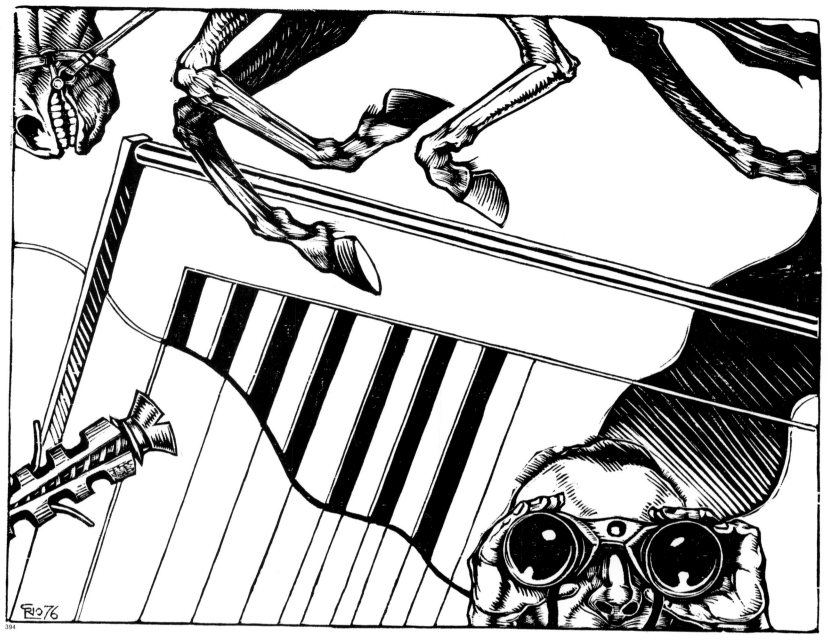

394

395

396

397

Magazine Illustrations

ARTIST / KÜNSTLER / ARTISTE:

397 Heiner A. Hoier
398 Mariet Numan
399, 400 Milou Hermus

DESIGNER / GESTALTER / MAQUETTISTE:

397 Dietmar Meyer

ART DIRECTOR / DIRECTEUR ARTISTIQUE:

397 Dietmar Meyer
398, 399 Dick de Moei
400 Bob Post

AGENCY / AGENTUR / AGENCE – STUDIO:

398, 399 Avenue

PUBLISHER / VERLEGER / EDITEUR:

397 Theobald & Sondermann
398, 399 De Geillustreerde pers b.v.
400 Playboy Enterprises, Inc.

397 Double spread with a black-and-white illustration from the magazine *Warum!* (Why!). The report is about prejudices and their consequences. (GER)
398 Spread from the magazine *Avenue,* with an excerpt from the book ''The hazards of being male'' illustrated here. In black and white. (NLD)
399 Full-page illustration to a story in *Avenue.* Only red shades. (NLD)
400 Full-page illustration to a story in *Avenue.* (NLD)

397 Doppelseite mit Schwarzweiss-Illustration aus der Zeitschrift *Warum!* In dem Bericht geht es um Vorurteile und ihre Ursachen. (GER)
398 Seite aus der Zeitschrift *Avenue,* die hier einen Auszug aus dem Buch «The hazards of being male» (Was es heisst, ein Mann zu sein) illustriert. In Schwarzweiss. (NLD)
399 Ganzseitige Illustration zu einer Geschichte in *Avenue.* Nur Rottöne. (NLD)
400 Ganzseitige Illustration zu einer Geschichte in *Avenue.* (NLD)

397 Page double avec des illustrations en noir et blanc du magazine *Warum!* Dans ce raport on discute les préjugés et leurs raisons. (GER)
398 Page figurant dans un extrait d'un livre (Etre un homme et ce que cela signifie). Elément du magazine *Avenue.* En noir et blanc. (NLD)
399 Illustration pleine page accompagnant un conte publié dans *Avenue.* Tons rouges. (NLD)
400 Illustration pleine page tirée du magazine *Avenue.* (NLD)

398

399

401

403

401, 402 Illustration and complete double spread with a report about the anthropologist Margaret Mead who has used the potentiality of the brain to better effect than most people, acquiring extraordinary consciousness. From *Quest*. (USA)
403 Double spread from the magazine *Duepiù* with an article about the beauty of Italian women and their characteristics from region to region. Blue hair-clouds. (ITA)
404, 405 Illustrations from the magazine *The News* with recipes which originated in New York. Both illustrations in colour. (USA)

401, 402 Illustration und komplette Doppelseite mit einem Bericht über die Anthropologin Margaret Mead, eine Frau, die die Möglichkeiten des Gehirns besser ausnutzt als die meisten Menschen und dadurch zu einem aussergewöhnlichen Bewusstsein gelangt. Aus *Quest*. (USA)
403 Doppelseite aus der Zeitschrift *Duepiù* mit einem Artikel über die Schönheit der Italienerin und Aufzählung der Besonderheiten nach geographischen Regionen. Haarwolke in Blau. (ITA)
404, 405 Illustrationen aus der Zeitschrift *The News* mit aus New York stammenden Rezepten, hier für ein Muschel- und ein Hummergericht. Beide farbig. (USA)

401, 402 Illustration et page double complète présentant un rapport sur l'anthropologiste Margaret Mead, une femme qui sait exploiter ses facultés intellectuelles plus que la plupart des autres et qui a par cela une conscience extraordinaire. Elément de *Quest*. (USA)
403 Page double du magazine *Duepiù*. L'article aborde le sujet de la beauté des femmes italiennes tout en énumérant les particularités par régions géographiques. (ITA)
404, 405 Illustrations du magazine *The News* présentant quelques recettes newyorkais: ici une spécialité composée de fruits de mer et de crustacés. En polychromie. (USA)

ARTIST / KÜNSTLER / ARTISTE:

401, 402 Fred Otnes
403 Adelchi Galloni
404, 405 Cathy Hull

ART DIRECTOR / DIRECTEUR ARTISTIQUE:

401, 402 Noel Werrett
403 Dino Mazzola
404, 405 Tom Ruis

PUBLISHER / VERLEGER / EDITEUR:

401, 402 Ambassador International Cultur Foundation
403 Arnoldo Mondadori
404, 405 The News

402

Magazine Illustrations

404

405

274673

S e Coe

407

ARTIST / KÜNSTLER / ARTISTE:

406 Sue Coe
407 Etienne Delessert
408, 409 Gary Viskupic

ART DIRECTOR / DIRECTEUR ARTISTIQUE:

406 Barbara Bosley Richer
407 Jean Parmentier
408, 409 Paul Back

AGENCY / AGENTUR / AGENCE – STUDIO:

407 Carabosse

PUBLISHER / VERLEGER / EDITEUR:

406 Ms.Magazine Corp.
407 Bayard Presse
408, 409 Newsday Inc.

408

406 Illustration to the book "The Ice Age" reprinted in *Ms Magazine.* (USA)
407 Colour illustration from an issue of the youth magazine *Record* containing an article about the development of medicine: "The end of the widespread epidemics." (FRA)
408, 409 Complete double spread and illustration to an article in *L.I. Magazine* about former Nazis in the USA. The "past" and man in black and white, background in green, yellow and black. (USA)

406 Illustration zu dem Buch «The Ice Age» (das Eiszeitalter) aus *Ms Magazine.* (USA)
407 Farbige Illustration aus dem Jugendmagazin *Record* zu einem Artikel über die Entwicklung der Medizin: «Das Ende der grossen Epidemien.» (FRA)
408, 409 Komplette Doppelseite und Illustration zu einem Artikel im *L.I. Magazine* über in den USA untergetauchte Nazis. Die «Vergangenheit» und Mann in Schwarzweiss, der Hintergrund in Grün, Gelb und Schwarz. (USA)

406 Illustration accompagnant un conte rendu du livre «L'époque glaciaire». (USA)
407 Illustration polychrome de *Record,* magazine pour les jeunes. Elle figure dans un article intitulé «La fin des grandes épidémies». (FRA)
408, 409 Page double complète et illustration d'un article paru dans *L.I.-Magazine.* L'article traite des Nazis disparus aux Etats-Unis. L'homme et «son passé» en noir et blanc sur un fond en vert, jaune et noir. (USA)

409

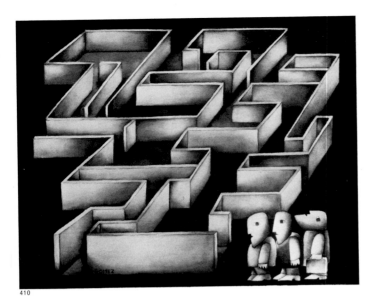

410

412

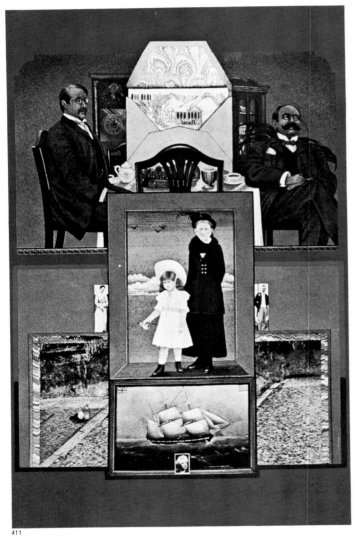

411

413

Magazine Illustrations
Zeitschriften-Illustrationen
Illustrations de périodiques

158

410 Illustration to an article about economic questions from the magazine *Ele e Ela*. In shades of blue and green. (BRA)
411 Black-and-white illustration under the title "Buchbasar" (Book Bazaar) from *Pardon*. "Writers have always had a hard time." (GER)
412 Illustration to a short story in the magazine *Freundin*. In full colour. (GER)
413 Spread from a story about a lustful wife. From *National Lampoon*. (USA)
414 First double spread of an article about psychoanalysis in *Boston* magazine. (USA)
415, 416 Two spreads from the magazine *Quest*. Twenty artists have attempted to portray and elucidate the actual moment of finding oneself. These drafts are accompanied by statements made on the same subject by famous authors. (USA)

414

ARTIST / KÜNSTLER / ARTISTE:

410 Vilma Gomez
411 Katrin Lindley
412 Valeri Pavlov
413 Andy Lackow
414 Mark Fisher
415 André François
416 Gary Viskupic

DESIGNER / GESTALTER / MAQUETTISTE:

414 Ronn Campisi
415, 415 Noel Werrett/Bart Drury

ART DIRECTOR / DIRECTEUR ARTISTIQUE:

410 Vilma Gomez
411 Helga M. Colle-Tiz
412 Gerhard Kromschröder
413 Peter Kleinman
414 Ronn Campisi
415, 416 Noel Werrett

AGENCY / AGENTUR / AGENCE – STUDIO:

414 Ronn Campisi Design

PUBLISHER / VERLEGER / EDITEUR:

410 Bloch Editores
411 Burda-Verlag
412 Pardon Verlagsgesellschaft mbH
413 21st Century Communications, Inc.
414 Boston Magazine
415, 416 Ambassador International Cultur Foundation

POTENTIALS

André François

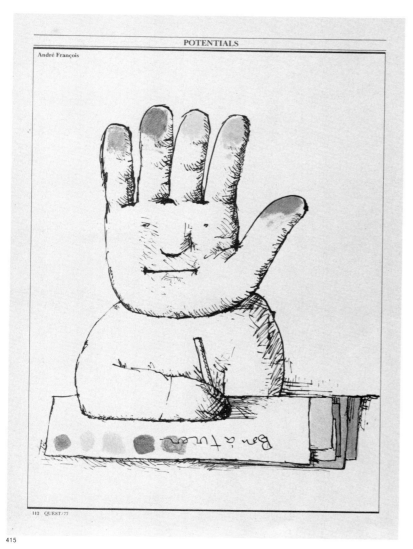

415

POTENTIALS

IT'S ALL AN ACT

Erving Goffman, in The Presentation of Self in Everyday Life:

The self, then, as a performed character, is not an organic thing that has a specific location, whose fundamental fate is to be born, to mature, and to die; it is a dramatic effect arising diffusely from a scene that is presented, and the characteristic issue, the crucial concern, is whether it will be credited or discredited.

In analyzing the self, then, we are drawn from its possessor, from the person who will profit or lose most by it, for he and his body merely provide the peg on which something of collaborative manufacture will be hung for a time. And the means for producing and maintaining selves do not reside inside the peg; in fact these means are often bolted down in social establishments. There will be a back region with its tools for shaping the body, and a front region with its fixed props. There will be a team of persons whose activity on stage in conjunction with available props will constitute the scene from which the performed character's self will emerge, and another team, the audience, whose interpretive activity will be necessary for this emergence. The self is a product of all of these arrangements, and in all of its parts bears the marks of this genesis.

The whole machinery of self-production is cumbersome, of course, and sometimes breaks down, exposing its separate components: back region control; team collusion; audience tact; and so forth. But, well oiled, impressions will flow from it fast enough to put us in the grips of one of our types of reality—the performance will come off and the firm self accorded each performed character will appear to emanate intrinsically from its performer.

Gary Viskupic

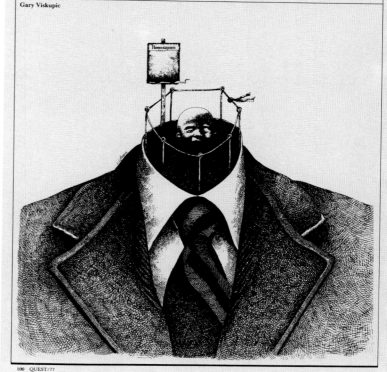

416

410 Illustration zu einem Artikel über Wirtschaftsfragen aus der Zeitschrift *Ele e Ela*. In Blau- und Grünschattierung. (BRA)
411 Schwarzweiss-Illustration unter der Rubrik «Buchbasar» aus *Pardon*. «Schon immer hatten Schriftsteller einen schweren Stand.» (GER)
412 Illustration zu einer Kurzgeschichte in der Zeitschrift *Freundin*. In Farbe. (GER)
413 Seite zu einer Geschichte über eine lüsterne Ehefrau. Aus *National Lampoon*. (USA)
414 Erste Doppelseite eines Artikels über Psychoanalyse, erschienen im Magazin *Boston*. (USA)
415, 416 Zwei Seiten aus der Zeitschrift *Quest*. Zwanzig Künstler haben versucht, den Moment des Sich-Selbst-Findens darzustellen. Die Entwürfe sind begleitet von Aussagen berühmter Autoren zu dem gleichen Thema. (USA)

410 Illustration accompagnant un article sur des questions économiques qui a été publié dans le magazine *Ele e Ela*. En divers tons bleus et verts. (BRA)
411 Illustration en noir et blanc figurant dans la rubrique du magazine *Pardon* consacré au livre. Ici on discute la situation difficile des écrivains. (GER)
412 Illustration accompagnant un conte du magazine *Freundin*. En polychromie. (GER)
413 Page tirée d'une histoire d'une épouse érotomane parue dans le magazine d'humour *National Lampoon*. (USA)
414 Page double introduisant un article sur la psychanalyse. (USA)
415, 416 Pages du magazine *Quest*. Vingt artistes ont cherché d'interpréter le moment de la découverte de soi. Les illustrations sont accompagnées de citations de divers écrivains même sujet. (USA)

417

ARTIST / KÜNSTLER:

417 Les Katz
418 Randy Enos/Les Katz/Ray Kursar
419 Andy Lackow
420 Randy Enos
421 Richard Egielski

ART DIRECTOR:

417–421 Peter Kleinman

PUBLISHER / VERLEGER:

417–421 21st Century Communications

Magazine Illustrations
Zeitschriften-Illustrationen
Illustrations de périodiques

417 Full-page colour illustration from *National Lampoon*. (USA)
418, 420 *National Lampoon:* double spread and various ironic and cynical Christmas cards from different countries. The countries touched on are Brazil, China and Saudi-Arabia. (USA)
419 Colourful double spread from *National Lampoon* with editorial. (USA)
421 Full-page illustration in murky purple shades to an article about Richard Nixon's last days in office. From *National Lampoon*. (USA)

417 Illustration couleur pleine page intitulée «humour à la Barnard». De *National Lampoon*. (USA)
418, 420 Page double présentant une série de cartes de vœux de Noël provenant de divers pays et détail d'une carte. Les pays – ici le Brésil, la Chine et l'Arabie Saoudite – sont représentés de façon ironique. Elément de *National Lampoon*. (USA)
419 Editorial polychrome sur page double. De *National Lampoon*. (USA)
421 Illustration pleine page du magazine *National Lampoon* accompagnant un article sur la fin du règne de Nixon. Teintes pourpres sombres. (USA)

417 Ganzseitige Farbillustration mit dem Titel «Barnard-Humor» aus *National Lampoon*. (USA)
418, 420 Doppelseite mit ironischen Weihnachtskarten aus diversen Ländern und Detail einer Karte aus *National Lampoon*. Die betroffenen Länder sind hier Brasilien, China und Saudi-Arabien. (USA)
419 Farbige Doppelseite aus *National Lampoon* mit einem Leitartikel. (USA)
421 Ganzseitige Illustration in düsteren Purpurtönen aus einem Artikel über die letzten Tage Richard Nixons im Amt. Aus *National Lampoon*. (USA)

418

419

420

421

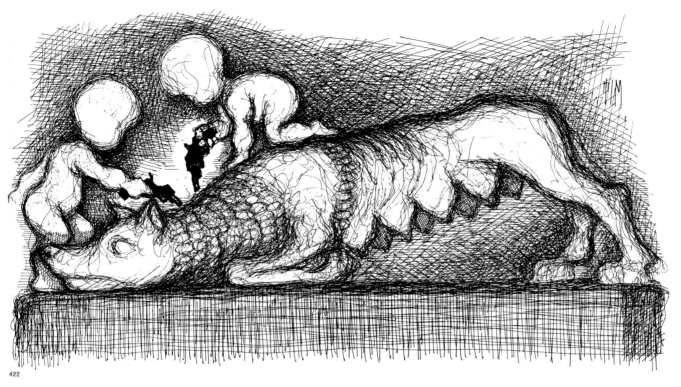

422

ARTIST / KÜNSTLER / ARTISTE:
422–424, 427 Tim

DESIGNER / GESTALTER / MAQUETTISTE:
425, 426 Ronn Campisi/Terry Koppel

ART DIRECTOR / DIRECTEUR ARTISTIQUE:
422–424, 427 Jean-Jacques Hauwy
425, 426 Ronn Campisi/Terry Koppel

PUBLISHER / VERLEGER / EDITEUR:
422–424, 427 Express-Union
425, 426 The Boston Globe

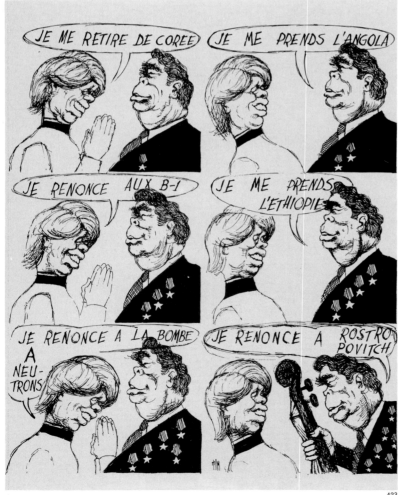

423

424

425

426

422 Illustration from *L'Express* dealing with Italy, 1978. (FRA)
423 Illustration from *L'Express* under the title "Contrasting Concessions". (I shall retreat from Korea – I take Angola; I shall renounce the B-1 – I'll take Etheopia; I shall renounce the bomb – neutron bomb, I renounce Rostropovich). (FRA)
424 A further illustration from *L'Express* about Begin und Sadat. (FRA)
425, 426 Two double spreads from a year-end special edition of the *Boston Sunday Globe*. Fig. 425 shows fashion trends, recalls the Pope's election, the strike of the *New York Times*, US foreign policy, Rhodesia and Iran, the television series "Holocaust", demonstration of nuclear power plant opponents. Fig. 426: First double spread of review. (USA)
427 "André Malraux after Goya." Black-and-white illustration from *L'Express*. (FRA)

422 Illustration aus *L'Express* zum Thema Italien 1978. (FRA)
423 Illustration aus *L'Express* unter dem Titel «Gegenseitige Zugeständnisse». (Ich ziehe mich aus Korea zurück – Ich nehme mir Angola; Ich verzichte auf die B-1 – Ich nehme mir Äthiopien; Ich verzichte auf die Bombe – Neutronenbombe; Ich verzichte auf Rostropovitsch.) (FRA)
424 Eine weitere Illustration aus *L'Express* hier zu Sadats Reise nach Jerusalem. (FRA)
425, 426 Zwei Doppelseiten aus einer Jahresend-Spezialausgabe des *Boston Sunday Globe*. Abb. 425 zeigt Mode, erinnert an die Papstwahl, den Streik der *New York Times*, die US-Aussenpolitik, Rhodesien und den Iran, die TV-Serie Holocaust, Demonstration der Atomkraftgegner. Abb. 426 ist die erste Doppelseite des Rückblicks mit Leitartikel. Sie bezieht sich auf die US-Wirtschaftslage, den Tod Hubert Humphreys, das «Steuersenkungs-Fieber» und Baseball. (USA)
427 «André Malraux in der Manier Goyas.» Schwarzweiss-Illustration aus *L'Express*. (FRA)

422 Illustration accompagnant un article intitulé «Pitié pour l'Italie». De *L'Express*. (FRA)
423 Pleine page du magazine *L'Express* illustrant de façon ironique les négotiations Salt II. (FRA)
424 Illustration publiée dans *L'Express* à l'occasion du voyage historique de Sadat à Jerusalem. (FRA)
425, 426 Deux pages doubles d'un numéro spécial de la fin de l'année du magazine *Boston Sunday Globe*. Fig. 425: aperçu rétrospectif sur la mode, l'élection du pape, la grève ayant atteint le *New York Times*, la politique extérieure des Etats-Unis, les événements en Rhodésie et en Iran, la présentation de Holocaust à la TV, démonstration des anti-nucléaires. Fig. 426: première page double de la rétrospective avec editorial, se référant à la situation économique des Etats-Unis, la mort de Hubert Humphrey, réduction des impôts et au baseball. (USA)
427 Illustration en hommage à la mémoire d'André Malraux, auteur de *L'Espoir* et du *Musée Imaginaire*. Elément publié dans le magazine *L'Express*. (FRA)

Magazine Illustrations
Zeitschriften-Illustrationen
Illustrations de périodiques

427

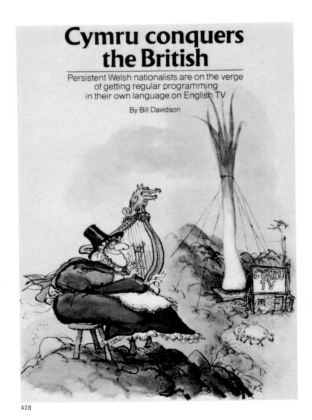

428

429

430

ARTIST / KÜNSTLER / ARTISTE:

428 Ronald Searle
429, 430 James Marsh
431 Tilman Michalski
432 Brian Zick/Star Studios
433 Bob Smith

DESIGNER / GESTALTER / MAQUETTISTE:

432 Mike Salisbury
433 Bob Smith

ART DIRECTOR / DIRECTEUR ARTISTIQUE:

428 Jerry Alten
429 Farhad Hormozi
430 David Jones
431 Eberhard Henschel
432 Mike Salisbury
433 Ralph Weinstock

AGENCY / AGENTUR / AGENCE – STUDIO:

429 Lock Means K.E.Y.
432 Mike Salisbury Design
433 Bob Smith Illustrations

PUBLISHER / VERLEGER / EDITEUR:

428 Triangle Publications, Inc.
430 Woman's Own Magazine
431 Burda Verlag GmbH
432 Chic Magazine
433 Players International Publications

428 Page from *TV Guide* to an article proposing a television channel for the (almost) 1 million Welsh people who still speak the so-called Cymreag, a consonant-laden Celtic tongue. In full colour. (USA)
429 Colour illustration to a yet unpublished book. (USA)
430 Illustration to an unusual story in *Woman's Own*. Dark shades of colour, brown border. (GBR)
431 Spread from a short story in the magazine *Freundin* about an antique dealer disguised as a vicar in order to somehow acquire a rare chest of drawers. (GER)
432 First double spread from an article in *Chic Magazine*. (USA)
433 Colour illustration to an article in *Players*. (USA)

428 Seite aus *TV Guide* zu einem Artikel über einen eigenen Fernsehkanal für die fast 1 Million Walliser, die noch die keltische (wallisische) Sprache sprechen. In Farbe. (USA)
429 Farbige Illustration für ein noch nicht veröffentlichtes Buch: Wie man sein Denkvermögen am besten auswertet. (USA)
430 Illustration zu einer Erzählung, in der es um ein Mädchen mit hellseherischen Fähigkeiten geht. Aus der Frauenzeitschrift *Woman's Own*. Düstere Farbtöne, brauner Rahmen. (GBR)
431 Seite zu einer Kurzgeschichte in der Zeitschrift *Freundin*. Es geht darin um einen als Pfarrer verkleideten Antiquitätenhändler, der sich in den Besitz einer seltenen Kommode bringen möchte. (GER)
432 Erste Doppelseite zu einem Artikel über die Gefahr der Ausbreitung von Geschlechtskrankheiten. Aus *Chic Magazine*. (USA)
433 Farbige Illustration zu einem Artikel über einen rebellischen Baseball-Spieler in der Zeitschrift *Players*. (USA)

428 Page du magazine *TV Guide*. On y discute la possibilité d'un canal de TV spécial pour les téléspectateurs gallois qui parlent encore la langue celte, le gallois. (USA)
429 Illustration pour un livre encore inédit: la meilleure manière d'utiliser son mental. En polychromie. (USA)
430 Illustration d'un récit publié dans le magazine *Woman's Own* au sujet d'une jeune femme possédant le don de double vue. Tons sombres, cadre brun. (GBR)
431 Page d'un récit publié dans le magazine *Freundin*. On raconte l'histoire d'un antiquaire déguisé en pasteur parce qu'il veut s'emparer d'une commode rare. (GER)
432 Première page double d'un article discutant le danger de la propagation des maladies vénériennes. De *Chic Magazine*. (USA)
433 Illustration (polychrome) d'un article sur un joueur de baseball rebelle. Elément du magazine *Players*. (USA)

431

432

433

434

ARTIST / KÜNSTLER / ARTISTE:

434, 435 James Marsh
436 Ken Laidlaw
438 Charles Santore

436

437

434 Illustration, approximately actual size, to an article in the *Sunday Telegraph Magazine* about UFO's seen in the sky over Wales. (GBR)
435 First double spread from an article in *Club International*. (GBR)
436 Colourful double spread from *Eltern* (Parents) with poems related to dreams. (GER)
437 Double spread from a youth magazine with a test (''Do you always know what you want?''). Pink pullover, light blue trousers, pink/blue arch, yellow background.
438 First double spread from a story published in *Good Housekeeping* magazine. Mostly in pink and blue shades. (USA)

434 Illustration, ungefähr Originalgrösse, aus einem Artikel im *Sunday Telegraph Magazine* über unidentifizierte Objekte, die am Himmel über Wales gesichtet wurden. (GBR)
435 Erste Doppelseite eines Artikels über Jahrmarktsvergnügen aus *Club International*. (GBR)
436 Farbige Doppelseite aus der Zeitschrift *Eltern* mit Gedichten zum Träumen. (GER)
437 Doppelseite aus einer Jugendzeitschrift mit einem Test («Weisst Du immer, was Du willst?»). Rosa Pullover, hellblaue Hose, Bogen rosa/blau vor gelbem Hintergrund.
438 Erste Doppelseite zu einer Geschichte mit dem Titel «Ich... und der Junge von nebenan». Vorwiegend Rosa- und Blautöne. Aus dem Magazin *Good Housekeeping*. (USA)

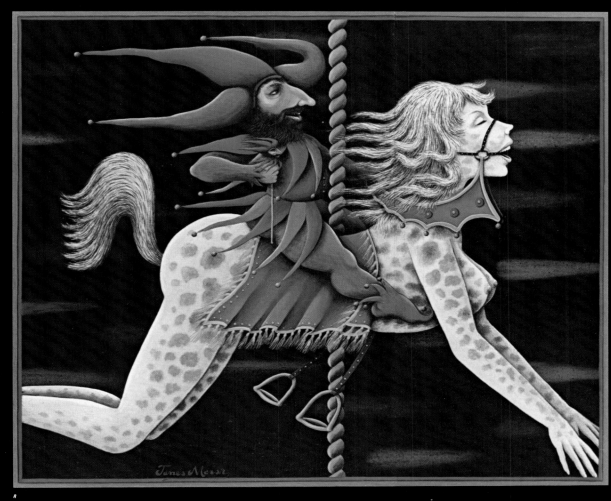

435

438

434 Illustration (approx. grandeur nature) pour un article du *Sunday Telegraph Magazine* consacré aux ovnis aperçus dans le ciel du pays de Galles. (GBR)
435 Page double initiale d'un article de *Club International*. Sujet: plaisirs des foires. (GBR)
436 Page double du magazine *Eltern* (parents) avec des poèmes pour rêver. En couleurs. (GER)
437 Page double d'un magazine pour la jeunesse présentant un test: Sais-tu toujours ce que tu veux? Pullover rose, pantalons bleus, fond jaune.
438 Page double initiale d'un récit intitulé «Moi... le jeune d'à côté». Prédominance de tons bleus et roses. Elément de *Good Housekeeping*. (USA)

ART DIRECTOR / DIRECTEUR ARTISTIQUE:

434 Roger Gould
435 David Jones
436 Noelle Thieux
438 Herb Bleiweiss

PUBLISHER / VERLEGER / EDITEUR:

434 Sunday Telegraph Magazine
435 Club International
436 Gruner & Jahr AG & Co
438 Good House Keeping

Magazine Illustrations

43

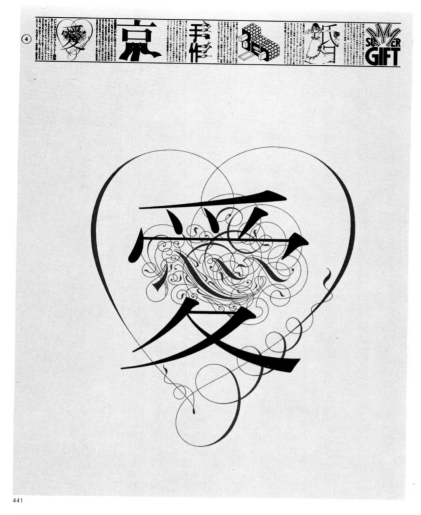

441

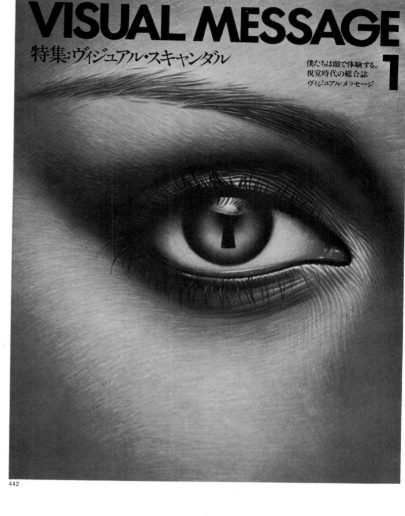

VISUAL MESSAGE

特集:ヴィジュアル・スキャンダル

僕たちは眼で体験する。
視覚時代の総合誌
ヴィジュアル メッセージ

1

442

443

439, 440 Illustration and complete cover of a special edition of the graphic design magazine *Idea*, for the annual exhibition of the Art Directors Club, New York. (JPN)
441, 443 Pages from the trade magazine *Illustrative Letterforms, Fantasy*, produced by a group of graphic designers. Design and lettering in Fig. 441 are ruby-red and blue-violet, Fig. 443 with ruby-red design on white, and white on a brilliant blue background. Most pages of the magazine are printed in one or two colours. (JPN)
442 Cover of the first edition of the new magazine *Visual Message*. Black lettering on peach-coloured skin, eye grey-black around the edges. (JPN)

439, 440 Illustration und kompletter Umschlag einer Spezialausgabe des Graphik-Magazins *Idea* anlässlich der jährlichen Ausstellung des Art Directors Club, New York. (JPN)
441, 443 Seiten aus dem Fachmagazin *Illustrative Letterforms, Fantasy*, das von einer Graphiker-Gruppe herausgegeben wird. Design und Schrift in Abb. 441 weinrot und blauviolett, Abb. 443 mit weinrotem Design auf Weiss, und weiss auf leuchtend blauem Hintergrund. Die meisten Seiten des Magazins sind mit einer oder zwei Farben gestaltet. (JPN)
442 Umschlag der ersten Ausgabe der neuen Zeitschrift *Visual Message* (visuelle Botschaft). Schwarze Schrift auf pfirsichfarbener Haut, grauschwarz umrandetes Auge. (JPN)

439, 440 Illustration et couverture d'un numéro spécial du magazine d'arts graphiques *Idea*. Le numéro présente une sélection de l'exposition annuelle de l'Art Directors Club, New York. (JPN)
441, 443 Pages du magazine professionnel *Illustrative Letterforms, Fantasy*, publié par un groupement de graphistes. Design et typographie (fig. 441) en rouge foncé et bleu-violet, fig. 443: design en rouge foncé sur fond blanc, et blanc sur fond bleu brillant. (JPN)
442 Couverture du premier numéro d'un nouveau magazine – *Visual Message* (message visuel). Typo noire sur peau rose, maquillage gris foncé. (JPN)

440

ARTIST / KÜNSTLER / ARTISTE:

439, 440 Mick Haggerty
441 Kenzo Nakagawa/Tack Miyoshi
442 Yohsuke Ohnishi
443 Kenzo Nakagawa/Hiro Nobuyama

DESIGNER / GESTALTER / MAQUETTISTE:

439, 440 Takenobu Igarashi
441, 443 Kenzo Nakagawa/Hiro
  Nobuyama/Satch Morikami
442 Takahisa Kamijo

ART DIRECTOR / DIRECTEUR ARTISTIQUE:

439, 440 Takenobu Igarashi
441, 443 Kenzo Nakagawa
442 Takahisa Kamijo

AGENCY / AGENTUR / AGENCE – STUDIO:

439, 440 Takenobu Igarashi Design
441, 443 Network Design Group
442 Kamijo Studio

PUBLISHER / VERLEGER / EDITEUR:

439, 440 Seibundo Shinkosha Publishing Co.
441, 443 Network Design Group
442 Visual Message Co.

Trade Magazines

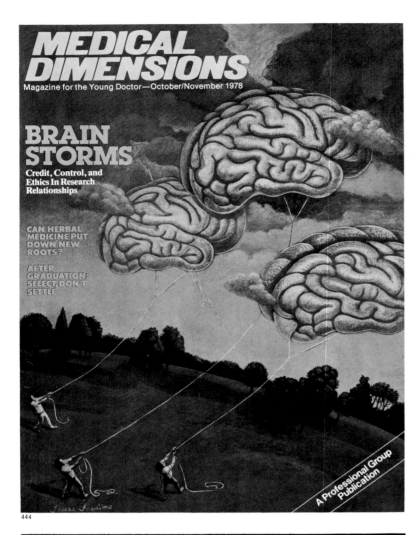

MEDICAL DIMENSIONS

Magazine for the Young Doctor—October/November 1978

BRAIN STORMS

Credit, Control, and Ethics In Research Relationships

CAN HERBAL MEDICINE PUT DOWN NEW ROOTS?

AFTER GRADUATION: SELECT, DON'T SETTLE

A Professional Group Publication

444

G. Moss

445

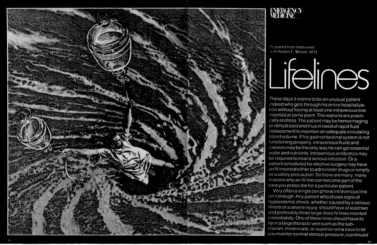

EMERGENCY MEDICINE

Prepared from interviews with Robert F. Wilson, M.D.

Lifelines

These days it seems to be an unusual patient indeed who gets through his entire hospitalization without having at least one intravenous line inserted at some point. The reasons are practically endless. The patient may be hemorrhaging or dehydrated and thus in need of rapid fluid replacement to maintain an adequate circulating blood volume. If his gastrointestinal system is not functioning properly, intravenous fluids and calories may be the only way he can get essential water and nutrients. Intravenous antibiotics may be required to treat a serious infection. Or a patient scheduled for elective surgery may have an IV inserted either to administer drugs or simply as a safety precaution. So there are many, many reasons why an IV line can become part of the care you prescribe for a particular patient.

Very often a single peripheral intravenous line isn't enough. Any patient who shows signs of hypovolemic shock, whether caused by a serious illness or a severe injury, should have at least two and preferably three large-bore IV lines inserted immediately. One of these lines should have its tip in a large thoracic vein such as the subclavian, innominate, or superior vena cava to let you monitor central venous pressure./continued

446

DEC. 1978/JAN. 1979

NEW ENGINEER

THE HANDICAPPED: A NEW STANDARD TO BREAK THE BARRIERS

The Educator Factor: Special Programs for the Disadvantaged Require Faculty Training and Support

The Official Rules: Who Was Murphy Anyhow?

Off Hours: The Ritual of New Year's

A Professional Group Publication

447

Trade Magazines
Fachzeitschriften
Magazines professionnels

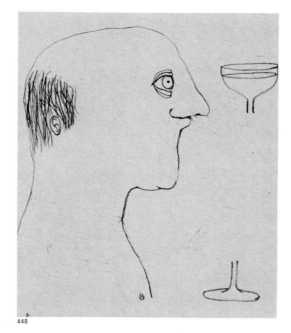

448

449

450

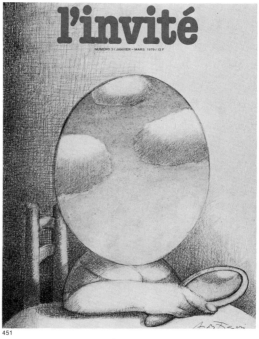

451

444 Cover in colour from *Medical Dimensions* relating to the editorial about the brain. (USA)
445 Black-and-white illustration with an article on photography in *DA* magazine. (USA)
446 First double spread to an article published in *Emergency Medicine*. In full colour. (USA)
447 Cover of the magazine *New Engineer*. Full colour. (USA)
448, 449 Detail of a black-and-white illustration and cover in full colour from the gourmet magazine *Epicurean*. (AUS)
450 Cover of the magazine *Juris Doctor*, with a 1978 salary survey inside. (USA)
451 Cover of *L'Invité*. Black and white with blue. (FRA)
452 Cover of the architectural trade magazine *L'Architecture d'Aujourd'hui*. In full colour. (FRA)
453 Cover in colour of the magazine *Print*. (USA)

444 Farbiger Umschlag von *Medical Dimensions*, hier mit Bezug auf den Leitartikel über das Gehirn. (USA)
445 Schwarzweiss-Illustration mit einem Artikel über Photographie aus der Fachzeitschrift *DA*. (USA)
446 Erste Doppelseite zu einem Artikel mit dem Titel «Lebenslinien» in *Emergency Medicine*. In Farbe. (USA)
447 Farbiger Umschlag des Magazins *New Engineer*. Im Leitartikel geht es um Hilfen für Behinderte. (USA)
448, 449 Detail einer Schwarzweiss-Illustration und farbiger Umschlag des Feinschmecker-Magazins *Epicurean*. (AUS)
450 Umschlag des Magazins *Juris Doctor*. Hier mit einer Verdienst-Übersicht für 1978 im Magazin. (USA)
451 Umschlag von *L'Invité*. Schwarzweiss mit Blau. (FRA)
452 Farbiger Umschlag der Architektur-Fachzeitschrift *L'Architecture d'Aujourd'hui*. (FRA)
453 Farbiger Umschlag des Magazins *Print*. (USA)

444 Couverture polychrome de *Medical Dimensions*, se référant ici à l'éditorial consacré au cerveau. (USA)
445 Illustration pleine page accompagnant un article sur la photographie. (USA)
446 Première page double d'un article intitulé «Lignes de vie». Du magazine *Emergency Medicine*. Polychromie. (USA)
447 Couverture polychrome d'un magazine, ici se référant à un article sur l'assistance aux handicappés. (USA)
448, 449 Détail d'une illustration noir-blanc et couverture polychrome d'un magazine culinaire. (AUS)
450 Couverture du magazine *Juris Doctor* contenant un aperçu sur les salaires en 1978. (USA)
451 Couverture de *L'Invité*, un magazine offert par les hôtels. Noir-blanc et bleu. (FRA)
452 Couverture couleur de *L'Architecture d'Aujourd'hui*. (FRA)
453 Couverture couleur du magazine *Print*. (USA)

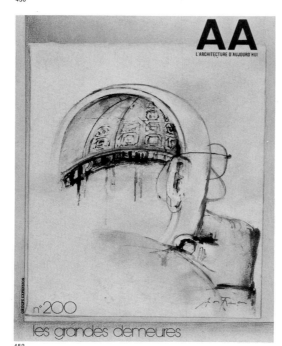

452

453

171

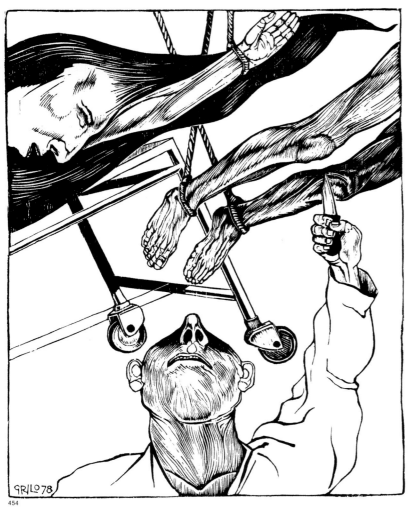

454

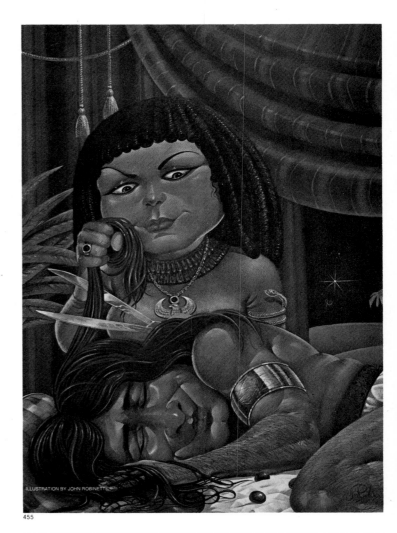

455

Trade Magazines
Fachzeitschriften
Magazines professionnels

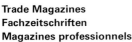

454 Black-and-white illustration from the medical journal *Sinmed*. (BRA)
455 Full-colour illustration to an article on how to save your hair, here with reference to the tale of Samson, whose secret strength lay in his unshorn and flowing locks. From *Body Forum* magazine. (USA)
456 Cover of an edition of *Designer* dealing with tourism. Black and white. (GBR)
457 Full-colour double spread from *Body Forum* magazine. (USA)
458, 459 Detail of the black-and-white illustration and complete double spread from a critical article in *Warum!* (Why!) about the importance of security for Germans. (GER)
460 Cover of *Savings & Loan News* referring to the involuntary urban housing movement. (USA)
461 Black-and-white drawing from *Politicks* magazine: blind man with chain locked to saxophone on Broadway. (USA)

454 Schwarzweiss-Illustration aus der medizinischen Fachzeitschrift *Sinmed*. (BRA)
455 Farbige Illustration zu einem Artikel über Haarpflege in *Body Forum* mit Anspielung auf Samson, dessen Kraft nach der Legende in seinen langen Haaren lag. (USA)
456 Umschlag einer Ausgabe von *Designer* zum Thema Tourismus. Schwarzweiss. (GBR)
457 Farbige Doppelseite aus *Body Forum*. «Lecithin – Gehirnnahrung?» (USA)
458, 459 Detail der Schwarzweiss-Illustration und komplette Doppelseite zu einem kritischen Artikel über das Streben nach Sicherheit in Deutschland. Aus *Warum!* (GER)
460 Umschlag der *Savings & Loan News*. Thema: Wohnungswechsel in Städten. (USA)
461 Schwarzweiss-Zeichnung aus *Politicks*. «Blinder Mann auf dem Broadway an ein Saxophon geket-tet.» (USA)

454 Illustration en noir et blanc tirée d'un périodique médical. (BRA)
455 Illustration (en couleurs) figurant dans un article de *Body Forum* sur les soins des cheveux. On fait allusion à Samson dont la force surhumaine résidait dans sa chevelure. (USA)
456 Couverture d'un numéro de *Designer*, se référant au tourisme. En noir et blanc. (GBR)
457 Page double en couleurs de *Body Forum*: «Lécithine – aliment du cerveau?» (USA)
458, 459 Détail de l'illustration noir-blanc et page double complète figurant dans un article critique sur les efforts des allemands qui tendent à plus de sécurité. (GER)
460 Couverture de *Savings & Loan News*. Sujet: changement de logement en ville. (USA)
461 «Homme aveugle qui se trouve attaché à son saxophone au milieu du Broadway.» Dessin en noir et blanc du magazine *Politicks*. (USA)

456

172

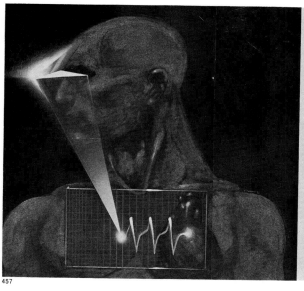
457

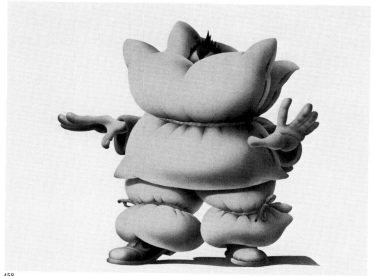
458

459

ARTIST / KÜNSTLER / ARTISTE:

454 Rubem Campos Grilo
455 John Robinette
456 Steve Burgess
457 Linda Wright
458, 459 Jochen Widmann
460 Lee Duggan
461 Marshall Arisman

DESIGNER / GESTALTER / MAQUETTISTE:

455, 457 Art Jones
458, 459 Dietmar Meyer
460 Jim Lienhart

ART DIRECTOR / DIRECTEUR ARTISTIQUE:

455, 457 Art Jones
456 Beryl McAlhone
458, 459 Dietmar Meyer
460 Jim Lienhart
461 Mary Morgan

PUBLISHER / VERLEGER / EDITEUR:

454 SINMED
455, 457 Body Forum Magazine
456 SIAD
458, 459 Theobald & Sondermann
460 Saving & Loan News
461 Politicks Magazine

460

461

462, 463 Black-and-white illustration and cover in colour from the medical journal *Emergency Medicine*. (USA)
464 Cover of the trade magazine *Industrial Launderer,* dealing here with dirty waste water. In colour. (USA)
465 Double spread in colour from an article with advice for the practising doctor confronted with orthopaedic problems. (USA)
466—469 Colour covers of the trade magazine *Industrial Launderer.* The themes are industrial protective clothing, visit of a committee to a prison, a launderers' congress and the still acceptable soil content of wiping cloth. (USA)
470 Black-and-white illustration from *Postgraduate Medicine* to an article about the effects of alcohol. (USA)

ARTIST / KÜNSTLER / ARTISTE:

462 Margaret Cusack
463, 465 Edwin Herder
464, 466—469 Jeff Davis
470 Alan E. Cober

462

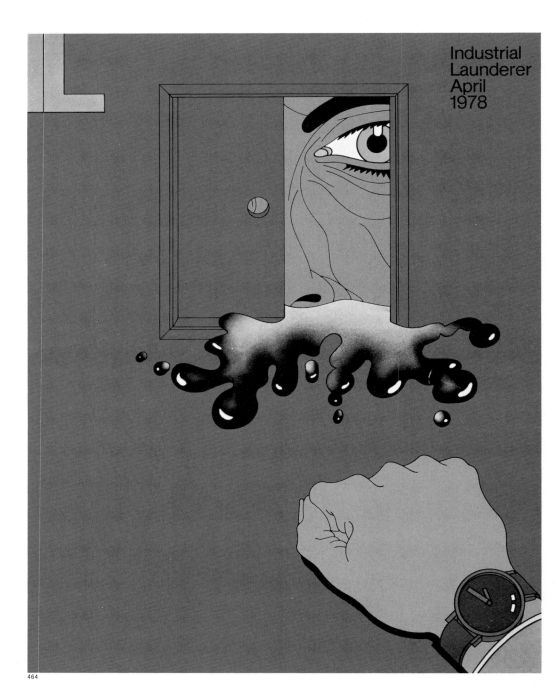

Industrial
Launderer
April
1978

464

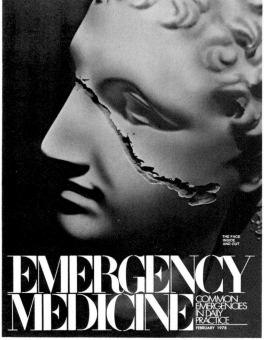

EMERGENCY MEDICINE COMMON EMERGENCIES IN DAILY PRACTICE FEBRUARY 1978

463

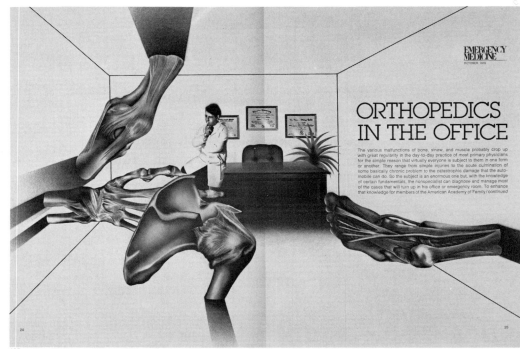

ORTHOPEDICS
IN THE OFFICE

465

462, 463 Schwarzweiss-Illustration und farbiger Umschlag der medizinischen Fachzeitschrift *Emergency Medicine*. (USA)
464 Umschlag der Wäscherei-Fachzeitschrift *Industrial Launderer* zum Thema Abwässer. In Farbe. (USA)
465 Farbige Doppelseite zu einem Artikel mit Ratschlägen für den praktischen Arzt bei orthopädischen Problemen, aus der Fachzeitschrift für junge Ärzte *Emergency Medicine*. (USA)
466—469 Farbige Umschläge der Wäscherei-Fachzeitschrift *Industrial Launderer*. Die Themen sind Schutzkleidung, ein Wäscherei-Kongress, Besuch eines Komitees im Gefängnis und der noch annehmbare Verschmutzungsgrad von Wäschestücken. (USA)
470 Schwarzweiss-Illustration von *Postgraduate Medicine* zu einem Artikel über die Auswirkungen des Alkohols. (USA)

462, 463 Illustration en noir et blanc et couverture polychrome d'un périodique médical. (USA)
464 Couverture du magazine *Industrial Launderer*, se référant ici aux eaux d'égout. En polychromie. (USA)
465 Page double (en polychromie) accompagnant un article qui s'adresse au médecin général et discute les problèmes orthopédiques. Elément d'un périodique médical. (USA)
466—469 Couvertures polychromes de divers numéros de *Industrial Launderer*. Elles se réfèrent aux vêtements de protection, un congrès des blanchisseurs, la visite d'un comitée dans un prison et à l'encrassement encore acceptable des vêtements. (USA)
470 Illustration en noir et blanc figurant dans un article du magazine *Postgraduate Medicine*. Il aborde le problème de l'alcool et ses effets néfastes. (USA)

466

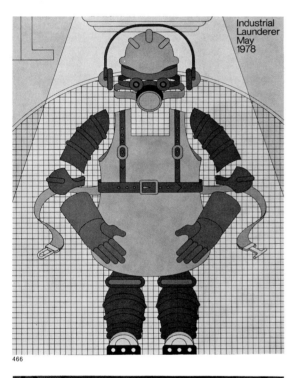

467

468

470

469

DESIGNER / GESTALTER / MAQUETTISTE:

462 Barbara Spina
463, 465 Diane Greene
464, 466—469 Jack Lefkowitz
470 John deCesare

ART DIRECTOR / DIRECTEUR ARTISTIQUE:

462, 463, 465 Tom Lennon
464, 466—469 Jack Lefkowitz
470 Tina Adamek

AGENCY / AGENTUR / AGENCE – STUDIO:

464, 466—469 Jack Lefkowitz Inc.
470 deCesare Design

PUBLISHER / VERLEGER / EDITEUR:

462, 463, 465 Fischer-Medical Publications
464, 466—469 Institute of Industrial Launderer
470 McGraw-Hill, Inc.

Trade Magazines
Fachzeitschriften
Magazines professionnels

471

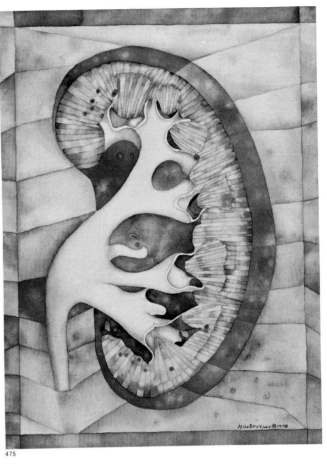

475

472

ARTIST / KÜNSTLER / ARTISTE:

471, 472 Dick Prins
473, 474 Dick Drayton
475 Alice Brickner
476, 477 Frank Bozzo
478, 479 Eugene Mihaesco

DESIGNER / GESTALTER / MAQUETTISTE:

471, 472 Jan Lepair
473, 474 Nicolas Sidjakov
475–479 John deCesare

ART DIRECTOR / DIRECTEUR ARTISTIQUE:

471, 472 Jan Lepair
473, 474 Nicolas Sidjakov
475–479 Tina Adamek

AGENCY / AGENTUR / AGENCE – STUDIO:

471, 472 Lepair Design
473, 474 Sidjakov & Berman Associates
475–479 deCesare Design

PUBLISHER / VERLEGER / EDITEUR:

471, 472 Honeywell Bull
473, 474 Crown Zellerbach
475–479 McGraw-Hill, Inc.

473

474

476

477

Trade Magazines / House Organs

479

478

471, 472 Detail of the illustration and complete cover of *Honeywell Bull's* house magazine *Partner.* (NLD)
473, 474 Double spread and cover of *Resource,* the house magazine of *Crown Zellerbach.* All illustrations in colour. (USA)
475 Full-page illustration from *Postgraduate Medicine,* a medical journal. In water-colours. (USA)
476, 477 Detail of the illustration and complete cover of the magazine *Postgraduate Medicine.* (USA)
478, 479 Illustration, double spread. *Postgraduate Medicine.* (USA)

471, 472 Detail der Illustration und kompletter Umschlag der Hauszeitschrift *Partner* von *Honeywell Bull.* (NLD)
473, 474 Doppelseite und Umschlag von *Resource,* Hauszeitschrift eines Herstellers von Maschinen für Waldrodung und Aufforstung. Alle Abbildungen in Farbe. (USA)
475 Ganzseitige Illustration aus *Postgraduate Medicine.* (USA)
476, 477 Detail der Illustration und kompletter Umschlag der Fachzeitschrift *Postgraduate Medicine.* Das Thema: Anämie. (USA)
478, 479 Illustration und komplette Doppelseite mit einem Artikel über Schizophrenie, aus *Postgraduate Medicine.* (USA)

471, 472 Détail de l'illustration et couverture complète du journal d'entreprise de *Honeywell Bull.* (NLD)
473, 474 Page double et couverture d'un numéro de *Resource,* journal d'entreprise d'un fabricant de machines pour le déboisement et le reboisement. Illustrations en couleurs. (USA)
475 Illustration pleine page d'un périodique médical. (USA)
476, 477 Détail de l'illustration et couverture complète d'un périodique médical. Sujet: l'anémie. (USA)
478, 479 Illustration et couverture complète d'un périodique médical, se référant ici à la schizophrénie. (USA)

ARTIST / KÜNSTLER / ARTISTE:

480, 481 Lowren West
482, 483 Padraig Creston

DESIGNER / GESTALTER / MAQUETTISTE:

480, 481 Harry Sehring/Creative Annex
482, 483 Any Dubois

ART DIRECTOR / DIRECTEUR ARTISTIQUE:

480, 481 Len Slonevsky/Don Kahn/Paul Jerr
482, 483 Jacques Tribondeau

AGENCY / AGENTUR / AGENCE – STUDIO:

482, 483 McCann-Erickson

PUBLISHER / VERLEGER / EDITEUR:

480, 481 Lederle Laboratories
482, 483 Esso France

480

481

480, 481 Cover and detail of an illustration from *Bookshelf*, a magazine dealing with medical publications, produced by *Lederle Laboratories*. (USA)
482, 483 Complete cover and detail of the illustration from *Pétrole Progrès*, the house magazine of *Esso* France, to which 25 000 people subscribe. (FRA)

480, 481 Umschlag und Detail der Illustration von *Bookshelf*, einem Magazin über medizinische Publikationen, das von *Lederle Laboratories* herausgegeben wird. (USA)
482, 483 Kompletter Umschlag und Detail der Illustration von *Pétrole Progrès*, Hauszeitschrift der *Esso* Frankreich. Thema ist der Ersatz der pflanzlichen Öle durch Mineralöle. Obgleich sie nur auf das Fachgebiet Öl ausgerichtet ist, hat die Zeitschrift 25 000 Abonnenten. (FRA)

480, 481 Couverture et détail de l'illustration d'un numéro de *Bookshelf*, magazine annonçant les nouvelles publications médicales. (USA)
482, 483 Couverture complète et détail de l'illustration d'un numéro de *Pétrole Progrès*, journal d'entreprise d'*Esso France*. On y aborde le sujet des huiles de pétroles remplaçant les huiles végétales. Quoique centré sur les aspects de l'industrie du pétrole, il compte 25 000 abonnés. (FRA)

482

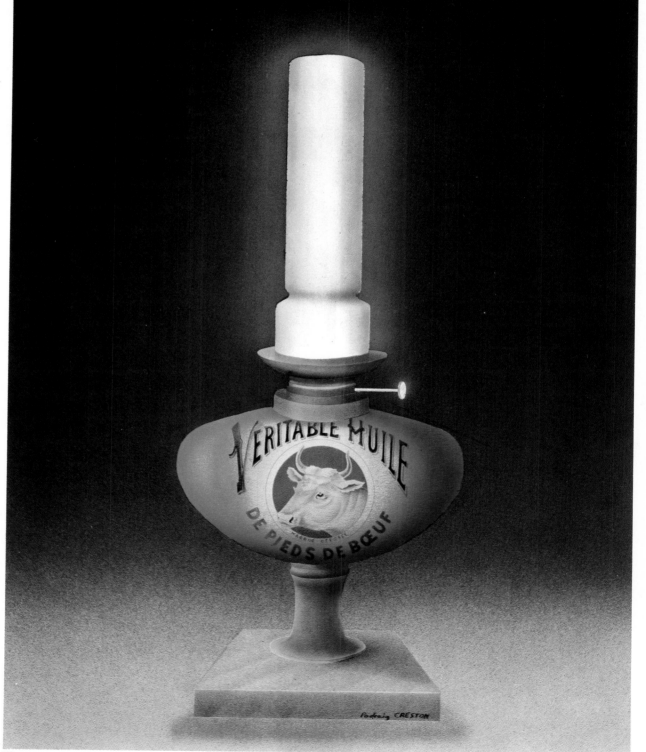

483

484

484, 485 Illustrations from *Pétrole Progrès,* the house magazine of *Esso* France. Fig. 484 shows the factory of tomorrow: clean and profitable. Fig. 485 illustrates an article about the utilization of energy. (FRA)
486 Cover of *Currency,* the house magazine of the *Reserve Bank of Australia.* The letters are in full colour. (AUS)
487 Cover of *Home Cooking,* the house magazine of *Kikkoman.* (JPN)
488 Illustration from a *Pétrole Progrès* cover. *Esso* house magazine. (FRA)
489 Illustration to the theme of industrial hygiene. From *Pétrole Progrès.* (FRA)

484, 485 Illustrationen aus *Pétrole Progrès,* Hauszeitschrift von *Esso* Frankreich. Abb. 484 zeigt den Betrieb von morgen: sauber und gewinnbringend. Abb. 495 illustriert einen Artikel über die Verwendung der Energie. (FRA)
486 Umschlag von *Currency,* Hauszeitschrift der *Reserve Bank of Australia.* Die Buchstaben sind mehrfarbig. (AUS)
487 Umschlag von *Home Cooking,* Hauszeitschrift von *Kikkoman.* (JPN)
488 Illustration des Umschlags von *Pétrole Progrès, Esso*-Hauszeitschrift. (FRA)
489 Illustration zum Thema Industrie-Hygiene. Aus *Pétrole Progrès.* (FRA)

484, 485 Illustrations de *Pétrole Progrès,* journal d'entreprise d'*Esso France.* Fig. 484 montre l'avenir envisagé pour l'entreprise: propre et rentable; fig. 485: article sur le bon usage de l'énergie. (FRA)
486 Couverture de *Currency,* journal d'entreprise d'une banque australienne. Les caractères sont en différentes couleurs. (AUS)
487 Couverture d'un numéro du journal d'entreprise de *Kikkoman.* (JPN)
488 Illustration de couverture de *Pétrole Progrès* d'*Esso France.* (FRA)
489 Illustration de *Pétrole Progrès* au sujet de l'hygiène industrielle. (FRA)

485

ARTIST / KÜNSTLER:

484 Jean Alessandrini
485 Claude Chevalley
486 John Copeland
487 Tadashi Ohashi
488 Josse Goffin
489 AND Partners (Photo Botti)

DESIGNER / GESTALTER:

484, 485, 488, 489 Any Dubois
486 John Copeland
487 Tadashi Ohashi

ART DIRECTOR:

484, 485, 488, 489 Jacques Tribondeau
486 Charles Jardine
487 Tadashi Ohashi

AGENCY / AGENTUR:

484, 485, 488, 489 McCann-Erickson

PUBLISHER / VERLEGER:

484, 485, 488, 489 Esso France
486 Reserve Bank of Australia
487 Kikkoman Shoyu Co., Ltd.

486

487

488

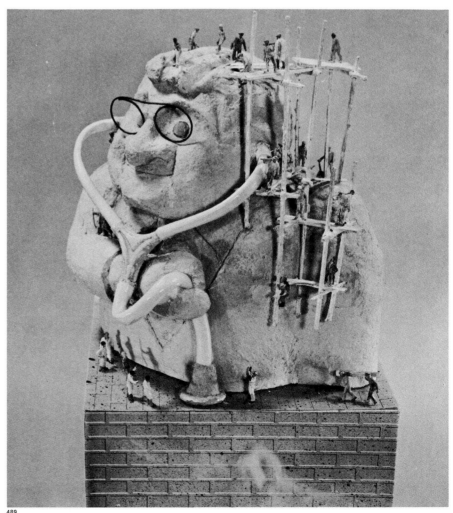

489

House Organs / Hauszeitschriften
Journaux d'entreprises

ARTIST / KÜNSTLER / ARTISTE:

490 Stanislaw Zagorski/Seymour Chwast/Emanuel Schongut
491 Stanislaw Zagorski/Bernard Bonhomme
492, 493 Seymour Chwast
494 Stanislaw Zagorski

DESIGNER / GESTALTER / MAQUETTISTE:

490–494 Richard Mantel

ART DIRECTOR / DIRECTEUR ARTISTIQUE:

490–494 Seymour Chwast

AGENCY / AGENTUR / AGENCE – STUDIO:

490–494 Push Pin Studios

PUBLISHER / VERLEGER / EDITEUR:

490–494 The Push Pin Graphic, Inc.

490, 491 Two examples from a number of double spreads from *Push Pin Graphic,* the Push Pin Studios' house magazine. Fig. 490 in black and white, Fig. 491 with the male figure in blue shades, pink rose, woman and hare in black and white. (USA)
492 Double spread from *Push Pin Graphic.* (USA)
493, 494 Cover pages in full colour from *Push Pin Graphic.* (USA)

490, 491 Zwei Beispiele von mehreren Doppelseiten unter dem Titel «Kostümfest» aus *Push Pin Graphic,* Hauszeitschrift der Push Pin Studios. Abb. 490 in Schwarzweiss, Abb. 491 mit Männergestalt in bläulichen Tönen und rosa Rose, Frau und Hase schwarzweiss. (USA)
492 «Das Leben auf Noahs Arche am 40. Tag.» Doppelseite aus *Push Pin Graphic.*(USA)
493, 494 Farbige Umschlagseiten von *Push Pin Graphic.* Die Themen der Ausgaben dieser Hauszeit-schrift sind Schlaf (Abb. 493) und Mode (Abb. 494). (USA)

490, 491 Deux pages doubles d'un numéro de *Push Pin Graphic,* revue d'entreprise des *Push Pin Studios.* Ce numéro était consacré au «bal costumé». Fig. 490 en noir et blanc; fig. 491: figure masculine en tons bleus avec rose rouge, figure féminine et lapin en noir-blanc. (USA)
492 «Le 40e jour sur l'arche de Noé.» Page double de *Push Pin Graphic.* (USA)
493, 494 Couvertures polychromes de *Push Pin Graphic.* On y discute les sujets du sommeil (fig. 493) et de la mode (fig. 494). (USA)

182

LIFE ABOARD NOAH'S ARK ON THE FORTIETH DAY.

492

BACK TO SLEEP ISSUE

Push Pin Graphic

NUMBER 74

AUGUST 1978

SEYMOUR CHWAST

493

SPECIAL FASHION ISSUE

Push Pin Graphic

NUMBER 75

OCTOBER 1978

STANISLAW ZAGORSKI

494

495 Double spread in black and white from an edition of *Push Pin Graphic*, the house magazine of the Push Pin Studios. (USA)
496, 497 Double spreads from an edition of *Push Pin Graphic* dealing with clowns and all their theatrical paraphernalia. (USA)
498 Draft of the cover from the clown edition of *Push Pin Graphic*. (USA)

495 Doppelseite in Schwarzweiss aus einer dem Wohnen gewidmeten Ausgabe von *Push Pin Graphic*, Hauszeitschrift der Push Pin Studios. (USA)
496, 497 Doppelseiten aus einer Ausgabe von *Push Pin Graphic* über Clowns. Hier die typischen Requisiten der Clowns und «Gesichter». (USA)
498 Entwurf für den Umschlag der Clown-Ausgabe von *Push Pin Graphic*. (USA)

MORMON TABERNACLE CHOIR'S LIVING ROOM BY RICHARD MANTEL

495

ARTIST / KÜNSTLER / ARTISTE:

495 Richard Mantel
496 Emanuel Schongut
497 Seymour Chwast
498 John Collier

DESIGNER / GESTALTER / MAQUETTISTE:

495–498 Richard Mantel

ART DIRECTOR / DIRECTEUR ARTISTIQUE:

495–498 Seymour Chwast

496

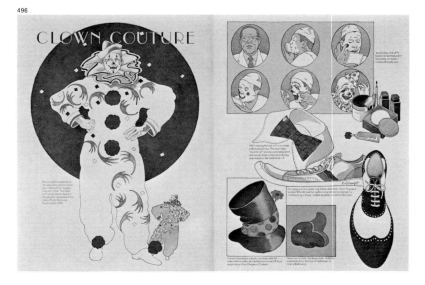

497

495 Page double en noir et blanc figurant dans un numéro de *Push Pin Graphic* qui est consacré à la «belle maison». (USA)
496, 497 Extraits d'un numéro de *Push Pin Graphic* consacré aux «Clowns». Doubles pages illustrées en couleurs: accessoires de clowns et synthèse d'un visage de clown. (USA)
498 Projet de couverture pour un numéro de *Push Pin Graphic* consacré aux «Clowns». (USA)

AGENCY / AGENTUR / AGENCE—STUDIO:
495—498 Push Pin Studios

PUBLISHER / VERLEGER / EDITEUR:
495—498 The Push Pin Graphic, Inc.

498

ARTIST / KÜNSTLER / ARTISTE:

499, 502, 504 Emanuel Schongut
500 Seymour Chwast
501 Larry Klein
503 Eduard Prüssen

DESIGNER / GESTALTER / MAQUETTISTE:

499, 502, 504 Richard Mantel
500 Seymour Chwast/Martin S. Moskof
501 Shlomo Krudo
503 Eduard Prüssen

499

500

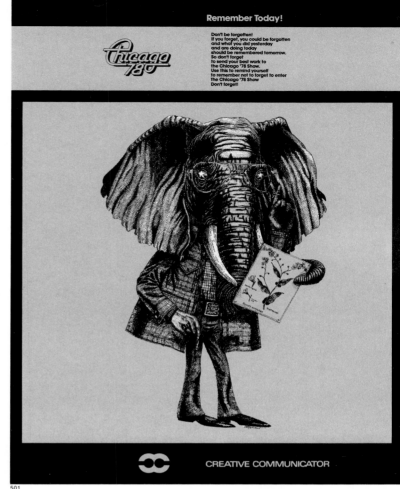

501

502

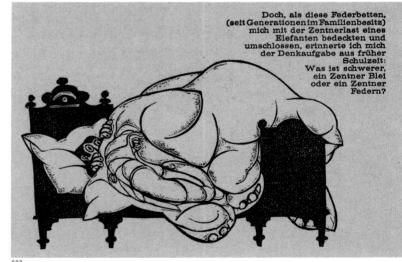

Doch, als diese Federbetten,
(seit Generationen im Familienbesitz)
mich mit der Zentnerlast eines
Elefanten bedeckten und
umschlossen, erinnerte ich mich
der Denkaufgabe aus früher
Schulzeit:
Was ist schwerer,
ein Zentner Blei
oder ein Zentner
Federn?

503

504

ART DIRECTOR / DIRECTEUR ARTISTIQUE:

499, 502, 504 Seymour Chwast
500 Richard Mantel
501 Shlomo Krudo/Dorothy Kienast

AGENCY / AGENTUR / AGENCE – STUDIO:

499, 502, 504 Push Pin Studios

PUBLISHER / VERLEGER / EDITEUR:

499, 502, 504 The Push Pin Graphic, Inc.
500 Nelson Doubleday, Inc.
501 Creative Communicator
503 Donkey-Press

499, 504 Illustration and complete cover of an "animal" edition of *Push Pin Graphic*. (USA)
500 Cover of *Tube*, a television magazine for children. In full colour. (USA)
501 Cover of *Creative Communicator*, organ of an artists' association in Chicago. (USA)
502 Double spread from an "animal" edition of *Push Pin Graphic*. (USA)
503 From *Donkey-Press*, small format "house magazine" of E. Prüssen, graphic designer. (GER)

499, 504 Illustration und kompletter Umschlag einer «Tier»-Ausgabe von *Push Pin Graphic*. (USA)
500 Farbiger Umschlag von *Tube*, einem Fernsehmagazin für Kinder. (USA)
501 Umschlag von *Creative Communicator*, Organ der Künstler-Vereinigungen in Chicago. (USA)
502 Doppelseite aus einer «Tier»-Ausgabe von *Push Pin Graphic*. (USA)
503 Aus *Donkey-Press*, kleinformatige «Hauszeitschrift» des Graphikers E. Prüssen. (GER)

499, 504 Illustration et couverture complète d'un numéro de *Push Pin Graphic* qui est entièrement consacré aux «Animaux». (USA)
500 Couverture polychrome de *Tube*, revue de TV pour la jeunesse. (USA)
501 Couverture de l'organe officiel de l'association des artistes de Chicago. (USA)
502 Page double extrait d'un numéro de *Push Pin Graphic* consacré aux «Animaux». (USA)
503 Extrait de *Donkey-Press*, «journal d'entreprise» de l'artiste E. Prüssen. (GER)

505–507 Double spread and two covers from *U&lc.*, house magazine of the *International Typeface Corporation.* (USA)
508–510 Double spreads from *U&lc.*, the house magazine of the *International Typeface Corporation.* Figs. 509 and 510 pertain to the revising of posters which introduce on this occasion prize-winning typographical designs. The new drafts are shown in large format, the originals in small format with an explanatory text. (USA)
511 Page from *Technology Review* with diagram showing the development of a new product. (USA)
512 Cover from *Ciba-Geigy Magazin.* Red "building stones for the Third World" on grey surface. (SWI)

505–507 Doppelseite («etwas für jedermann») und zwei Umschläge von *U&lc.*, Hauszeitschrift der Typographen-Vereinigung International Typeface Corporation. (USA)
508–510 Doppelseiten aus *U&lc.*, Hauszeitschrift der International Typeface Corporation. Thema von Abb. 508: «Von Angesicht zu Angesicht». In Abb. 509 und 510 geht es um die Überarbeitung von Plakaten, die hier prämierte typographische Designs vorstellen. Die neue Lösung wird grossformatig gezeigt, die ursprüngliche Lösung klein darüber mit erklärendem Text. (USA)
511 Seite aus *Technology Review* mit Diagramm der Entwicklung eines neuen Produkts. (USA)
512 Umschlag von *Ciba-Geigy Magazin.* Rote Bausteine auf grauem Grund. (SWI)

505
506   507

ARTIST / KÜNSTLER / ARTISTE:

505 Lionel Kalish
507 John Alcorn
512 Christian Lang

DESIGNER / GESTALTER / MAQUETTISTE:

505–510 Herb Lubalin
511 Bernie LaCasse
512 Christian Lang

ART DIRECTOR / DIRECTEUR ARTISTIQUE:

505–510 Herb Lubalin
511 Nancy C. Pokross
512 Christian Lang

505–507 Page double («il y a quelque chose pour chacun») et couvertures de *U&lc.*, journal de l'association internationale des typographes. (USA)
508–510 Pages doubles de *U&lc.*, organe de l'association internationale des typographes. Fig. 8: «Face
à face»; fig. 509 et 510: la retouche d'un projet d'affiche. On y présente des conceptions typographiques
primées. La conception finale est montrée en grand face à la conception originale (en format réduit) avec
texte explicatif. (USA)
511 Page de *Technology Review* avec diagramme sur le développement d'un nouveau produit. (USA)
512 Couverture du magazine *Ciba-Geigy*. Briques rouges sur fond gris. (SWI)

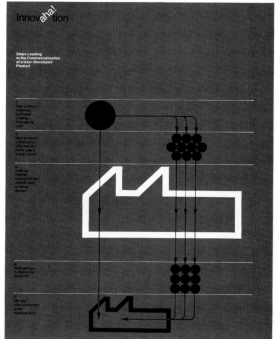

511

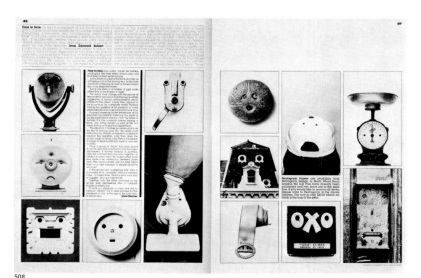

508

509

512

510

AGENCY / AGENTUR / AGENCE – STUDIO:

505–510 LSC&P Design Group, Inc.
511 MIT Design Services
512 Zentrale Werbung Ciba-Geigy

PUBLISHER / VERLEGER / EDITEUR:

505–510 International Typeface Corporation
511 Massachusetts Institute of Technology
512 Publizitätsdienst Ciba-Geigy AG

House Organs
Hauszeitschriften
Journaux d'entreprises

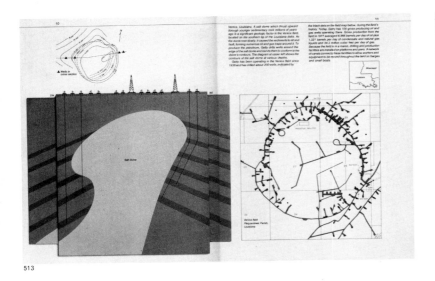

513

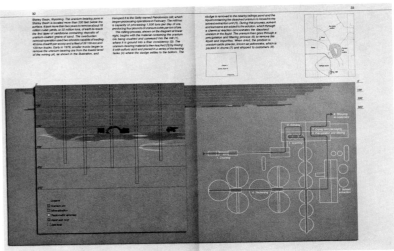

514

ARTIST / KÜNSTLER / ARTISTE:

513, 514 Paul Bice
515–518 Alfred Lutz

DESIGNER / GESTALTER / MAQUETTISTE:

513, 514 Claire Denador
515–518 Alfred Lutz

ART DIRECTOR / DIRECTEUR ARTISTIQUE:

513, 514 Robert Miles Runyan/Dick Rice
515–518 Alfred Lutz

AGENCY / AGENTUR / AGENCE – STUDIO:

513, 514 Runyan + Rice

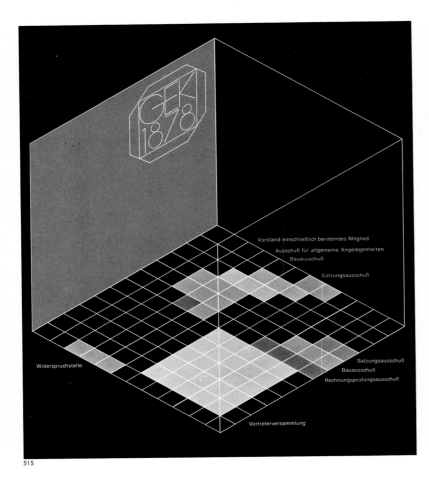

515

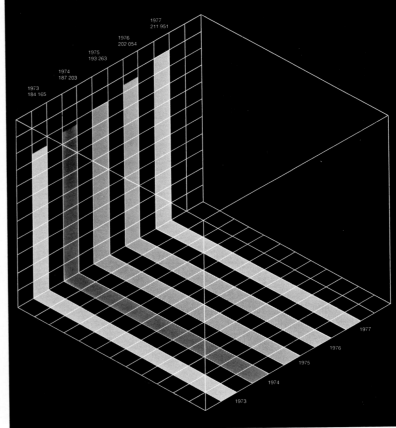

516

Annual Reports

513, 514 Double spreads from the 1977 annual report of the *Getty Oil Company*. A cross-section of a drilling field is shown here: Fig. 513 shows the salt dome and its contours at various depths, and the oil field; Fig. 514 shows the uranium-bearing zone and the milling process. Colours are used to distinguish the various strata. (USA)
515–518 Three pages and a complete double spread from the annual report of the *Schwäbisch Gmünder Ersatzkasse*. Fig. 515: the self-governing body or organ; Fig. 516: the development of membership; Figs. 517 and 518: the revenue. All illustrations with white lines on a black surface with other areas in colour. (GER)

513, 514 Doppelseiten aus dem Jahresbericht 1977 der *Getty Oil Company*. Hier ein Bohrfeld im Querschnitt (Erd- und Salzkammerbereich in Beige- und Brauntönen, Oberfläche blau) und Lageplan der Brunnen (Abb. 513). Abb. 514 illustriert den Abbau von Uranvorkommen und dessen Verarbeitung. Uran, Sand und Vererzung sind farbig gekennzeichnet. (USA)
515–518 Drei Seiten und eine komplette Doppelseite aus einem Jahresbericht der *Schwäbisch Gmünder Ersatzkasse*. Hier die Selbstverwaltung, dargestellt in Abb. 515, die Entwicklung des Mitgliederbestandes in Abb. 516 und die Einnahmen in Abb. 517 und 518. Alle Darstellungen mit weissen Linien auf schwarzem Grund mit farbigen Feldern. (GER)

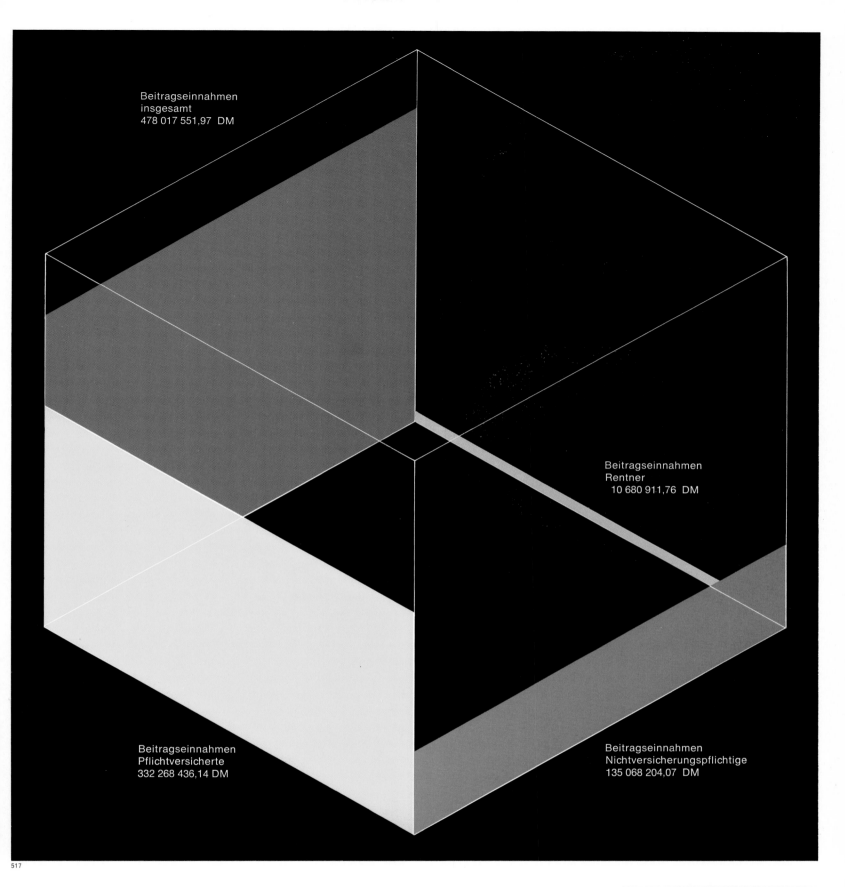

Beitragseinnahmen
insgesamt
478 017 551,97 DM

Beitragseinnahmen
Rentner
10 680 911,76 DM

Beitragseinnahmen
Pflichtversicherte
332 268 436,14 DM

Beitragseinnahmen
Nichtversicherungspflichtige
135 068 204,07 DM

517

513, 514 Page double du rapport annuel 1977 d'une compagnie pétrolière. Fig. 513: terrain de forage vu en coupe (couche de terre et de sel fossile en tons bruns et beiges, surface bleue) et plan des puits. Fig. 514 illustre l'exploitation d'uranium et sa transformation. Uranium, sable et minerai sont marqués en couleurs. (USA)
515—518 Trois pages simples et page double complète figurant dans le rapport annuel d'une banque de Schwäbisch Gmünd. Fig. 515: illustration de l'auto-gestion, fig. 516: le développement du nombre des membres, fig. 517 et 518: les recettes. Représentations uniformes avec des lignes blanches sur fond noir, cases en couleurs. (GER)

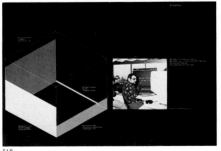

518

519

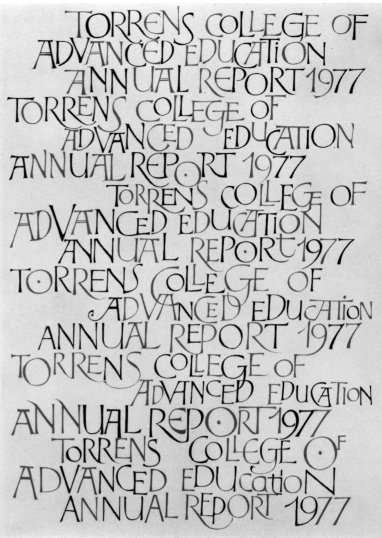

520

522

523

519 Cover of the business report of the *AG für das Werbefernsehen*. (SWI)
520 Cover of the annual report of a college. Letters in red, brown, green and ochre. (USA)
521, 525 Double spread and cover of the annual report of the *Prince Bernhard Foundation*. (NLD)
522–524 Double spreads and cover illustration of the 1977 annual report of a paper and cardboard manufacturer. (USA)

519 Couverture du rapport de gestion de la SA pour la publicité à la télévision. (SWI)
520 Couverture du rapport annuel d'un lycée. Caractères en rouge, brun, vert, ocre. (USA)
521, 525 Page double et couverture du rapport annuel d'une fondation. (NLD)
522–524 Pages doubles et illustration de couverture du rapport annuel d'une papeterie. Les couleurs rappellent les œuvres de Robert Motherwell, Robert Rauschenberg et Jasper Johns. (USA)

519 Umschlag des Geschäftsberichtes der *AG für das Werbefernsehen*. (SWI)
520 Umschlag des Jahresberichtes eines College. Buchstaben rot, braun, grün und ocker. (USA)
521, 525 Doppelseite und Umschlag eines Jahresberichtes der *Prinz Bernhard Stiftung*. (NLD)
522–524 Doppelseiten und Umschlagillustration aus dem Jahresbericht 1977 eines Papier- und Kartonagenherstellers. Die Farben erinnern an die Werke amerikanischer Maler, wie z.B. Robert Motherwell, Robert Rauschenberg und Jasper Johns. (USA)

521

524

525

Annual Reports

ARTIST / KÜNSTLER / ARTISTE:

519 Kurt Wirth
520 John Copeland
521, 525 Jeroen Henneman
522–524 Robert Cunningham

DESIGNER / GESTALTER / MAQUETTISTE:

519 Kurt Wirth
520 John Copeland
521, 525 Hans Versteeg
522–524 Norman Perman

ART DIRECTOR / DIRECTEUR ARTISTIQUE:

519 Kurt Wirth
521, 525 Hans Versteeg
522–524 Norman Perman/Davis Crippen

AGENCY / AGENTUR / AGENCE – STUDIO:

519 Kurt Wirth
521, 525 Dots Design
522–524 Norman Perman Inc.

526

527

530

532

ARTIST / KÜNSTLER / ARTISTE:

526–528 Magda Cianciara
529 Steven Martin/June Wynn
530 Paul Orenstein
531 Alfred Lutz
532, 533 Archie Lieberman

ART DIRECTOR / DIRECTEUR ARTISTIQUE:

526–528 Magda Cianciara
529 Tom Ohmer
530 Robert Burns
531 Alfred Lutz
532, 533 Norman Perman/Paul Faberson

DESIGNER / GESTALTER / MAQUETTISTE:

526–528 Magda Cianciara
529 Bruce Dobson
530 Lawrence Finn
531 Alfred Lutz
532, 533 Norman Perman

Annual Reports

information under the Toxic Substances Control Act (TSCA) and the Consumer Product Safety Act (CPSA). TRAC brings together Company experts in various technical disciplines and the law, and it reviews information on suspected hazards from all sources, external and internal. All Company employees have been instructed how to report information to TRAC which they believe may indicate a substantial new hazard. And TRAC has twin responsibilities: to report to the federal government risk information judged reportable under TSCA or CPSA and to make recommendations on actions to minimize or eliminate potential hazards.

An environmental surveillance program was begun in 1978 under which periodic independent reviews are carried out to make sure that environmental programs being implemented at our plants comply with Company policy and with applicable laws and regulations. A pilot program in business risk management was initiated which aims at identifying potential environmental hazards in our various businesses and alternatives for dealing with them. To assist in meeting the complex reporting requirements of the environmental laws, we developed a computerized data base containing more than 400,000 pieces of information on nearly 10,000 materials that Allied Chemical handles.

These and other management programs are proving effective because they are backed up by extensive training efforts to equip our people to use them. Attendance at environmental training workshops held for Allied Chemical managers and professionals in 1978 totaled more than 1,700. Numerous special training programs have been developed for our business areas.

528

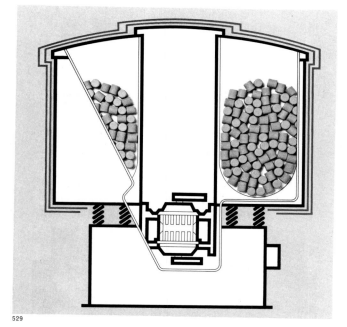

529

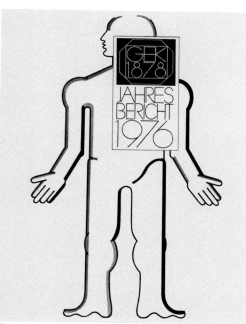

531

AGENCY / AGENTUR / AGENCE – STUDIO:

526–528 Art for Industry
529 Advertising Designers, Inc.
530 Burns, Cooper, Hynes Ltd.
532, 533 Norman Perman Inc.

526–528 Pages from the annual report of *Allied Chemical*. Fig. 526 introduces the financial review; Figs. 527 and 528 deal with environment, also in colour. (USA)
529 Page from the annual report of Sweco Inc. (USA)
530 Cover of the annual report, 1978, of a building firm. (CAN)
531 Cover of the 1976 annual report of a bank. (GER)
532, 533 Cover and unfolding double spread from the annual report of International Minerals and Chemical Corp. (USA)

526–528 Seiten aus dem Jahresbericht 1978 der *Allied Chemical*. Abb. 526 leitet den finanziellen Rückblick ein; Abb. 527 und 528 zum Thema Umwelt, ebenfalls farbig. (USA)
529 Seite aus einem Jahresbericht der Sweco Inc. (USA)

530 Umschlag des Jahresberichtes 1978 einer Baufirma. (CAN)
531 Umschlag des Jahresberichtes 1976 einer Bank. (GER)
532, 533 Umschlag und ausklappbare Doppelseite aus dem Jahresbericht der International Minerals & Chemical Corp. (USA)

526–528 Page du rapport annuel d'une compagnie de produits chimiques. Fig. 526: page initiale du rapport financiaire; fig. 527 et 528: pages en polychromie au sujet de l'environnement. (USA)
529 Page d'un rapport annuel de la Sweco, Inc. (USA)
530 Couverture du rapport d'une société de construction. (CAN)
531 Couverture du rapport annuel 1976 d'une banque. (GER)
532, 533 Couverture et page double à repli figurant dans le rapport annuel d'une entreprise de l'industrie chimique. (USA)

533

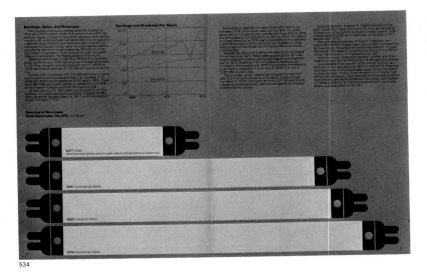

534

535

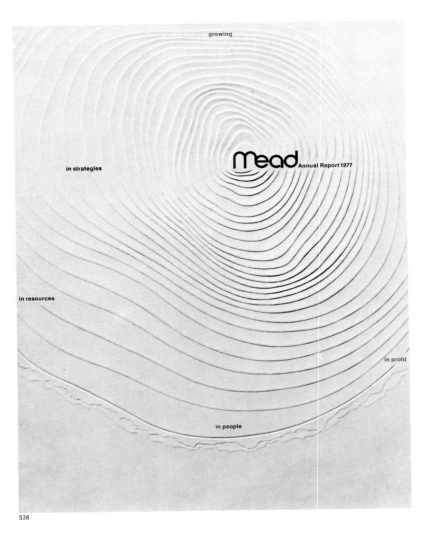

536

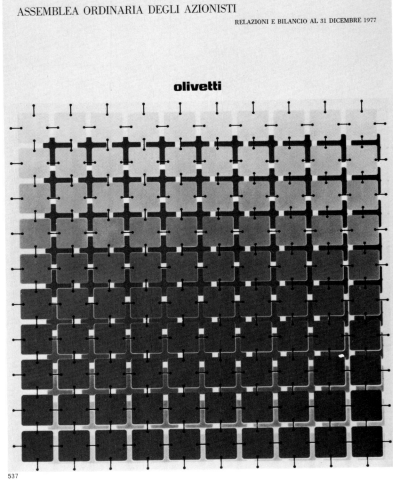

ASSEMBLEA ORDINARIA DEGLI AZIONISTI

RELAZIONI E BILANCIO AL 31 DICEMBRE 1977

olivetti

537

539

ARTIST / KÜNSTLER / ARTISTE:

534, 535 Susan Slover
536 Bruce Davidson
537 Giovanni Ranzini
538 Alfredo Gambaro
539 Ed Kysar

DESIGNER / GESTALTER / MAQUETTISTE:

534, 535 Susan Slover
536 Sheldon Seidler/Bill Mihalik
537 Ottavio Cengic
539 James Marrin

534, 535 Double spreads from an annual report of the *Southern Company* electric power suppliers. Light brown ground, illustrations in two colours. (USA)
536 Cover of a *Mead* annual report. Main feature is the blind embossing on white cardboard reminding one of the annual rings of a tree. (USA)
537, 538 Cover and detail of a cover illustration from the *Olivetti* shareholders' reports. In black and white. (ITA)
539 Double spread from an annual report of the Charles Stark Draper Laboratories Inc., manufacturers of instruments for air and space travel. (USA)

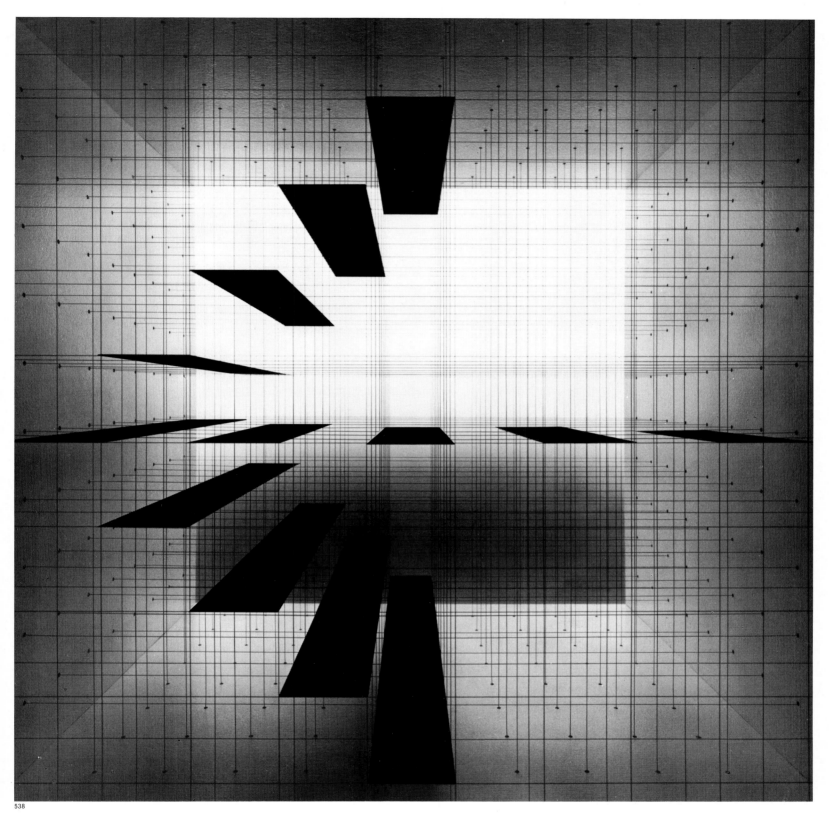

538

ART DIRECTOR / DIRECTEUR ARTISTIQUE:

534, 535 Robert E. Cargill
536 Sheldon Seidler
537, 538 Franco Bassi
539 Tom Ohmer

AGENCY / AGENTUR / AGENCE – STUDIO:

534, 535 Cargill and Assoc. Inc.
536 Sheldon Seidler Inc.
537, 538 Olivetti, Ufficio Pubblicità
539 Advertising Designers, Inc.

Annual Reports

534, 535 Doppelseiten aus einem Jahresbericht des Elektrizitätswerkes *Southern Company*. Hellbrauner Untergrund, Illustrationen zweifarbig.(USA)
536 Umschlag eines Jahresberichtes von *Mead*. Die Blindprägung des weissen Kartons erinnert an die Jahresringe eines Baumes, Haupt-Rohstofflieferant dieser Firma. (USA)
537, 538 Umschlag und Detail einer Umschlag-Illustration von Aktionärsberichten der Firma *Olivetti*. In Schwarzweiss. (ITA)
539 Doppelseite aus einem Jahresbericht der Charles Stark Draper Laboratories, Inc., Hersteller von Geräten für die Luft- und Raumfahrt. (USA)

534, 535 Pages doubles tirées du rapport annuel d'une compagnie d'électricité. Illustrations en deux couleurs sur fond brun clair. (USA)
536 Couverture du rapport de gestion d'une papeterie. Gaufrage à sec sur carton blanc, rappelant les cernes d'un arbre, matière première de cette entreprise. (USA)
537, 538 Couverture et détail de l'illustration d'une autre couverture en noir-blanc de rapports destinés aux actionnaires d'*Olivetti*. (ITA)
539 Page double figurant dans le rapport annuel d'une entreprise qui fabrique des appareils et équipements pour l'aviation et l'astronautique. (USA)

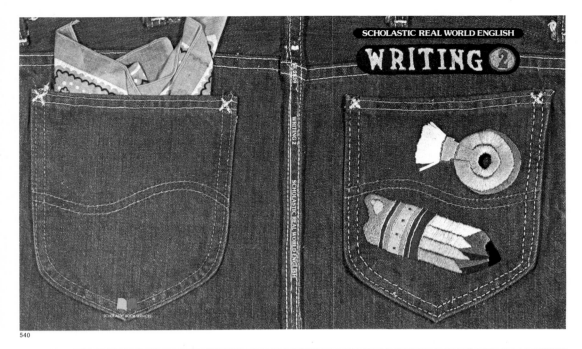

540

542

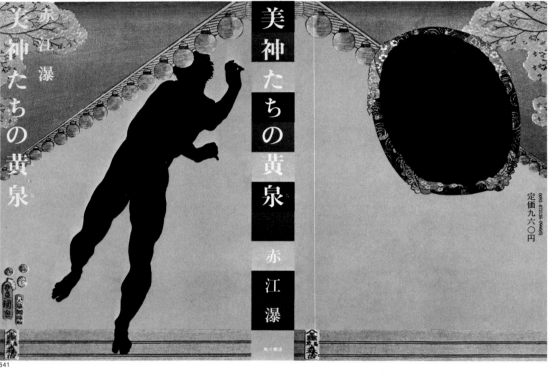

541

543

ARTIST / KÜNSTLER / ARTISTE:

540 Richard Lucik
541 Tadanori Yokoo
542 Isadore Seltzer
543 Kenji Sumura
544 Bengt Fosshag
545 Art Goodman
546, 547 Friedrich Hechelmann

DESIGNER / GESTALTER / MAQUETTISTE:

540 Skip Sorvino
541 Tadanori Yokoo
542 Andrew Kner
543 Kenji Sumura
544 Karl W. Henschel/Bengt Fosshag
545 Saul Bass/Art Goodman
546, 547 Friedrich Hechelmann

PUBLISHER / VERLEGER / EDITEUR:

540 Scholastic Book Services
541 Kadokawa Shoten Publishing Co.
542 RC Publications
543 Bompiani Editore
544 Rowohlt Verlag
545 Harcourt Brace Jovanovich, Inc.
546, 547 Nord-Süd Verlag

540 Cover of a school text book for English lessons. Mostly red shades on jeans-blue. (USA)
541 Complete cover of a Japanese book. The colours are red, black, green and blue. (JPN)
542 Cover of an annual about exhibition design from a series of books, entitled *Print Casebooks*. (USA)
543 Cover of a book about a gentleman thief. (ITA)
544 Colour cover of an book about chess. (GER)
545 Cover of a book, with green cliffs and a blue sky, entitled ''The Longest War''. (USA)
546, 547 Complete cover and excerpt therefrom for a children's book about a gigantic young lady. (SWI)

540 Umschlag eines Schulbuches für den Englischunterricht. Vorwiegend Rottöne auf Jeans-Blau. (USA)
541 Kompletter Umschlag eines japanischen Buches in Rot, Schwarz, Grün und Blau. (JPN)
542 Umschlag eines Jahrbuches über Ausstellungs-Design aus einer Buchreihe mit dem Titel *Print Casebooks*. (USA)
543 Umschlag eines Buches über einen Gentleman-Dieb. (ITA)
544 Farbiger Umschlag eines Sachbuches über Schach. (GER)
545 Umschlag eines Buches mit dem Titel «Der längste Krieg». Grüne Felsen vor blauem Himmel. (USA)
546, 547 Kompletter Umschlag und Ausschnitt daraus für ein Kinderbuch, das von einem Riesenfräulein handelt. (SWI)

540 Couverture d'un manuel pour l'enseignement de la langue anglaise. Prédominance de tons rouges sur fond bleu. (USA)
541 Recto et verso d'un livre japonais. En rouge, noir, vert et bleu. (JPN)
542 Couverture d'un répertoire annuel d'expositions de design, figurant dans une série intitulée *Print Casebooks*. (USA)
543 Couverture d'un roman policier. (ITA)
544 Couverture polychrome d'un livre sur l'échec. (GER)
545 Couverture d'un livre intitulé «La guerre la plus longue». Rochers verts, ciel bleu. (USA)
546, 547 Couverture complète et détail de l'illustration: livre d'enfant traitant d'une fille géante. (SWI)

544

545

546

AGENCY / AGENTUR:

540 Scholastic Book Services
543 Studio K
544 Studio Sign
545 Saul Bass/Herb Yager & Associates

547

ARTIST / KÜNSTLER / ARTISTE:

548–550 Etienne Delessert
552 Edward Gorey
553, 554 Oskar Weiss

DESIGNER / GESTALTER / MAQUETTISTE:

548, 549 Jean Olivier Héron
550 Etienne Delessert
551 Donna Schenkel
552 Eduard Gorey
553, 554 Oskar Weiss

ART DIRECTOR / DIRECTEUR ARTISTIQUE:

548, 549 Jean Olivier Héron
550 Etienne Delessert
552 Kurt Jenny
553, 554 Oswald Dubacher

AGENCY / AGENTUR / AGENCE – STUDIO:

550 Carabosse SA
551 MIT Press Design Department

PUBLISHER / VERLEGER / EDITEUR:

548, 549 Gallimard
550 Mary-Josée
551 MIT Press
552 Diogenes Verlag
553, 554 Ex Libris Verlag

William Camus
Les Oiseaux de Feu
et autres contes peaux-rouges

folio junior
Texte intégral illustré

548

Pierre Mac Orlan
Les clients du
Bon Chien Jaune

folio junior
Texte intégral illustré

549

DIE WEICHE SPEICHE / EDWARD GOREY

552

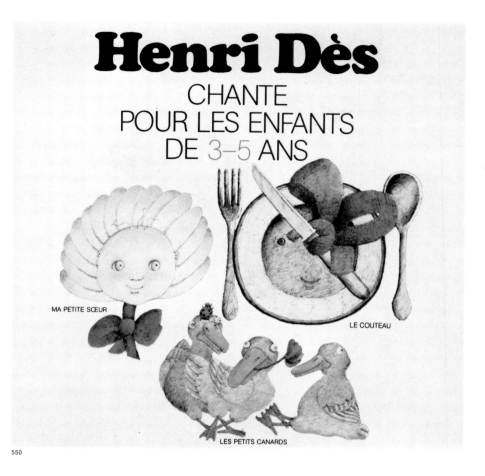

550

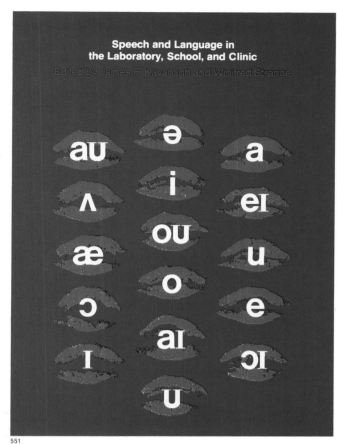

551

553

554

555

Book Covers
Buchumschläge
Couvertures de livres

The Detective of London

Robert Kraus and Bruce Kraus / illustrated by Robert Byrd

557

558

Grand bal
du printemps

Folio

Texte intégral

559

The Magic Circus

Wayne Anderson and Christopher Logue

560

YOK-YOK

6. **La chenille** ET TROIS AUTRES HISTOIRES

GALLIMARD · TOURNESOL

561

562

563

ARTIST / KÜNSTLER / ARTISTE:

562, 568 Cathy Hull
563, 564 John Martin
565 Milton Glaser
566 H.P. Wyss
567 Christopher McKimmie
569 Ken Laidlaw
570 Peter Bradford

DESIGNER / GESTALTER / MAQUETTISTE:

562, 568 Joe Montebellow
569 Sushma Baqaya

ART DIRECTOR / DIRECTEUR ARTISTIQUE:

563, 564 David Wyman
565 Harris Lewine
566 Oswald Dubacher
567 Christopher McKimmie
569 John Munday

AGENCY / AGENTUR / AGENCE – STUDIO:

563, 564 Camera Ready Art
565 Milton Glaser Inc.
567 University of Queensland Press
569 Andrew Archer Associates
570 Peter Bradford & Associates

PUBLISHER / VERLEGER / EDITEUR:

562, 568 Harper & Row
563, 564 Canadian Council on Children and Youth
565 Harcourt Brace Jovanovich, Inc.
566 Ex Libris Verlag
567 D.J. Murphy and R.B. Joyce
569 Transworld Publishers Ltd.
570 Thomas Y. Crowell

564

565

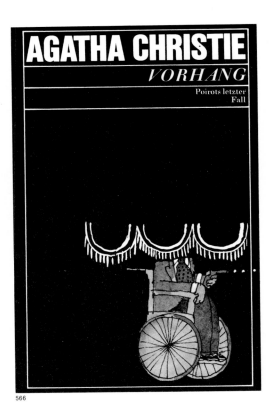

566

567

568

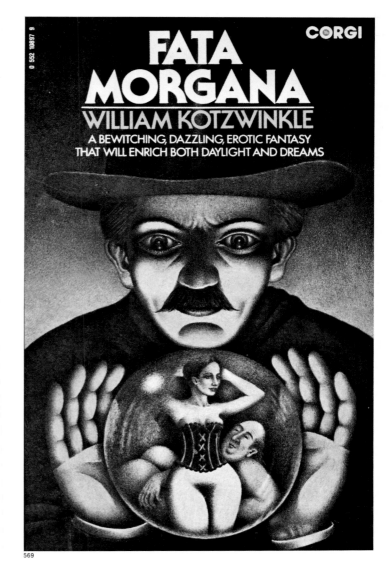

FATA MORGANA
WILLIAM KOTZWINKLE
A BEWITCHING, DAZZLING, EROTIC FANTASY
THAT WILL ENRICH BOTH DAYLIGHT AND DREAMS

CORGI

569

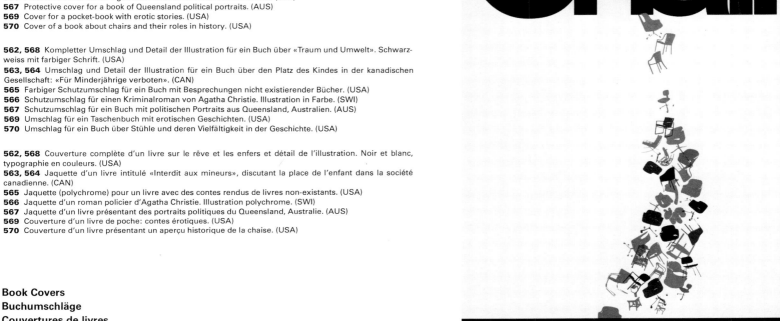

570

562, 568 Complete cover and detail of the illustration from a book dealing with the subconscious. Black and white with lettering in colour. (USA)
563, 564 Cover and detail of the illustration for a book about the place of the child in Canadian society. (CAN)
565 Protective cover of a book. In full colour. (USA)
566 Protective cover for an Agatha Christie novel. Illustration in colour. (SWI)
567 Protective cover for a book of Queensland political portraits. (AUS)
569 Cover for a pocket-book with erotic stories. (USA)
570 Cover of a book about chairs and their roles in history. (USA)

562, 568 Kompletter Umschlag und Detail der Illustration für ein Buch über «Traum und Umwelt». Schwarzweiss mit farbiger Schrift. (USA)
563, 564 Umschlag und Detail der Illustration für ein Buch über den Platz des Kindes in der kanadischen Gesellschaft: «Für Minderjährige verboten». (CAN)
565 Farbiger Schutzumschlag für ein Buch mit Besprechungen nicht existierender Bücher. (USA)
566 Schutzumschlag für einen Kriminalroman von Agatha Christie. Illustration in Farbe. (SWI)
567 Schutzumschlag für ein Buch mit politischen Portraits aus Queensland, Australien. (AUS)
569 Umschlag für ein Taschenbuch mit erotischen Geschichten. (USA)
570 Umschlag für ein Buch über Stühle und deren Vielfältigkeit in der Geschichte. (USA)

562, 568 Couverture complète d'un livre sur le rêve et les enfers et détail de l'illustration. Noir et blanc, typographie en couleurs. (USA)
563, 564 Jaquette d'un livre intitulé «Interdit aux mineurs», discutant la place de l'enfant dans la société canadienne. (CAN)
565 Jaquette (polychrome) pour un livre avec des contes rendus de livres non-existants. (USA)
566 Jaquette d'un roman policier d'Agatha Christie. Illustration polychrome. (SWI)
567 Jaquette d'un livre présentant des portraits politiques du Queensland, Australie. (AUS)
569 Couverture d'un livre de poche: contes érotiques. (USA)
570 Couverture d'un livre présentant un aperçu historique de la chaise. (USA)

Book Covers
Buchumschläge
Couvertures de livres

VASILIJ GROSSMAN ROSTRUM
ALLT FLYTER

571

BERYL BAINBRIDGE / ROSTRUM
UTFLYKTEN MED VINFABRIKEN

572

HELMUT ZENKER
KASSBACH
ELLER DET ALLMÄNNA INTRESSET FÖR MARSVIN / ROSTRUM

573

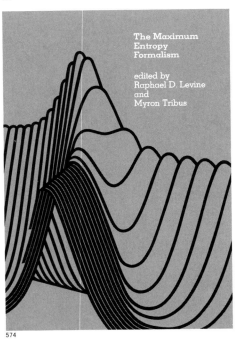

The Maximum
Entropy
Formalism

edited by
Raphael D. Levine
and
Myron Tribus

574

JURIJ TRIFONOV ROSTRUM
VÄNINGSBYTET

575

A Journey through Texas
Or, a Saddle-Trip on the Southwestern Frontier
Frederick Law Olmsted
Foreword by Larry McMurtry

576

ARTIST / KÜNSTLER / ARTISTE:

571–573, 575 Dan Jonsson
576 Ed Lindlof
577, 578 Michael D. Brown
579 Laszlo Kubinyi
580 Wendell Minor
581 Stanislaw Zagorski

DESIGNER / GESTALTER /
MAQUETTISTE:

571–573, 575 Dan Jonsson
574 Diane Jaroch
576 Richard Hendel
577, 578 Michael D. Brown
579 Meri Shardin
580 Wendell Minor
581 Stanislaw Zagorski

ART DIRECTOR / DIRECTEUR
ARTISTIQUE:

571–573, 575 Majbritt Hagdahl
576 Richard Hendel
577, 578 Michael D. Brown
579 Riki Levinson
580 Frank Metz
581 Harris Lewine

AGENCY / AGENTUR / AGENCE –
STUDIO:

574 MIT Press Design Department
576 Ed Lindlof
577, 578 Michael D. Brown Inc.
580 Wendell Minor Design

PUBLISHER / VERLEGER / EDITEUR:

571–573, 575 Forum
574 MIT Press
576 University of Texas Press
577, 578 Crossing Press
579 E.P. Dutton
580 Summit Books Inc.
581 Harcourt Brace Jovanovich, Inc.

577

571–573, 575 Cover illustrations in black and white for a series of books from the *Forum* publishing company. (SWE)
574 Protective cover for a scientific book. Violet lines on a grey background. (USA)
576 Protective cover for a book in which the author traces his journey through Texas. It belongs among the Texan classics and is of particular interest to historians. Illustration in black and white, orange title on greybrown. (USA)
577, 578 Cover of a book about an unusual aspect of politics and detail of the illustration. Black on light brown. (USA)
579 Protective cover with colour illustration for a book of tales in which cats play the main roles as they dominate human beings in terms of wit and spirit. (USA)
580 Colour cover for a biography of E.A. Poe. (USA)
581 Cover illustration for a novel written by Georges Simenon. Blue, red and green shades. (USA)

571–573, 575 Umschlagillustrationen in Schwarzweiss für eine Buchreihe des *Forum*-Verlags. (SWE)
574 Schutzumschlag für ein wissenschaftliches Buch. Violette Linien auf grauem Hintergrund. (USA)
576 Schutzumschlag für ein Buch, in dem der Autor seine Reise durch Texas schildert. Es gehört zu den Klassikern in Texas und gilt als wertvolles Nachschlagwerk für Historiker. Illustration in Schwarzweiss, Titel orange auf Graubraun. (USA)
577, 578 Umschlag für ein Buch über «programmierte Politik» und Detail der Illustration. Schwarz auf Hellbraun. (USA)
579 Schutzumschlag mit farbiger Illustration für ein Buch mit Geschichten, in denen Katzen, den Menschen an Witz und Geist überlegen, die Hauptrolle spielen. (USA)
580 Farbiger Umschlag für eine Biographie von E.A. Poe. (USA)
581 Umschlagillustration für einen Roman von Georges Simenon («Die Familienlüge»). Blau-, Rot- und Grüntöne. (USA)

571–573, 575 Illustrations de couverture (en noir et blanc) pour une série de livres des éditions *Forum*. (SWE)
574 Jaquette pour un livre scientifique. Lignes violettes sur fond en gris. (USA)
576 Jaquette d'un livre dans lequel l'auteur retrace un voyage à travers le Texas. Dans le Texas, ce livre compte parmi les classiques et il est considéré comme ouvrage de référence de valeur pour les historiens. Illustration noir-blanc, titre orange. (USA)
577, 578 Couverture d'un livre sur la «politique programmée» et détail de l'illustration. Noir sur fond brun clair. (USA)
579 Jaquette avec illustration en couleur pour un livre de contes dans lesquels des chats, supérieurs aux hommes en ce qui concerne l'esprit, jouent le rôle principal. (USA)
580 Couverture polychrome d'une biographie d'Edgar Allan Poe. (USA)
581 Illustration de couverture d'un roman de Georges Simenon. Tons bleus, rouges et verts. (USA)

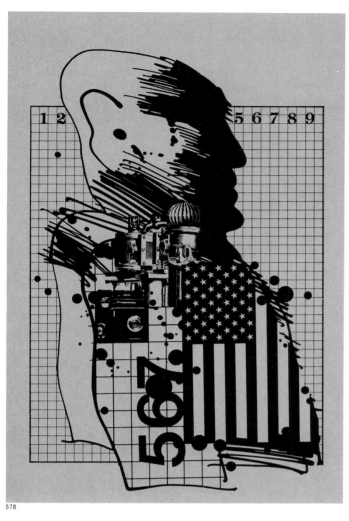

578

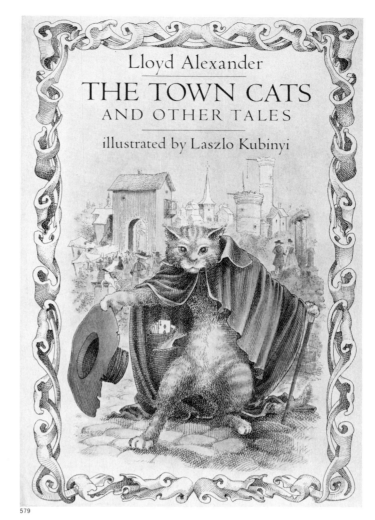

579

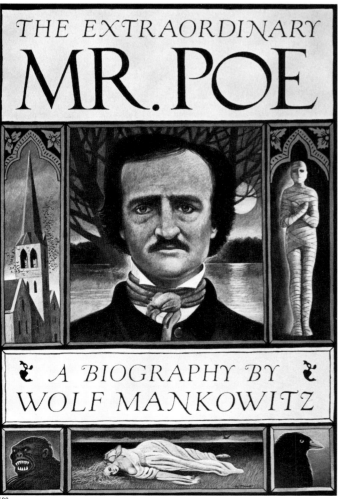

580

581

4

Calendars

Trade Marks and Symbols

Letterheads

Packaging

Gramophone Record Covers

Film & TV Advertising

Kalender

Schutzmarken

Briefköpfe

Packungen

Schallplatten-Umschläge

Film- & Fernsehwerbung

Calendriers

Marques et emblèmes

En-têtes

Emballages

Pochettes de disques

Publicité télévisée

582

MAY
monday

OCTOBER
wednesday

JANUARY
saturday

SEPTEMBER
wednesday

28

JUNE
thursday

JANUARY
thursday

JANUARY
thursday

ARTIST / KÜNSTLER / ARTISTE:

582 Michael Foreman/John McConnell/Stephen
Bertrand/John Faulkner/Heathcote Williams/
Marcia Bueno Sussekind
583 Guida Joseph
584, 589 John Gorham

DESIGNER / GESTALTER / MAQUETTISTE:

582 Gill Metcalf
583 Jan Lepair
584–589 John McConnell

ART DIRECTOR / DIRECTEUR ARTISTIQUE:

582 David Hillman
583 Jan Lepair
584–589 John McConnell

AGENCY / AGENTUR / AGENCE – STUDIO:

582, 584–589 Pentagram
583 Lepair Design

583

Juli

17 maandag
18 dinsdag
19 woensdag
20 donderdag
21 vrijdag
22 zaterdag
23 zondag

24 maandag
25 dinsdag
26 woensdag
27 donderdag
28 vrijdag
29 zaterdag
30 zondag

Op grote voet leven

en morgen?

...weer kans op regen...

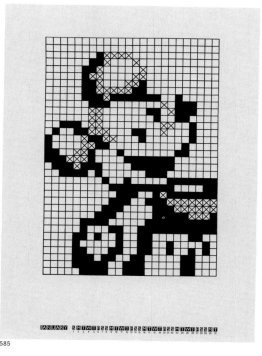

584

586

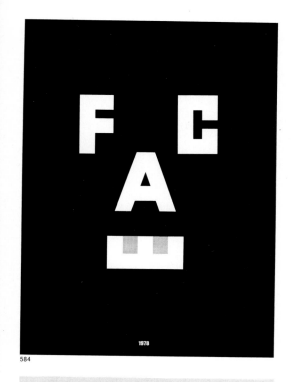

584

585

587

588

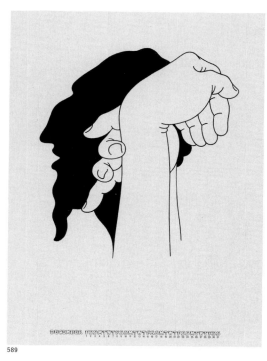

589

582 Eight pages from a calendar published by Inter-Action, a charity organization. It is produced in book form, and each day has an illustration devoted to it drawn by an artist or a friend of the organization. The aim of Inter-Action is to activate the public either by means of a helping programme for neighbours or through cultural performances and other events. (GBR)
583 Double spread from a bank's desk calendar. Each page contains a humorous sketch or illustration pertaining to a certain quirk of speech. (NLD)
584–589 Cover page and five monthly sheets from a calendar of the *Face Photosetting* printing company. All black and white. (GBR)

582 Acht Blätter aus einem Kalender, der von der Wohltätigkeits-Organisation Inter-Action herausgegeben wurde. Er ist in Buchform gestaltet und enthält für jeden Tag eine Illustration eines Künstlers oder Freundes der Organisation. Ziel von Inter-Action ist die Aktivierung der Bevölkerung, sei es durch Nachbarschafts-Hilfeprogramme oder kulturelle und andere Veranstaltungen. (GBR)
583 Doppelseite aus der Agenda einer Bank. Jede Seite enthält eine humoristische Zeichnung oder Illustration zu einer Redewendung wie hier «auf grossem Fuss leben». (NLD)
584–589 Deckblatt und fünf Monatsblätter aus einem Kalender der Druckerei *Face Photosetting*. Alle schwarzweiss. (GBR)

582 Huit feuillets d'un calendrier, publié par Inter-Action, une organisation de bienfaisance. Les illustrations accompagnant chaque journée ont été créées par divers artistes ou par des amis de l'organisation. Inter-Action a pour but d'activer la population, soit par des programmes d'entr'aide ou par des manifestations culturelles ou générales. (GBR)
583 Page double de l'agenda d'une banque. Sur chaque page on trouve un dessin ou une illustration humoristique se référant à des locutions courantes, comme p.ex. «vivre sur un grand pied». (NLD)
584–589 Feuille de couverture et cinq feuilles mensuelles figurant dans le calendrier d'une imprimerie. Noir-blanc. (GBR)

590

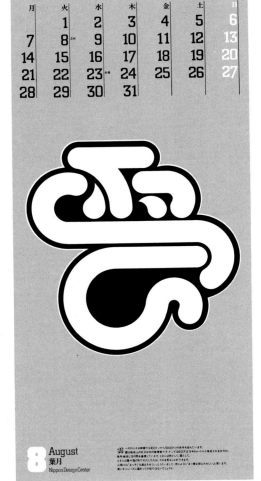

591

592

593

594

ARTIST / KÜNSTLER / ARTISTE:

590, 591 Kenzo Nakagawa/Satch Morikami/
Hiro Nobuyama/Tack Miyoshi
592–594 Tadashi Ohashi
595 Kozo Mio

DESIGNER / GESTALTER / MAQUETTISTE:

592–594 Tadashi Ohashi
595 Ikko Tanaka/Tokiyoshi Tsubouchi

ART DIRECTOR / DIRECTEUR ARTISTIQUE:

590, 591 Kenzo Nakagawa
595 Ikko Tanaka

AGENCY / AGENTUR / AGENCE – STUDIO:

590, 591 Nippon Design Center

Calendars
Kalender
Calendriers

590, 591 Two sheets from a wall calendar of the Nippon Design Center. (JPN)
592–594 Sheet and detail therefrom as well as a full-colour illustration from a women's magazine wall calendar. (JPN)
595 Illustration from a monthly sheet of the *Toyo Ink* wall calendar with graphic designs by twelve artists. (JPN)

590, 591 Zwei Blätter aus einem Wandkalender des Nippon Design Center. (JPN)
592–594 Blatt und Detail daraus sowie eine weitere farbige Illustration aus dem Wandkalender eines Frauenmagazins. (JPN)
595 Illustration eines Monatsblattes aus einem Wandkalender der *Toyo Ink* mit Graphiken von zwölf Künstlern. (JPN)

590, 591 Deux feuilles tirées d'un calendrier mural du Nippon Design Center. (JPN)
592–594 Feuillet, détail de l'illustration et illustration d'un calendrier mural d'un magazine féminin. (JPN)
595 Composition du calendrier mural d'un fabricant d'encres d'imprimerie avec des œuvres graphiques de douze artistes. (JPN)

ARTIST / KÜNSTLER / ARTISTE:

596, 597 Tomi Ungerer
598, 599 Don Weller
600, 601 U. G. Sato

DESIGNER / GESTALTER / MAQUETTISTE:

596, 597 Atelier Pütz
598, 599 G. S. Rosentswieg
600, 601 U. G. Sato

ART DIRECTOR / DIRECTEUR ARTISTIQUE:

596, 597 Robert Pütz
598, 599 G. S. Rosentswieg
600, 601 U. G. Sato

597

598

596

599

AGENCY / AGENTUR / AGENCE – STUDIO:

596, 597 Robert Pütz GmbH & Co.
598, 599 The Graphics Studio
600, 601 Design Farm

596, 597 Detail of the illustration and complete sheet from "Tomi Ungerer's Regenbogen-Kalender" (Tomi Ungerer's Rainbow Calendar), produced by the *Argos Verlag*. (GER)
598, 599 Complete double spread and illustration from a desk agenda of the Graphic Process Co., "A Slice of Los Angeles". (USA)
600, 601 Full-colour illustrations from a Design Farm wall calendar. Fig. 600: "Peace", and Fig. 601: "Tearing". (JPN)

596, 597 Detail der Illustration und komplettes Blatt aus «Tomi Ungerer's Regenbogen-Kalender», herausgegeben vom *Argos Verlag*. (GER)
598, 599 Komplette Doppelseite und Illustration aus einer Tisch-Agenda der Graphic Process Co. unter dem Motto «Ein Stück von Los Angeles». (USA)
600, 601 Farbige Illustrationen aus einem Wandkalender von Design Farm. Hier «Friede» (Abb. 600) und «Zerreissen» (Abb. 601). (JPN)

596, 597 Détail de l'illustration et feuillet complet du «calendrier de l'arc-en-ciel de Tomi Ungerer», publié par les editions *Argos*. (GER)
598, 599 Page double complète et illustration d'un agenda de table de la Graphic Process Co. qui a paru sous le titre «Aspects de Los Angeles». (USA)
600, 601 Illustrations polychromes figurant dans un calendrier mural de Design Farm. Fig. 600: «paix», fig. 601: «déchirer». (JPN)

600

601

215

ARTIST / KÜNSTLER / ARTISTE:

602, 604 James Marsh
603, 605–607 Christine Chagnoux

ART DIRECTOR / DIRECTEUR ARTISTIQUE:

602, 604 Jill Mumford
603, 605–607 Engel Ph. Verkerke

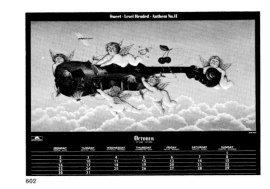

602

603

604

605

606

602, 604 Complete sheet and illustration to an instrumental piece by the Sweet pop group taken from a wall calendar of the *Polydor* record company. (GBR)
603, 605—607 Complete sheet and full-colour illustrations from a wall calendar devoted exclusively to cats drawn by Christine Chagnoux. "Christine's Cats." (NLD)

602, 604 Vollständiges Blatt und Detail der Illustration zu einem Instrumentalstück der Pop-Gruppe Sweet aus einem Wandkalender der Schallplattenfirma *Polydor*. (GBR)
603, 605—607 Vollständiges Blatt und farbige Illustrationen aus einem Wandkalender, der ausschliesslich Katzenbilder der Künstlerin Christine Chagnoux enthält. «Christine's Cats.» (NLD)

602, 604 Feuillet complet et détail de l'illustration accompagnant une pièce de musique du groupe Sweet. Elément d'un calendrier mural de *Polydor*. (GBR)
603, 605—607 Feuillet complet et illustrations (en polychromie) d'un calendrier mural qui est entièrement consacré aux chats de l'illustratrice Christine Chagnoux. (NLD)

607

Calendars
Kalender
Calendriers

608

609

608, 609, 612 Three full-colour illustrations from a wall calendar devoted to the art of printing, from the *Eindhovensche Drukkerij*. (NLD)
610 Three-monthly sheet from a *Vega Press* calendar. Illustration in colour. (AUS)
611 Party calendar sheet for December from the *Network Design Group*. (JPN)
613, 614 Illustration for the autumn sheet and complete winter sheet from a wall calendar of the *Roland Offsetmaschinenfabrik*. All illustrations show the same landscape during the different seasons of the year. Full colour. (GER)

608, 609, 612 Drei farbige Illustrationen aus einem der Druckkunst gewidmeten Wandkalender der *Eindhovenschen Drukkerij*. (NLD)
610 Drei-Monats-Blatt aus einem Kalender der *Vega Press*. Illustration in Farbe. (AUS)
611 Party-Kalenderblatt für den Monat Dezember von der *Network Design Group*. (JPN)
613, 614 Illustration für das Herbstblatt und komplettes Winterblatt aus einem Wandkalender der *Roland Offsetmaschinenfabrik*. Alle Illustrationen des Kalenders zeigen die gleiche Landschaft zu verschiedenen Jahreszeiten. In Farbe. (GER)

608, 609, 612 Illustrations polychromes figurant dans un calendrier mural qui est consacré entièrement à l'art typographique. (NLD)
610 Feuillet d'un calendrier de la *Vega Press*. En polychromie. (AUS)
611 Feuillet d'un calendrier des fêtes. (JPN)
613, 614 Illustration de la feuille d'automne et feuille d'hiver complète figurant dans un calendrier mural d'un fabricant de machines offset. On y voit le même paysage au cours des saisons. En polychromie. (GER)

610

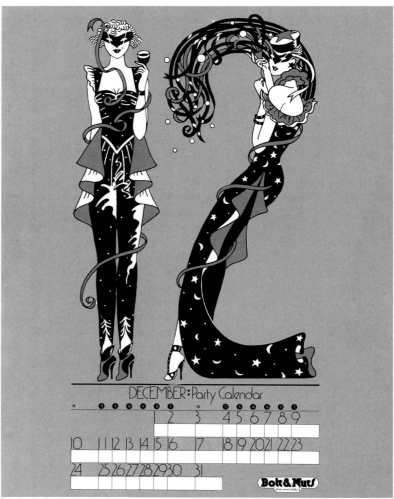
611

612

ARTIST / KÜNSTLER / ARTISTE:

608, 609, 612 Ad van Hoof
610 Ken Cato
611 Kumiko/Hiro/Tack/Sumiko
613, 614 Felix Gluck

DESIGNER / GESTALTER / MAQUETTISTE:

608, 609, 612 Marie-Louise Mannaerts
610 Ken Cato
611 Kenzo Nakagawa/Hiro Nobuyama/
    Satch Morikami
613, 614 Olaf Leu/Fritz Hofrichter

ART DIRECTOR / DIRECTEUR ARTISTIQUE:

608, 609, 612 P. Moll
610 Ken Cato
611 Kenzo Nakagawa
613, 614 Olaf Leu/Fritz Hofrichter

AGENCY / AGENTUR / AGENCE – STUDIO:

608, 609, 612 Kreatieve Groep, Eindhoven
610 Cato Hibberd Design Pty Ltd
611 Network Design Group
613, 614 Olaf Leu Design

613

614

615

DESIGNER / GESTALTER / MAQUETTISTE:

615 Ikko Tanaka/Tetsuya Oht
616 Nancy Long
618 Fernando Alvarez Cozzi
619 Pekka Martin
620 Hans Huwer
621 Rubén Fontana/Gustavo Pedroza
622 Fernando Medina
623 Bülent Erkmen
624 Tatsuomi Majima
625 Bryan L. Peterson
626 Hermann Schardt
627 Rolf Harder

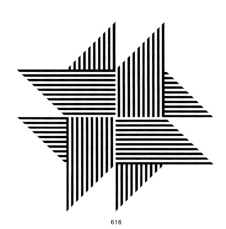

616

615 Symbol of the World Crafts Council. (JPN)
616 Symbol of a firm of marketing consultants. (USA)
617 Trademark of the *Charles Jourdan* company. (GBR)
618 Symbol of the Wool Secretariat in Uruguay. (URU)
619 Symbol for the wood and pulp industries. (FIN)
620 Signet for the town of Neunkirchen. (GER)
621 Symbol of an Italian bank. (ARG)
622 Symbol of a construction company. (SPA)
623 Trademark of car tyres produced under a licence issued by
B.F. Goodrich. (TUR)
624 Symbol of a construction company. (JPN)
625 Symbol for *Williams*, piano and organ makers. (USA)
626 Logo for a printing house. (GER)
627 Logo for the *International Design & Woodcraft* company,
manufacturers of furniture. (CAN)

615 Symbol für den World Crafts Council. (JPN)
616 Symbol für eine Marketing-Beratungsfirma. (USA)
617 Schutzmarke des Hauses *Charles Jourdan*. (GBR)
618 Symbol für das Woll-Sekretariat in Uruguay. (URU)
619 Symbol für die holzverarbeitenden Industrien. (FIN)
620 Signet für die Stadt Neunkirchen. (GER)
621 Symbol für eine italienische Bank. (ARG)
622 Symbol für ein Bauunternehmen. (SPA)
623 Schutzmarke für Autoreifen, die unter der Lizenz von
B.F. Goodrich hergestellt werden (TUR)
624 Symbol für ein Bauunternehmen. (JPN)
625 Symbol für *Williams*, Klavier- und Orgelhersteller. (USA)
626 Logo für die Industriedruck AG. (GER)
627 Logo für *International Design & Woodcraft,* Hersteller von
Möbeln. (CAN)

615 Symbole du conseil mondial des arts et métiers. (JPN)
616 Marque d'un bureau de conseillers en gestion. (USA)
617 Marque de fabrique de *Charles Jourdan*. (GBR)
618 Symbole de l'industrie lainière de l'Uruguay. (URU)
619 Symbole des industries de transformation du bois. (FIN)
620 Symbole de la ville Neunkirchen. (GER)
621 Symbole d'une banque italienne. (ARG)
622 Symbole d'une entreprise de construction. (SPA)
623 Marque de fabrique pour un pneu fabriqué sous la licence de
Goodrich. (TUR)
624 Symbole d'une entreprise de construction. (JPN)
625 Symbole d'un fabricant de pianos et d'orgues. (USA)
626 Logo d'une imprimerie. (GER)
627 Logo d'un fabricant de meubles. (CAN)

620

621

ART DIRECTOR / DIRECTEUR ARTISTIQUE:

615 Ikko Tanaka
619 Pekka Martin
622 Fernando Medina
623 Bülent Erkmen
624 Tatsuomi Majima
625 Bryan L. Peterson
627 Rolf Harder

AGENCY / AGENTUR / AGENCE – STUDIO:

618 Perrier Publicidad
619 SEK Advertising Ltd.
621 Fontana/Pedroza
622 Fernando Medina Diseño
624 Dentsu Advertising
627 Rolf Harder & Assoc.

**Trade Marks
Schutzmarken
Marques et emblèmes**

617

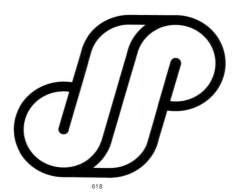

618

619

621

622

623

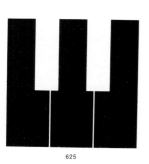

625

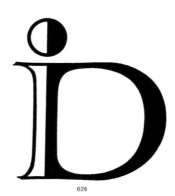

626

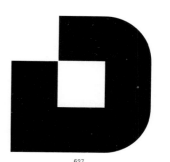

627

628

629

630

632

633

634

636

637

638

DESIGNER / GESTALTER / MAQUETTISTE:

628 Bill Bundzak
629 Fernando Alvarez Cozzi
630 Steff Geissbuhler
631 Paul Ibou
632 Jim Polowy
633 Pekka Martin
634 Burton Kramer
635 Gali Hus
636 Maurizio Milani
637 Jim Lienhart
638 Peter Adam
639 Fernando Medina
640 Juan Carlos Distéfano/Rubén Fontana
641 August Maurer

ART DIRECTOR / DIRECTEUR ARTISTIQUE:

628 Bill Bundzak
630 Steff Geissbuhler
632 Jim Polowy
633 Pekka Martin
634 Burton Kramer
636 Armando Milani
637 Jim Lienhart
638 Gottschalk & Ash
639 Fernando Medina
641 August Maurer

AGENCY / AGENTUR / AGENCE – STUDIO:

628 Young Goldman Young Inc.
630 Chermayeff & Geismar Assoc.
632 Jim Polowy Graphic Design
633 SEK Advertising Ltd.
634 Studio Armando Milani
636 Studio Armando Milani
638 Gottschalk & Ash, Ltd.
639 Fernando Medina Diseño
640 Fontana/Pedroza
641 Ciba-Geigy Zentrale Werbung

631

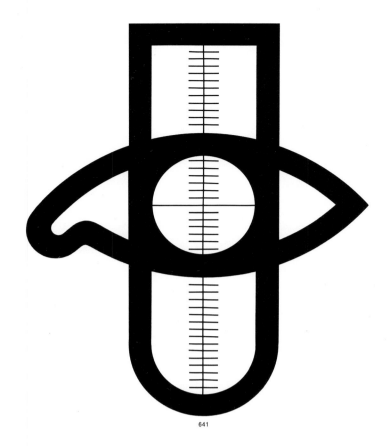

641

635

639

640

628 Symbol of the *Coplay* company, producers of cement. (USA)
629 Symbol of Industrias Forestales (forestry industries). (URU)
630 Logo of *Banco d'Italia.* (USA)
631 Symbol of the printers *De Bièvre.* (BEL)
632 Symbol of Victor's Tailor Shop. (USA)
633 Symbol of an indoor sports stadium. (FIN)
634 Symbol of the Canadian Broadcasting Corp. (CAN)
635 Symbol of an Israeli electricity company, based on a Hebraic character. (ISR)
636 Trademark of a silversmith. (USA)
637 Symbol of the *Ellerman* insurance company. (USA)
638 The *Rug Tufters* trademark, a company in the carpet business. (USA)
639 Symbol of the artists' association Asociación de Artistas Plasticós de Madrid. (SPA)
640 Symbol of a credit bank. (ARG)
641 Symbol of the chemical analysts at a world congress. (SWI)

628 Symbol der Firma *Coplay,* ein Unternehmen aus der Zementbranche. (USA)
629 Symbol für Industrias Forestales (Forstindustrien). (URU)
630 Logo der *Banco d'Italia.* (USA)
631 Symbol für die Druckerei *De Bièvre.* (BEL)
632 Symbol für die Schneiderei Victor's Tailor Shop. (USA)
633 Symbol für eine Sporthalle. (FIN)
634 Symbol für die kanadische Rundfunkgesellschaft Canadian Broadcasting Corp. (CAN)
635 Symbol für eine israelische Elektrizitäts-Gesellschaft, das auf einem hebräischen Buchstaben basiert. (ISR)
636 Schutzmarke für einen Silberschmied. (USA)
637 Symbol für das Versicherungsunternehmen *Ellerman.* (USA)
638 Schutzmarke für *Rug Tufters,* ein Unternehmen aus der Teppich-Branche. (USA)
639 Symbol für den Künstlerverband Asociación de Artistas Plasticós de Madrid. (SPA)
640 Symbol einer Kreditbank. (ARG)
641 Symbol der chemischen Analytiker bei einem Weltkongress. (SWI)

628 Symbole de *Coplay,* une cimenterie. (USA)
629 Symbole de l'administration des eaux et forêts. (URU)
630 Logo du *Banco d'Italia.* (USA)
631 Symbole d'une imprimerie. (BEL)
632 Symbole d'un atelier de tailleur. (USA)
633 Symbole pour un centre de sport. (FIN)
634 Symbole de la radiodiffusion et télévision canadienne. (CAN)
635 Symbole d'une compagnie d'électricité israélienne, dérivé d'un caractère hébreu. (ISR)
636 Marque de fabrique d'un orfèvre. (USA)
637 Symbole d'une compagnie d'assurances. (USA)
638 Marque de fabrique d'un fabricant de tappis et de moquettes. (USA)
639 Symbole de l'association des artistes plastiques de Madrid. (SPA)
640 Symbole d'une banque de crédit. (ARG)
641 Symbole créé pour les analystes chimiques lors d'un congrès mondial. (SWI)

642

643

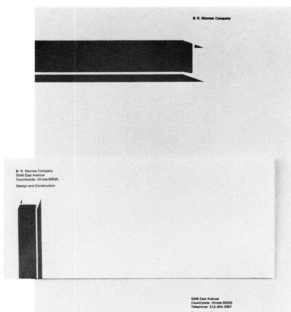

645

646

648

649

642 Stationery of the Richmond Civic Opera. (USA)
643 Stationery of a market research company. (USA)
644 Stationery of the Metropolitan Museum of Art, New York. (USA)
645 Writing-paper of a design and construction company. Symbol in vivid orange. (USA)
646 Writing-paper of the design company Cosgrove Assoc. Red and blue logo. (USA)
647 Stationery of the *Atlantic Records* disc company, for an advertising publication. (USA)
648–650 Three examples of drafts for stationery designed by eight well-known designers at the invitation of the Gilbert Paper Company. This paper quality, specially made for designers, contains 25 per cent cotton, which guarantees high-quality printing. Fig. 648 shows Herb Lubalin's draft; Fig. 649 the photographic design by Henry Wolf with the letterhead in embossed printing; Fig. 650: the design by Saul Bass, who used blind embossing for the symbol. (USA)
651 Writing-paper and airmail envelope of a design company run by four people. (GBR)
652 Stationery of Remond Design. (USA)
653 Logotype for a company. (DEN)

642 Briefpapier der Richmond Civic Opera. (USA)
643 Briefbogen einer Marktforschungsfirma. (USA)
644 Briefbogen des Metropolitan Museum of Art, New York, mit Hinweis auf die Tutanchamon-Schätze. (USA)
645 Briefpapier einer Design- und Konstruktionsfirma. Symbol in kräftigem Orange. (USA)
646 Briefbogen für die Designer Cosgrove Associates. Logo rot und blau. (USA)
647 Briefbogen für die Werbepublikation *Feature* der Schallplattenfirma *Atlantic Records*. (USA)
648–650 Drei von insgesamt acht Briefpapierentwürfen, um die der Papierhersteller Gilbert Paper Company bekannte Designer gebeten hatte. Die speziell für Designer geschaffene Papierqualität besteht zu 25 Prozent aus Baumwolle, die eine hohe Druckqualität garantieren soll. Abb. 648 zeigt den Entwurf von Herb Lubalin, Abb. 649 den von Henry Wolf, der seine Aufgabe photographisch löste, mit Briefkopf in Prägedruck, und Abb. 650 die Arbeit von Saul Bass, der für sein Symbol Blindprägung verwendete. (USA)
651 Briefbogen und Luftpostumschlag einer Design-Firma, die aus vier Mitarbeitern besteht. (GBR)
652 Briefpapier von Remond Design. (USA)
653 Schriftzug für eine Firma. (DEN)

642 En-tête du Richmond Civic Opera. (USA)
643 En-tête d'une société d'étude du marché. (USA)
644 Papier à lettres du Metropolitan Museum of Art de New York: référence aux trésors de Tout Ankh Amon. (USA)
645 En-tête d'une société de design et de construction. Symbole exécuté en orange vif. (USA)
646 En-tête pour le bureau de design Cosgrove Associates. Logo rouge et bleu. (USA)
647 En-tête pour la revue publicitaire *Feature* du producteur de disques *Atlantic Records*. (USA)
648–650 Trois des huit en-têtes que la papeterie Gilbert Paper Company avait commandés à des artistes graphiques de renom. Le papier spécialement fabriqué pour les graphistes comprend 25% de coton, garant d'une qualité d'impression élevée. La fig. 648 montre la création de Herb Lubalin, la 649 celle de Henry Wolf exécutée en photo et en gaufrage, la 650 celle de Saul Bass, qui a eu recours au gaufrage à sec pour imprimer son symbole. (USA)
651 Feuille de papier à lettres et enveloppe avion d'une équipe de design comprenant quatre spécialistes. (GBR)
652 En-tête de Remond Design. (USA)
653 Paraphe pour une société. (DEN)

ARTIST / KÜNSTLER / ARTISTE:

642 Robert C. Carter
643 Joe Scorsone
646 Jerry Campbell
647 Todd Schorr
648 Herb Lubalin
649 Henry Wolf
650 Saul Bass
651 Bob Blechman
652 Barbara Redmond

DESIGNER / GESTALTER / MAQUETTISTE:

642 Robert C. Carter
643 Joe Scorsone
646 Jerry Cosgrove
647 Sandi Young
648 Herb Lubalin
649 Henry Wolf
650 Saul Bass
651 Paul Anthony
652 Barbara & Patrick Redmond
653 Niels Hartmann

ART DIRECTOR / DIRECTEUR ARTISTIQUE:

642 Robert C. Carter
643 Tony Leonie
646 Jerry Cosgrove
647 Bob Defrin
648–650 Herb Lubalin
651 Alan Fletcher
652 Barbara Redmond
653 Niels Hartmann

AGENCY / AGENTUR / AGENCE – STUDIO:

642 Carter Design
643 Friebel Studios
644 Goslin/Barnett Inc.
646 Cosgrove Associates Inc.
647 Atlantic Records
648–650 LSC&P Design Group
651 Pentagram
652 Barbara & Patrick Redmond Design
653 Niels Hartmann

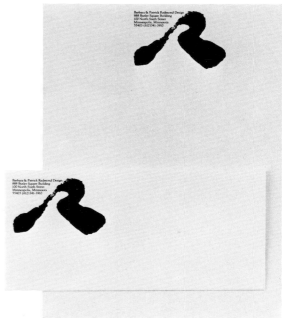

654

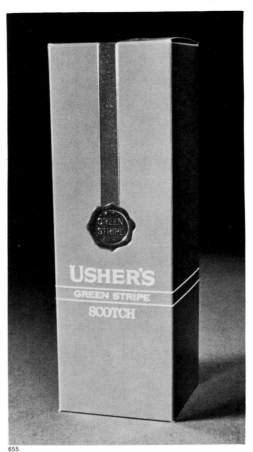

655

656

654 Bottle styling for *John Barr* whisky. Gold label. (GBR)
655 Packaging for *Usher's* Scotch whisky. (USA)
656 Gift package for sake. Bluish-violet porcelain bottle with golden rice plant, symbol of a good harvest. (JPN)
657 Typical bottle of *Rhinecastle* wines. (AUS)
658 Bottle styling for *Claytons Kola Tonic*. (AUS)
659–662 Detail of labels for *Ueker an der Egg*, Riesling and Sylvaner (Fig. 659); the Portuguese red wine *Vasco da Gama* (Fig. 660); and *Wyfelder Burgherrewy* Riesling and Sylvaner (Fig. 662); and bottle styling for these wines (Fig. 661). *Ueker an der Egg* in a brown bottle with label in beige, brown and gold; *Vasco da Gama* with red cap and label in the colours of a map; *Wyfelder Burgherrewy* in green bottle with yellow label in brown and gold shades. (SWI)
663 Gift package and bottle styling for *Finlandia* vodka. (USA)

Packaging
Packungen
Emballages

657

658

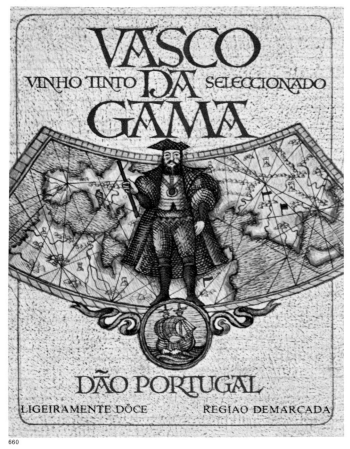

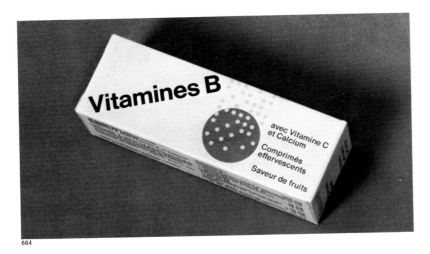

664

665

666

667

ARTIST / KÜNSTLER / ARTISTE:

665 William Mitchell
666, 671 Shigeru Akizuki
667 Werner Jeker
668 Z. de Zeeuw-Deventer B.V.
669, 670 Katsu Kimura

DESIGNER / GESTALTER / MAQUETTISTE:

664 Rolf Harder
665 William Mitchell
666, 671 Shigeru Akizuki
667 Werner Jeker
668 Data Doorn B.V.
669, 670 Katsu Kimura

ART DIRECTOR / DIRECTEUR ARTISTIQUE:

664 Rolf Harder
667 Werner Jeker
668 G. Eilander
669, 670 Katsu Kimura

AGENCY / AGENTUR / AGENCE – STUDIO:

664 Rolf Harder & Assoc.
665 Macy's Visual Merchandising Dept.
667 Werner Jeker
668 Nederlands Verpakkingscentrum
669, 670 Packaging Direction Co., Ltd.

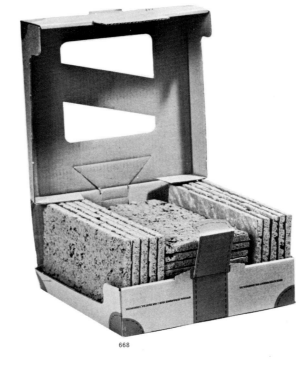

668

**Packaging
Packungen
Emballages**

664 Folding box for soluble vitamin B tablets *Redoxan B* with fruit flavour. Red tablets with pink dots. (CAN)
665 Boxes made of corrugated cardboard for the food and drink department of *Macy's*, an American department store. (USA)
666 Gift box for powdered coffee and cream in a soluble mixture. Beige and brown shades. (JPN)
667 A tin of *Lipton's* tea, which is produced in four different colours. Two sides of the tin are shown here. (SWI)
668 Package for *Brick*, a building product: "The wall in the box." Here an open and a closed box. (NLD)
669 Exterior packaging in brown shades with gold and bottle styling for the cosmetics company *Hinoki*, here for a lotion of the *Clinical* series. Lettering on the bottle in brown and gold, lid in white. (JPN)
670 Box in three different shades of green with white and red lettering, for Japanese tea. (JPN)
671 Folding box for two bottles of *Hachi Canon*, a wine from a Japanese castle. The wording is in French. (JPN)

664 Faltschachtel für Vitamin-B-Brausetabletten *Redoxan B* mit Fruchtgeschmack. Magentarote Tablette mit rosa Punkten. (CAN)
665 Schachteln aus Wellpappe für die Lebensmittel- und Getränkeabteilung des amerikanischen Warenhauses *Macy's*. (USA)
666 Geschenkschachtel für Pulverkaffee und Rahm in Puderform. Beige- und Brauntöne. (JPN)
667 Teedose von *Lipton's*, die in vier verschiedenen Farben hergestellt wird. Hier zwei Seiten der Dose. (SWI)
668 Verpackung für das Bauprodukt *Brick*: «Die Wand aus der Schachtel». Hier eine geöffnete und eine geschlossene Schachtel. (NLD)
669 Äussere Verpackung in Brauntönen mit Gold und Flaschengestaltung der Kosmetikfirma *Hinoki*, hier für eine Lotion der Linie *Clinical*. Beschriftung der Flasche in Braun und Gold, der Deckel in Weiss. (JPN)
670 Schachtel in drei verschiedenen Grüntönen mit weisser und roter Schrift für japanischen Tee. (JPN)
671 Faltschachtel für zwei Flaschen *Hachi Canon*, einen Wein von einem japanischen Schloss. Hier wird auf die Aufmachung der französischen Weine angespielt, der Text ist dementsprechend in französischer Sprache. (JPN)

664 Boîte pliante pour les comprimés effervescents de vitamine B *Redoxan B* au goût fruité. Comprimé magenta avec points roses. (CAN)
665 Boîtes de carton ondulé pour les départements alimentation et boissons des grands magasins américains *Macy's*. (USA)
666 Boîte-cadeau pour du café instantané et de la crème en poudre. Tons beiges et bruns. (JPN)
667 Boîte de thé de chez *Lipton's* fabriquée en quatre couleurs différentes. On voit ici deux côtés de la boîte. (SWI)
668 Emballage pour le produit de construction *Brick*: «Le mur qui sort de la boîte». On voit ici une boîte ouverte et fermée. (NLD)
669 Emballage extérieur, aux tons bruns avec de l'or, et étude de bouteille pour la société des cosmétiques *Hinoki*, en l'espèce pour une lotion de la gamme *Clinical*. Texte brun et or, couvercle blanc. (JPN)
670 Boîte à thé japonais avec lettrage en blanc et rouge sur un fond en trois verts différents. (JPN)
671 Boîte pliante pour le vin japonais *Hachi Canon*. L'inscription en est rédigée en français. (JPN)

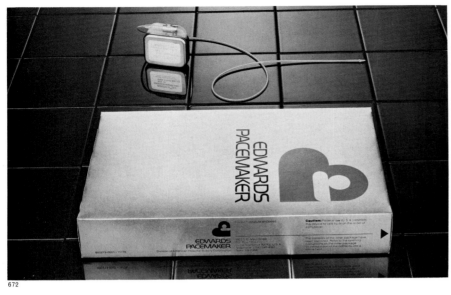

672

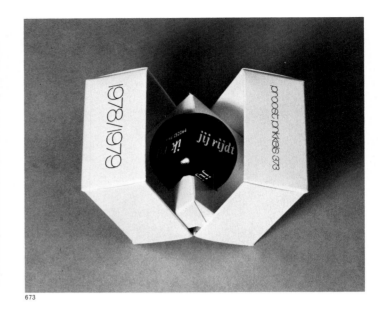

673

674

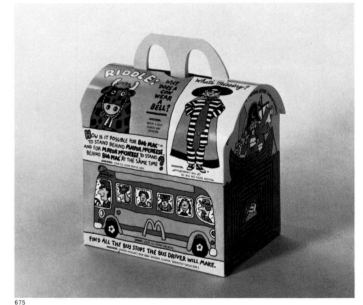

675

676

677

ARTIST / KÜNSTLER / ARTISTE:

672 Garry Sato
675 Simms Taback
676 Robert Marshall
677 Peter Calvitto
678 Kenkichi Yamano

DESIGNER / GESTALTER / MAQUETTISTE:

672 Shoji Teraishi
673 Hans Manusama
675 Simms Taback
676 Ian Kidd/Barrie Tucker
677 Ken Cato
678 Shigeru Akizuki
679 Derek Spaull

ART DIRECTOR / DIRECTEUR ARTISTIQUE:

672 Douglas Boyd
675 Denis Johnson
676 Tucker & Kidd
677 Ken Cato
678 Shigeru Akizuki
679 Derek Spaull

AGENCY / AGENTUR / AGENCE – STUDIO:

672 Douglas Boyd Design
676 Tucker & Kidd
677 Cato Hibberd Design Pty Ltd
679 Derek Spaull Graphics

678

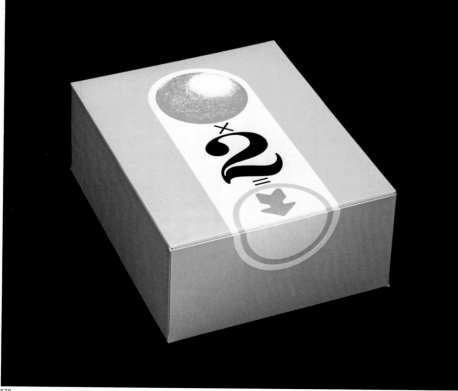

679

672 . Packaging and product design for an *Edwards* pacemaker. Shape of the heart is in blue on white cardboard. (USA)
673 Packaging for an advertising gift for the New Year from the paper manufacturers *Proost en Brandt*. (NLD)
674 Packaging for *Xerox* photocopying paper. (USA)
675 A take-away carrier bag from *McDonald's* ("Happy Meals"). The bag is decorated in many different colours. (USA)
676 Cardboard packaging and box for 6 bottles of *Berri Estates* wine. (USA)
677 Packaging for *Robert-Timms* coffee. Gold on black. Plumage ranges in shades of yellow through to red. Green bird's head and blue tail feathers. (AUS)
678 Gift tin for *Fujiya* confectionery. (JPN)
679 Packaging (wrapping) for cough drops with orange flavouring. (AUS)

672 Verpackungsgestaltung und Produkt-Design für einen *Edwards*-Herzschrittmacher. Herzform blau auf weissem Karton. (USA)
673 Verpackungsgestaltung für ein Werbegeschenk zum Jahreswechsel von dem Papierhersteller *Proost en Brandt*. (NLD)
674 Verpackung für *Xerox*-Photokopierpapier. (USA)
675 Tragschachtel zum Mitnehmen von *McDonald's* «Happy Meals» (Fröhliche Mahlzeiten). In vielen verschiedenen Farben. (USA)
676 Versandkarton und Schachtel für 6 Flaschen *Berri-Estates*-Wein. (USA)
677 Verpackung für *Robert-Timms*-Kaffee. Gold auf Schwarz. Farbtöne des Gefieders von Gelb bis Rot, grüner Vogelkopf und blaue Schwanzfedern. (AUS)
678 Geschenkdose für Baumkuchen von *Fujiya*. (JPN)
679 Packungsgestaltung für Hustenbonbons mit Orangen-Geschmack. (AUS)

672 Conception de l'emballage et du produit pour les stimulateurs cardiaques *Edwards*. Dessin de cœur bleu sur carton blanc. (USA)
673 Emballage conçu pour un cadeau publicitaire distribué à l'occasion du Nouvel An par la papeterie *Proost en Brandt*. (NLD)
674 Emballage de papier de photocopie *Xerox*. (USA)
675 Carton de transport pour les «Happy Meals» (joyeux repas) à l'emporter de chez *McDonald's*. Fabriqué en un grand nombre de coloris différents. (USA)
676 Carton d'expédition et coffret contenant 6 bouteilles de vin de la marque *Berri Estates*. (USA)
677 Conditionnement de café pour *Robert Timms*. Noir sur or. Les couleurs du plumage vont du jaune au rouge; tête de l'oiseau en vert, queue bleue. (AUS)
678 Boîte-cadeau recevant des gâteaux *Fujiya*. (JPN)
679 Emballage de bonbons contre le toux parfumés à l'orange. (AUS)

680

681

682

683

ARTIST / KÜNSTLER / ARTISTE:

680–683 Giulio Cittato

DESIGNER / GESTALTER / MAQUETTISTE:

680 Allessandro Raffin/Giulio Cittato
681–683 Giulio Cittato
684 Jay Smith
685, 687 Helmut Schmid
686 Walter Bosshardt
688 Carmen Dunjko

AGENCY / AGENTUR / AGENCE – STUDIO:

680 Grafica Foto Pubblicitavia
684 Michael Peters & Partners
685, 687 Nippon International Agency
688 Burns, Cooper, Hynes Ltd.

ART DIRECTOR / DIRECTEUR ARTISTIQUE:

680–683 Giulio Cittato
684 Michael Peters
685, 687 Helmut Schmid
686 Walter Bosshardt
688 Robert Burns

Packaging/Packungen
Emballages

684

685

686

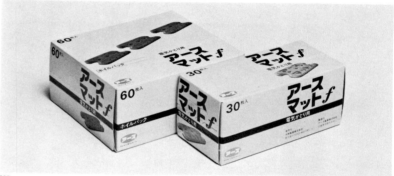

687

688

233

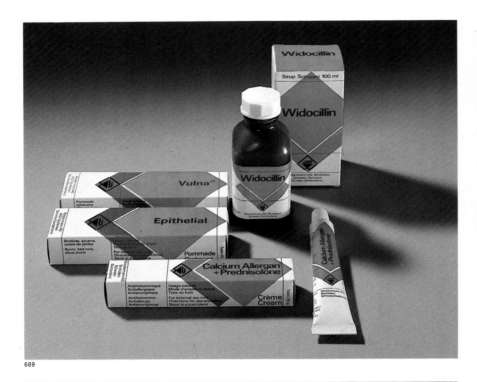

689

690

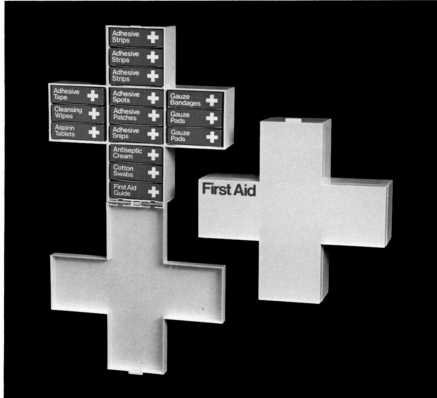

692

693

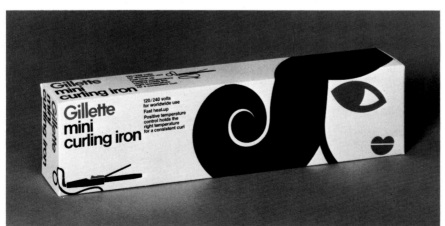

696

689 Packaging for Wiedenmann AG pharmaceutical products. (SWI)

690, 691 Gift paper and muffler with packing as an advertising present for the fur industry. Black and white. (GER)

692 Packaging for first-aid material. (USA)

693 Packaging for *Beecham* shampoos of the *Free & Lovely* range. One kind with stripes in orange shades, the other in blue shades. (AUS)

694, 695 Packaging for the *Pharmaton* range of cosmetics. Here a tube with packing for a special cream (Fig. 694), and a choice of tubes all with silver tops. Colours on the front part of the tubes: orange for a day cream, ochre for the special cream, olive-green for a hair lotion and blue for a soluble bath mixture. (SWI)

696 Packaging for *Gillette* curling-irons in the lower price range. Red and black lettering, blue eye, red mouth. (USA)

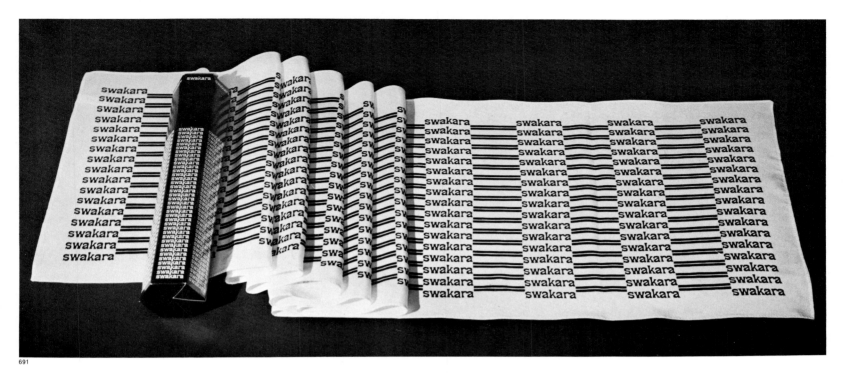

691

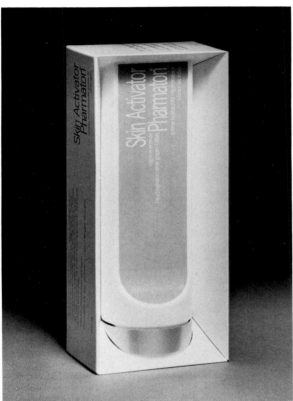

694

695

ART DIRECTOR / DIRECTEUR ARTISTIQUE:

689 Walter Bosshardt
690, 691 Lutz Reinhardt
692 David L. Romanoff
693 Ken Cato
694, 695 Francesco Milani/Lucas Häfliger
696 Morison S. Cousins

AGENCY / AGENTUR / AGENCE – STUDIO:

690, 691 Swakara-Team, J. W. Thompson
692 Romanoff Design Inc.
693 Cato Hibberd Design Pty Ltd
694, 695 Francesco Milani
696 Morison S. Cousins & Associates

ARTIST / KÜNSTLER / ARTISTE:

690, 691 Lutz Reinhardt
693 Cato Hibberd Design Pty Ltd
696 Johann Schumacher

DESIGNER / MAQUETTISTE:

689 Walter Bosshardt
690, 691 Lutz Reinhardt
692 David L. Romanoff
693 Ken Cato
694, 695 Lucas Häfliger
696 Johann Schumacher

689 Packungen für pharmazeutische Produkte von Wiedenmann AG. (SWI)
690, 691 Geschenkpapier und Schal mit Verpackung als Werbegeschenk für die Pelzindustrie. Schwarzweiss. (GER)
692 Packungsgestaltung für Erste-Hilfe-Mittel. (USA)
693 Packungsgestaltung für *Beecham*-Haarshampoos *Free & Lovely*. Eine Sorte mit Streifen in Orange-Tönen, die andere mit Blau-Tönen. (AUS)
694, 695 Packungsgestaltung für die Pflegekosmetik-Linie *Pharmaton*. Hier Tube mit Karton für eine Spezialcreme (Abb. 694) und eine Auswahl von Tuben, alle mit silbrigem Deckel (Abb. 695). Farben der Vorderseiten der Tuben: Orange für eine Tagescreme, Ocker für die Spezialcreme, Olivgrün für ein Haarwasser und Blau für einen Badezusatz. (SWI)
696 Packung für eine Mini-Locken-Brennschere der unteren Preisklasse von *Gillette*. Schrift rot und schwarz, blaues Auge, roter Mund. (USA)

689 Conditionnements de produits pharmaceutiques pour la Wiedenmann SA. (SWI)
690, 691 Papier-cadeau et foulard avec emballage réalisés comme cadeau publicitaire pour l'industrie de la fourrure. Noir et blanc. (GER)
692 Etude d'emballages pour du matériel de premiers secours. (USA)
693 Etude de conditionnements pour les shampooings *Free & Lovely* de *Beecham*. Une partie de la gamme à rayures orangées, une autre à tons bleus. (AUS)
694, 695 Etude de conditionnements pour la gamme de cosmétiques *Pharmaton*. On voit ici un tube et carton pour une crème spéciale (fig. 694) et un choix de tubes, tous au bouchon argenté (fig. 695). Couleurs des faces avant de ces tubes: orange pour une crème de jour, ocre pour la crème spéciale, vert olive pour une lotion capillaire et bleu pour un sel de bain. (SWI)
696 Emballage pour un mini-fer à boucler à prix modique de chez *Gillette*. Texte rouge et noir, œil bleu, lèvres rouges. (USA)

**Packaging
Packungen
Emballages**

697

697 Packaging for a plastic jug with eight cups. Shown here are the front, back and side of the packing. (NLD)
698 Packaging for various knives and cutlery. (USA)
699 Paper carrier bag for a men's clothes shop. In full colour. (USA)
700 Carrier bags with labels for perfumes. In brown. (GBR)
701 Packaging for *Christian Dior* panty-hose. The number of stocking rolls can be varied according to the size of the top. (JPN)
702 Folding box for a *Hiroo* lighter. In gold and brown. (JPN)
703 Packaging for a client's present from a design studio. Cardboard white, black and red, red tissue paper with silver fruit. (AUS)

697 Verpackung für eine Plastik-Kanne mit acht Bechern. Hier die Vorder-, Rück- und Seitenansicht des Kartons. (NLD)
698 Packungsgestaltung für verschiedene Messer und Bestecke. (USA)
699 Papiertaschen eines Geschäftes für Herrenbekleidung. Farbig. (USA)
700 Dunkelbraune Tragtaschen mit Etiketten für eine Parfumerie. (GBR)
701 Packungsgestaltung für Strumpfhosen von *Christian Dior*. Die Anzahl der Strumpfrollen kann durch die Grösse der Deckel variiert werden. (JPN)
702 Faltschachtel für ein *Hiroo*-Feuerzeug in Gold und Braun. (JPN)
703 Verpackung für das Kundengeschenk eines Design-Studios. Karton weiss, schwarz und rot, Seidenpapier rot mit silbriger Frucht. (AUS)

697 Emballage conçu pour un pichet et huit gobelets. On voit ici le carton de face, de dos et de côté. (NLD)
698 Conception d'emballages pour divers couteaux et couverts. (USA)
699 Sacs en papier d'un magasin de confection hommes. En couleurs. (USA)
700 Sacs de transport brun foncé, avec étiquettes, pour une parfumerie. (GBR)
701 Etude de conditionnement pour des collants *Christian Dior*. Le nombre de collants varie en fonction de la grandeur du couvercle. (JPN)
702 Boîte pliante pour un briquet *Hiroo* or et brun. (JPN)
703 Emballage pour le cadeau présenté par un studio de design à sa clientèle. Carton blanc, noir, rouge, papier de soie rouge avec fruit argenté. (AUS)

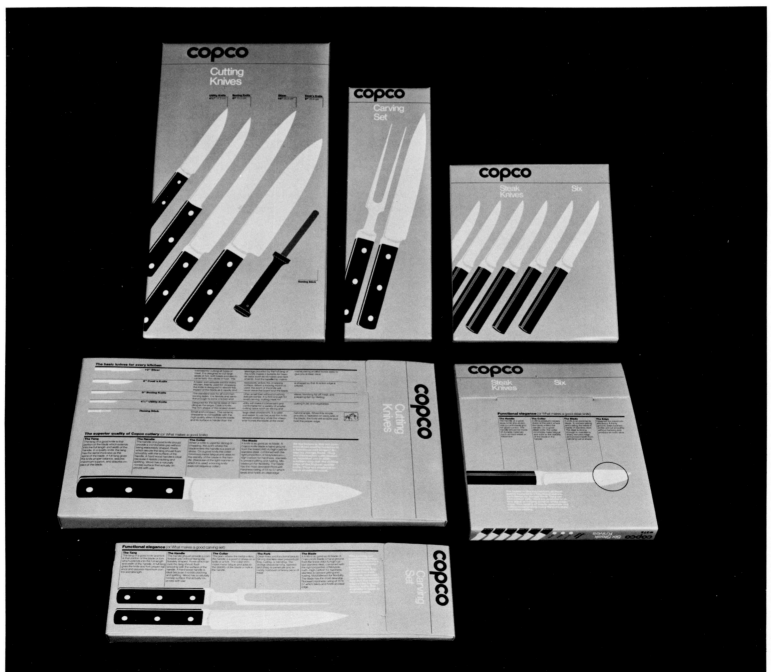

698

699

700

701

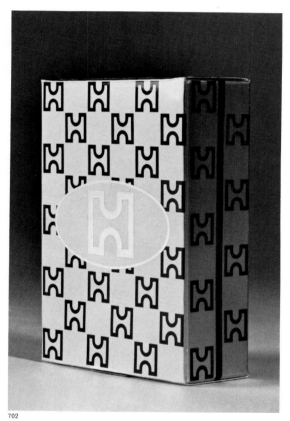

702

703

**Packaging
Packungen
Emballages**

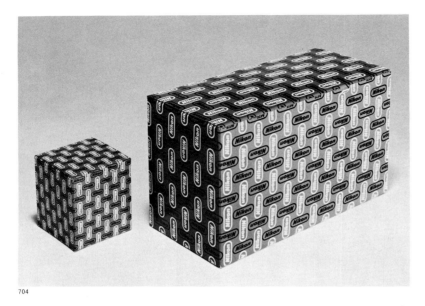

704

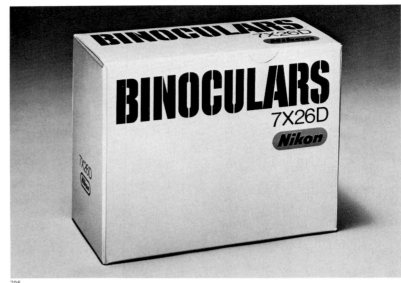

705

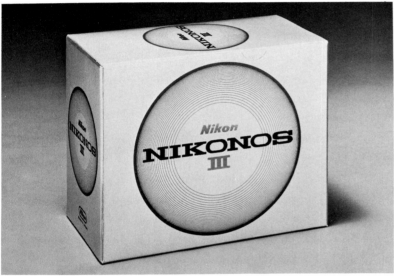

706

707

708

709

**Packaging
Packungen
Emballages**

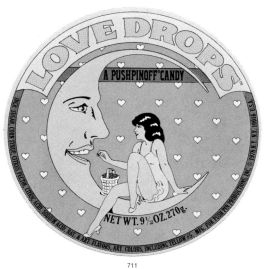

710

711

712

704–707 Packaging for *Nikon* products. (JPN)
708 Packaging for *Interparts*, products manufactured by *Chrysler* for the international market. White lettering on blue, red continents on white, blue lines. (USA)
709 Box covered with foil for an expensive industrial article manufactured by *Norton*. (USA)
710–712 Details of labels for tins of *Pushpinoff* confectioneries marketed by Push Pin Productions, Inc. Shown here are *Berry Nice* raspberry sweets, *Love Drops* and *Ming Mint Almonds*. The labels are all in pastel shades. (USA)
713, 714 Packaging for a *Stanley* hedge-clipper. Here a single box and a box for tool sets. (GBR)

704–707 Packungsgestaltung für *Nikon*-Produkte. (JPN)
708 Verpackung für *Interparts*, Produkte des Automobilherstellers *Chrysler* für den internationalen Markt. Weisse Schrift auf Blau, Erdteile rot auf Weiss, blaue Linien. (USA)
709 Mit Folie überzogene Schachtel für einen teuren Industrieartikel von *Norton*. (USA)
710–712 Detail der Etiketten für eine *Pushpinoff*-Bonbon-Verpackung. Hier für Himbeer-Bonbons *Berry Nice*, *Love Drops* (Liebestropfen) und *Ming Mint Almonds* (Mandeln mit Pfefferminz). In sogenannten Bonbon-Farben. (USA)
713, 714 Packungsgestaltung für eine *Stanley*-Heckenschere. Hier ein einzelner Karton und Karton für Geräte-Sets. (GBR)

704–707 Emballages conçus pour les produits *Nikon*. (JPN)
708 Emballage pour les produits *Interparts* du constructeur automobile *Chrysler* destinés au marché international. Texte blanc sur bleu, continents rouge sur blanc, lignes bleues. (USA)
709 Boîte recouverte d'une feuille plastique, pour un article industriel *Norton* de grand prix. (USA)
710–712 Détail des étiquettes pour un emballage de bonbons *Pushpinoff*: ici pour les bonbons à la framboise *Berry Nice*, les *Love Drops* (gouttes d'amour) et les *Ming Mint Almonds* (amandes à la menthe). En couleurs bonbon. (USA)
713, 714 Emballages conçus pour des cisailles à haie *Stanley*: un carton isolé et un carton pour jeux d'outils. (GBR)

ARTIST / KÜNSTLER / ARTISTE:

708 Gordon Mattichak
710–712 Seymour Chwast

DESIGNER / GESTALTER / MAQUETTISTE:

704–707 Yusaku Kamekura
708 Victor Jennings
709 Wayne M. Olsen
710–712 Seymour Chwast
713, 714 David Pearce

ART DIRECTOR / DIRECTEUR ARTISTIQUE:

704–707 Yusaku Kamekura
708 Gordon Mattichak/Gary Williams
709 Edward C. Kozlowski
713, 714 John McConnell

AGENCY / AGENTUR / AGENCE – STUDIO:

708 Chrysler Graphic Art Services
709 Edward C. Kozlowski Design Inc.
710–712 Push Pin Studios
713, 714 Pentagram

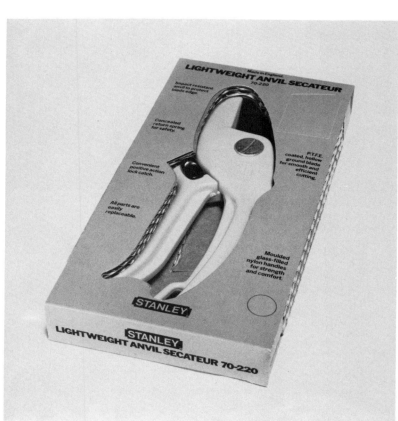

713

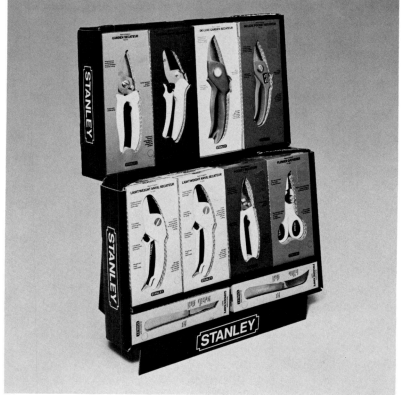

714

Record Covers
Schallplattenhülln
Pochettes de disques

ARTIST / KÜNSTLER / ARTISTE:

715 David Wilcox
716 Norman Catherine
717 James McMullan
718, 720 Seymour Chwast
719 Milton Glaser
721 Christopher Spollen

DESIGNER / GESTALTER / MAQUETTISTE:

715 Ron Coro/Johnny Lee
717, 718, 720 Paula Scher
719 Milton Glaser
721 Michael Sean Walsh

ART DIRECTOR / DIRECTEUR ARTISTIQUE:

715 Ron Coro/Johnny Lee
716 Norman Catherine
718–720 Paula Scher
721 Michael Sean Walsh

AGENCY / AGENTUR / AGENCE – STUDIO:

715 Elektra/Asylum Records
718, 720 Push Pin Studios
719 Milton Glaser Inc.

715

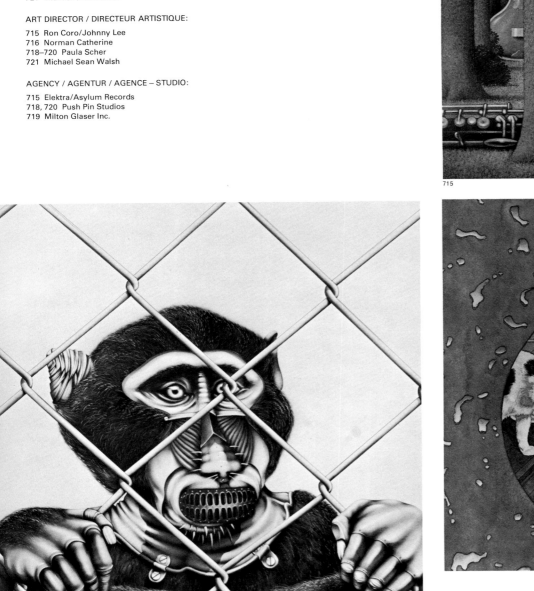

716

717

PUBLISHER / VERLEGER / EDITEUR:

715 Elektra/Asylum Records
716 Joburg Records
717–720 CBS Inc.
721 Pickwick International, Inc.

715 Record cover entitled *Out of the Woods* by the Oregon group. Illustration in shades of green and brown. (USA)
716 Full-colour illustration for a record cover for recordings by Ramsay Mackay with the title *Bosbok-rand*. A book was published to go with this record. (SAF)
717 Record cover for recordings by the Lake group. Light shades. (USA)
718 Full-colour record cover for recordings by the jazz violinist Stephane Grappelli. The title refers to one of the tracks. (USA)
719 Cover for a record by Maynard Ferguson entitled *Carnival*. Illustration in bright colours, continued on the reverse side. (USA)
720 Full-colour cover for a record by Dan Hartman. (USA)
721 Cover for a record of *Sousa's* best-known marches. (USA)

718

Maynard Ferguson **Carnival**

719

720

721

715 Hülle für eine Schallplatte der Gruppe Oregon. Titel: *Out of the Woods* (Aus dem Wald). Illustration in Grün- und Brauntönen. (USA)

716 Farbige Illustration für die Hülle einer Schallplatte mit dem Titel *Bosbokrand* von Ramsay Mackay, zu der auch ein Buch mit dem Titel *Letzte Briefe aus der Wildnis* gehört. (SAF)

717 Schallplattenhülle für Aufnahmen der Gruppe Lake. Helle Farbtöne. (USA)

718 Farbige Schallplattenhülle für Aufnahmen des Jazz-Geigers Stephane Grappelli. Der Titel *Uptown Dance* bezieht sich auf eines der Stücke. (USA)

719 Hülle für eine Schallplatte von Maynard Ferguson mit dem Titel *Carnival*. Illustration in leuchtenden Farben, die sich auf der Rückseite fortsetzt. (USA)

720 Farbige Hülle für eine Platte mit dem Titel *Instant Replay* von Dan Hartman. (USA)

721 Hülle für eine Schallplatte mit den bekanntesten Märschen von *Sousa*. (USA)

715 Pochette pour un disque du groupe Oregon intitulé *Out of the Woods* (Du fond des bois). Illustration exécutée en teintes vert et brun. (USA)

716 Pochette d'un disque de Ramsay Mackay intitulé *Bosbokrand*, diffusé en même temps qu'un livre intitulé «Dernières lettres de la brousse». (SAF)

717 Pochette pour un enregistrement du groupe Lake. Coloris clairs. (USA)

718 Pochette pour un enregistrement du violoniste de jazz Stephane Grappelli. Le titre *Uptown Dance* est celui de l'un des morceaux interprétés. (USA)

719 Pochette pour un disque de Maynard Ferguson intitulé *Carnival*. L'illustration aux couleurs vives occupe le recto et le verso. (USA)

720 Pochette couleur pour un disque intitulé *Instant Replay*, interprété par Dan Hartman. (USA)

721 Pochette pour un disque contenant les meilleures marches de *Sousa*. (USA)

722

723

724

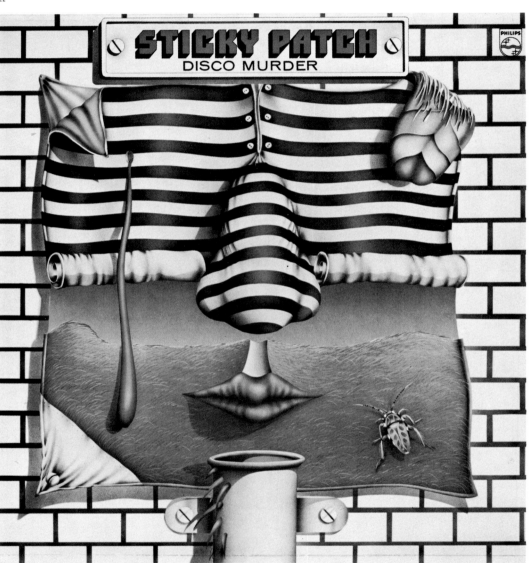

725

726

722 Full-colour cover for a Niitsu Akio record. (JPN)
723 Full-colour cover for Steve Hunter recordings. (USA)
724 Record cover in full colour for tracks recorded by the Target group. (USA)
725 Full-colour cover for a record by the Sticky Patch group. The title refers to one of the tracks. (SAF)
726 Full-colour cover for a record by the Brubeck Quartet. (USA)
727, 728 Detail and complete record cover for jazz-rock recordings by the drummer Lenny White. (USA)

722 Farbige Hülle für eine Schallplatte von Niitsu Akio. (JPN)
723 Farbige Hülle für Aufnahmen von Steve Hunter. (USA)
724 Schallplattenhülle in Farbe für Aufnahmen der Gruppe Target (Zielscheibe). (USA)
725 Farbige Hülle für eine Platte der Gruppe Sticky Patch. Der Titel *Disco Murder* bezieht sich auf ein Stück. (SAF)
726 Farbige Hülle für Aufnahmen des Brubeck-Quartetts. (USA)
727, 728 Detail und vollständige Schallplattenhülle für Jazz-Rock-Aufnahmen des Schlagzeugers Lenny White. (USA)

722 Pochette couleur pour un disque de Niitsu Akio. (JPN)
723 Pochette couleur d'un enregistrement de Steve Hunter. (USA)
724 Pochette en couleurs pour un enregistrement du groupe Target (Cible). (USA)
725 Pochette couleur pour un disque du groupe Sticky Patch, dont le titre *Disco Murder* est celui de l'un des morceaux. (SAF)
726 Pochette couleur d'un disque du quartette Brubeck. (USA)
727, 728 Détail et pochette complète d'un disque de jazz-rock du batteur Lenny White. (USA)

ARTIST / KÜNSTLER / ARTISTE:

722 Tadanori Yokoo
723 Don Punchatz
724 Lou Beach
725 Norman Catherine
726 Milton Glaser
727, 728 David Wilcox

DESIGNER / GESTALTER / MAQUETTISTE:

722 Tadanori Yokoo
723 Lynn Dreese Breslin
724 Chuck Beeson
726 Milton Glaser
727, 728 Abie Sussman

Record Covers
Scalplattenhülln
Pochettes de disques

727

728

243

721 — 734 ➡

736 — 741 ➡

729—735 Frames from animated films for *Sharp*, manufacturers of computers and business machines. Figs. 729–731 from *Sharp Sound*, Figs. 732–735 from *The Wonderful World*, an animated film which utilizes an atmosphere of magic and dream to suggest the quality and capabilities of *Sharp* products. (BRA)
736—741 Frames from the animated film entitled *At the Tip of Your Fingers* especially made for *Sharp*. The gist of this film is that man's sophisticated technology has imprisoned him but has also endowed him with greater powers, so that nowadays with just a touch of his finger-tip he can perform complex calculations with endless possibilities and combinations or bring to life the magic pictures of television. (BRA)
742—750 Nine frames from another *Sharp* animated film entitled *Colours and Sounds of Our Land*. This extremely colourful and romantic presentation of the natural beauties and resources of Brazil shows a technical product finally emerging from them. (BRA)

729—735 Bilder aus Trickfilmen für Sharp SA, Hersteller von Computern und Büromaschinen. Abb. 729–731 aus «Sharp-Klänge», Abb. 732–735 aus «Die wunderbare Welt», einem Trickfilm, der sich Zauber- und Traumatmosphäre zunutze macht, um Qualität und Leistungsvermögen der *Sharp*-Produkte zu suggerieren. (BRA)
736—741 Bilder aus dem Trickfilm «An Deiner Fingerspitze» für *Sharp*. Die Quintessenz dieses Films ist, dass die spitzfindige Technologie des Menschen ihn zum Sklaven gemacht, ihm aber auch grössere Fähigkeiten verliehen hat, so dass er mit einem Fingerspitzendruck imstande ist, komplexe Berechnungen anzustellen oder die magischen Bilder am Fernseher zum Leben zu erwecken. (BRA)
742—750 Neun Bilder aus einem weiteren *Sharp*-Trickfilm mit dem Titel «Farben und Klänge unseres Landes». Die farbenprächtige und romantische Darstellung der natürlichen Schönheiten und Reichtümer Brasiliens zeigt, wie zuletzt ein technisches Produkt daraus hervorgeht. (BRA)

729—735 Images de films d'animation réalisés pour le compte de la Sharp S.A., fabricant d'ordinateurs et de machines de bureau; fig. 729-731: «Sonorités *Sharp*»; fig. 732-735: «Ce monde merveilleux», un dessin animé plongeant le spectateur dans le rêve et la magie pour évoquer la qualité et les performances de produits *Sharp*. (BRA)
736—741 Images du dessin animé «A la pointe de tes doigts» réalisé pour *Sharp*. Le sujet: la technologie sophistiquée a enchaîné l'homme tout en décuplant ses aptitudes: ainsi, en effleurant une touche du bout de ses doigts, il est capable de réaliser des calculs complexes ou de faire naître des images magiques sur un écran de télévision. (BRA)
742—750 Neuf images d'un autre dessin animé *Sharp*, «Couleurs et sons de notre pays». La représentation romantique et haute en couleur des beautés et richesses naturelles du Brésil sert à présenter en fin de compte un produit technique qui en résulte. (BRA)

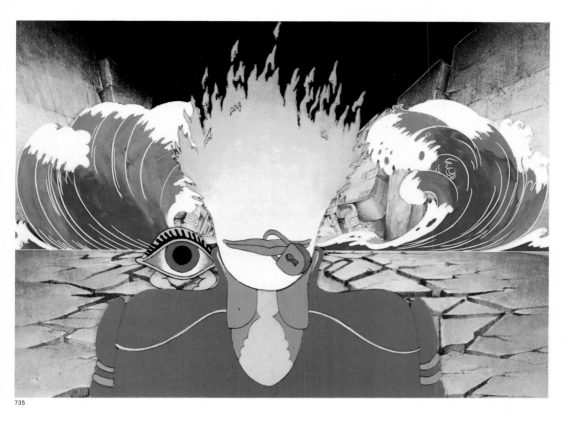

735

ARTIST / KÜNSTLER / ARTISTE:

729–750 Walbercy Ribas Camargo

DESIGNER / GESTALTER / MAQUETTISTE:

729–750 Walbercy Ribas Camargo

ART DIRECTOR / DIRECTEUR ARTISTIQUE:

729–750 Walbercy Ribas Camargo

AGENCY / AGENTUR / AGENCE – STUDIO:

729–750 Start Desenhos Animados Ltda./
          Praxis Propaganda Ltda.

PRODUCER / PRODUZENT / PRODUCTION:

729–750 Praxis Propaganda Ltda.

742 – 750 →

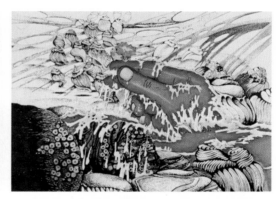

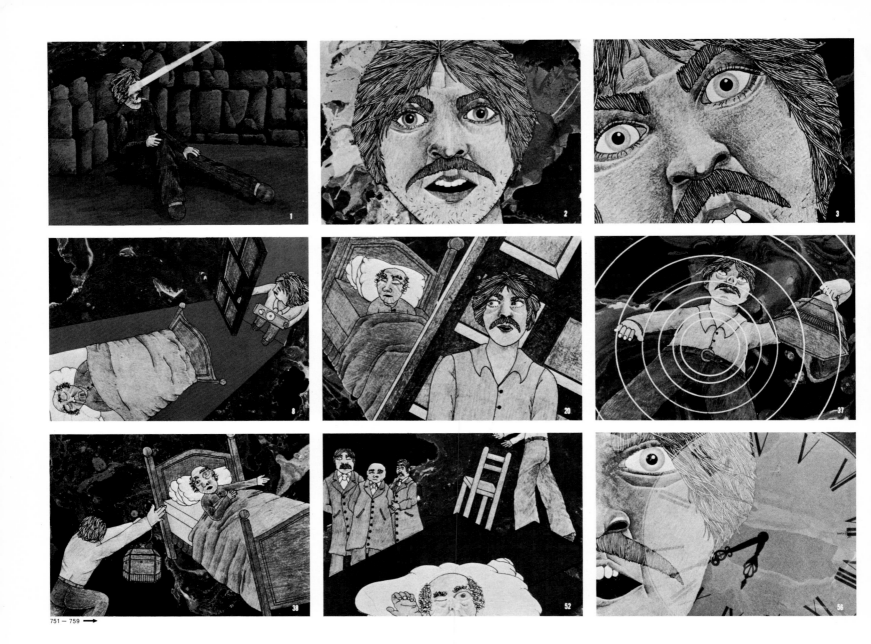

751 — 759 ➡

ARTIST / KÜNSTLER / ARTISTE:

751–759 Linda Sekelsky
760, 767–772 Keith S. Aldred
761–766 Marguerita

DESIGNER / GESTALTER / MAQUETTISTE:

751–759 Peter Oths
760, 767–772 Keith S. Aldred
761–766 Marguerita

ART DIRECTOR / DIRECTEUR ARTISTIQUE:

751–759 Peter Oths
760, 767–772 Keith S. Aldred
761–766 Marguerita

AGENCY / AGENTUR / AGENCE – STUDIO:

751–759 Listening Library, Inc.
760, 767–772 Granada Television Ltd.
761–766 Marguerita

PRODUCER / PRODUZENT / PRODUCTION:

751–759 Listening Library, Inc.
760, 767–772 Granada Television Ltd.
761–766 Marguerita

760

Film/Televison

246

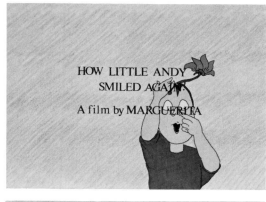

761—766 ⟶

751—759 Nine frames from an animated film version of Edgar Allan Poe's story *The Tell Tale Heart*. The colour illustrations were cut and mounted on black oil-and-water backgrounds to enhance the eerie atmosphere. (USA)
760, 767—772 Frames from an animated film used as an insert in the *Granada* television feature *Reports Action* to obtain volunteers for this programme. (GBR)
761—766 Sequence from the animated film *How Little Andy Smiled Again*, used in the *Sesame Street* programme of the Children's Television Workshop. (USA)

751—759 Neun Bilder aus einem Zeichentrickfilm nach einem Werk von Edgar Allan Poe. Die farbigen Illustrationen wurden alle auf schwarzem Hintergrund montiert, um eine unheimliche, mysteriöse Atmosphäre zu erzeugen. (USA)
760, 767—772 Sieben Bilder aus einem Zeichentrickfilm, der beim TV-Programm *Reports Action* zwischengeschaltet wird, um Freiwillige für dieses Programm zu gewinnen. (GBR)
761—766 Bilder aus dem Trickfilm *How Little Andy Smiled Again* (Wie der kleine Andy wieder lachte), der im Rahmen des Kinderprogramms *Sesam-Strasse* gesendet wurde. (USA)

751—759 Neuf cases d'une version du récit *The Tell Tale Heart* d'Edgar Allan Poe réalisée en animation. Les illustrations couleur ont été montées sur des arrière-plans noirs peints à l'huile et à l'aquarelle, qui font frémir d'angoisse. (USA)
760, 767—772 Cases d'un film d'animation intercalé dans l'émission TV *Reports Action* de *Granada* pour recruter des volontaires pour ce programme. (GBR)
761—766 Séquence du dessin animé *How Little Andy Smiled Again* (Comment petit Andy retrouva son sourire) utilisé dans le cadre de l'émission *Rue Sésame* du Children's Television Workshop. (USA)

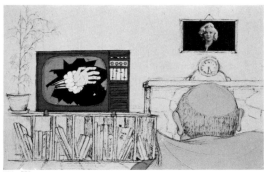

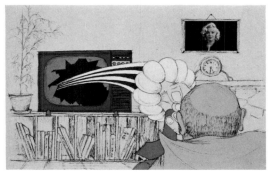

767—772 ⟶

247

Paper / Papier: Papierfabrik Biberist – Biber GS SK3, blade coated,
pure white 120 gm² and Biber Offset SK3, pure white, machine-
finished, 140 gm² / Biber GS SK3, hochweiss, satiniert, 120 gm²
und Biber-Offset SK3, hochweiss, maschinenglatt, 140 gm²

Printed by / gedruckt von: Merkur AG, Langenthal,
Karl Schwegler AG, Zürich, Tages-Anzeiger / Regina Druck,
Zürich, J. E. Wolfensberger AG, Zürich

Cover / Einband: Buchbinderei Schumacher AG, Bern / Schmitten
Glossy lamination / Glanzfoliierung: Durolit AG, Pfäffikon SZ